D0218016

YAMAY

1011143

ANIMAL LAW
IN ENGLAND AND WALES

By the same author:
  Garden Law
  Gun Law

To

LUCIFER AND PERSEPHONE

of the species *Felis catus*

ANIMAL LAW

by

Godfrey Sandys-Winsch, B.A. (Cantab.)
Solicitor

SECOND EDITION

LONDON:
Printed and Published by
SHAW & SONS LTD.,
Shaway House, SE26 5AE
1984

First Published – – – – *April*, 1978
Second Edition – – – – *March*, 1984

ISBN 07219 0801 2

© SHAW & SONS Ltd. 1984
Printed in Great Britain

CONTENTS

APPENDICES

PREFACE TO SECOND EDITION

The First Edition of this book was most kindly received, and I am grateful to reviewers and other readers for both their compliments and criticisms.

The most important legislation on animal law in the intervening years has been the Wildlife and Countryside Act 1981 whose provisions protecting wildlife, building on and expanding those in earlier Acts, are now in force. That Act has also amended the law protecting badgers, seals and deer.

A new Deer Act was passed in 1980 to prevent the poaching of deer, and the following year saw the enactment of the Zoo Licensing Act; however, there are no indications yet that the latter will soon be operative, and it is not further mentioned in this Edition. The Animal Health Act of 1981 has consolidated and replaced the Diseases of Animals Act 1950, the Ponies Act 1969, the Rabies Act 1974 and some subordinate legislation made under those Acts. The names of many new animals have been added to those to which the Dangerous Wild Animals Act of 1976 applies.

The main changes in the law contained in statutory instruments have been the revocation of the regulations governing respectively the breeding of sheep and the threshing of stacks. New regulations have been made about the export of animals and the import of equine animals, and other regulations have been amended.

Very little new case law has emerged.

To aid those readers needing to use legal references, I have in this Edition added a table of statutes with their sections and a table of statutory instruments with page references for both.

I gratefully acknowledge the help I have received from Mrs. Susan M. MacDonald of the Ministry of Agriculture, Fisheries and Food on import, export and other licences, and from Mr. F. Channing of the Department of the Environment on, mainly, the Wildlife and Countryside Act 1981.

The law is stated as at 1st October 1983.

GODFREY SANDYS-WINSCH.

LEASINGHAM,
LINCOLNSHIRE.

November 1983.

PREFACE TO FIRST EDITION

My aim in writing this book is to present in a reasonably compact and comprehensive form to anyone associated with animals the many facets of the law which affect them. It has not been an easy task in the sense that, if I had attempted to cover every detail of that law, I should have been writing for a long while yet and then not have achieved my aim. I therefore had to decide what should be omitted.

Broadly speaking, I have attempted to cover the law dealing with quadrupeds of all kinds, thus leaving out material on birds, fishes and insects; though seals and rare wild creatures have been included. Even so, a decision had to be made on the width of coverage for quadrupeds. For example, I calculate that there are roughly 1,000 pages of statute and regulations on diseases of animals alone which I could not hope to accommodate fully. And there are matters, peripheral in a sense, such as slaughterhouses, sheep and cattle subsidies, schemes and grants, artificial insemination and horse and greyhound racing, which I felt constrained to omit.

With such apologia, I offer this book to the reader in the hope that he will find it readable, useful and interesting.

I readily acknowledge the comprehensive guidance I have received from the publishers of, and the contributors to, the relevant titles in, the Fourth Edition of *Halsbury's Laws of England*. I also wish to thank the Animal Health Division of the Ministry of Agriculture, Fisheries and Food for their ready and indispensable advice on Chapters 3 and 9, and Mr. Bruce Lawson for his diligence in tracking down some of the more obscure regulations.

Apart from occasional references to Scotland, the law is that of England and Wales. It is stated as at 1st February

1978, though in one instance I have dealt with law which is
to come into force on a later unknown date.

GODFREY SANDYS-WINSCH.

LEASINGHAM,
LINCOLNSHIRE.

February 1978.

NOTES ON LEGAL REFERENCES

For those readers who wish to refer to legal sources, I have mentioned in the footnotes the Acts of Parliament, the statutory instruments and the titles of court cases which are relevant. Separate tables listing each of these in alphabetical order, with the pages on which they are referred to, are to be found on the pages following this page. The individual sections of Acts, but not sub-sections, paragraphs or provisoes, are so listed.

In the footnotes the following arrangements apply. The titles of Acts are abbreviated by the use of all or some of their initial letters which are repeated with the full titles in the Table of Statutes. The title of each of the statutory instruments is given in full, followed in brackets by the Statutory Instrument (S.I.) or Statutory Rule and Order (S.R.&O.) serial number for the year in which it was made; the serial number is repeated in brackets in the Table of Statutory Instruments. Except where a particular page reference in a report is quoted, references to court cases cite only the title and year of the case. Full references to case reports are given in the Table of Cases.

References to sections of the Acts and to statutory instruments do not mention that they may have been amended or substituted by other legislation. They are quoted or used as currently enacted.

As well as the standard abbreviations used for case reports and those for statutory instruments mentioned above, the following are used in the footnotes and tables:

Section or sections of an Act .... s. or ss.
Schedule to an Act or Statutory instrument ...... Sch.
Article or regulation number in a statutory
instrument. .... Art.

The footnotes also include the catalogue numbers (Cat. No.) of forms which are available from the publishers of this book.

TABLE OF STATUTES

TABLE OF STATUTORY INSTRUMENTS

xxix

TABLE OF CASES

A

ANIMAL LAW

OWNERSHIP, THEFT AND OWNERS' RESPONSIBILITIES

A. OWNERSHIP

In law the term "animals" includes all creatures not belonging to the human race. They are then broadly divided into two groups: domestic and wild. Domestic animals include all those domestic or tame animals as by habit or training live in association with man.[1] Wild animals include not only those which are savage by nature but also those of a more mild or timid nature which cannot be classed as domestic or tame. But a domestic animal which reverts to a wild state is no longer domestic but wild.[2]

Domestic animals are owned in the same way as inanimate objects such as cars and furniture. Ownership is retained

---

[1] *Halsbury's Laws of England*, 4th Ed., Vol. 2, para. 201.
[2] *Falkland Islands Co. v. R.* (1864).

[3]

when the animal is lost or strays, and the owner has the same legal rights against anyone detaining it as he would have for his own goods[1]; keeping and feeding another person's animal does not of itself permit retention of the animal until its keep is paid.[2] Generally, the young of domestic animals are owned by the mother's owner,[3] but in the case of a lease of livestock the young belong to the lessee in the absence of a clear indication to the contrary.[4]

The position about ownership of wild animals is more complicated. Unlike domestic animals, no one can have complete ownership of living wild animals, but in three cases there can be a qualified ownership. First, a person who lawfully takes, tames or reclaims a wild animal may claim it as his property until it regains its natural liberty, and may take legal remedies against another who takes it from him.[5] This right applies, for example, to hares, pheasants or partridges kept in a warren or enclosure.[6]

Secondly, the owner of land has a right to the young of wild animals born on his land until they can run (or fly) away, and may take legal action against a person taking them.[7] Thirdly, a landowner also has the right[8] to hunt, take and kill wild animals as long as they are on his land.[9] This right may be transferred by a letting of the sporting rights; the terms of the letting will determine whether the right extends to all wild animals or, as is often the case, only to game.[10]

Different rules operate for dead wild animals. These are fully owned by the owner or occupier[11] of the land where they lie or by the tenant of the sporting rights if these are

---

[1] *E.g.*, an action in court for detention or trover,

[2] *Binstead v. Buck* (1777).

[3] *Halsbury's Laws of England*, 4th Ed., Vol. 2, para. 203.

[4] *Tucker v. Farm & General Trust Ltd.* (1966).

[5] *Grymes v. Shack* (1610).

[6] *Mallock v. Eastly* (1685).

[7] *Case of Swans* (1592) 7 Co. Rep. 15b at 17b; *Blades v. Higgs* (1865).

[8] Concurrently with the right of an occupier to take hares and rabbits; *see* pp. 107–110.

[9] *Blades v. Higgs*, as above.

[10] *See*, further, p. 110.

[11] *I.e.*, the occupying owner or the tenant of the land if let.

let.[1] Exceptions arise where a landowner kills an animal from his land on that of another, or where a trespasser chases the animal from one person's land to that of another and kills it there; in both cases the carcase belongs to the killer.[2]

B. THEFT

Although for a long time it has been a crime to steal most kinds of domestic and tame animals, quite illogically a few kinds could not be stolen,[3] and it was not until the Theft Act was passed in 1968 that the law was rationalised. The position now is that all domestic animals, and wild animals which are tamed or ordinarily kept in captivity, can be the subject of theft if the person from whom they were taken had possession or control of them, or had a proprietary right or interest[4] in them.[5] A wild animal not within this description (or its carcase) can only be stolen if—

(1) it has been reduced into possession[6] by or on behalf of another person **and** possession of it has not since been lost or abandoned; **or**

(2) another person is in course of reducing it into possession.[7]

When, within these limits, animals can be stolen, it follows that they may also be the subjects of the offences of obtaining property by deception and receiving stolen goods.[8]

To advertise publicly a reward for the return of any animal

---

[1] *Fitzgerald v. Firbank* (1897).

[2] *Churchward v. Studdy* (1811); *Sutton v. Moody* (1697); *Blades v. Higgs* (1865).

[3] These were dogs, cats and "animals of a base nature" (whatever that may mean). (*Halsbury's Laws of England*, 4th Ed. Vol. 2, para. 230.)

[4] But not an equitable interest, which is an interest arising only from an agreement to transfer or grant an interest. (T.A. 1968, s. 5(1).).

[5] T.A. 1968, ss. 1(1), 4(1), 5(1).

[6] No statutory definition is given of the phrase "reduce into possession". It is suggested that this means the doing of some act by the other person to assert his ownership, *e.g.* caging or possibly trapping the animal, or putting the carcase in a game bag or car, or hiding it.

[7] T.A. 1968, s. 4(4).

[8] T.A. 1968, ss. 15(1), 22(1), 34(2)(*b*).

stolen or lost, using any words to the effect that no questions will be asked, or that the person producing the animal will be safe from apprehension or inquiry, or that any money paid for its purchase or advanced by way of loan on it will be repaid, is an offence for which the advertiser, printer and publisher can be prosecuted.[1]

C. OWNERS' RESPONSIBILITIES

The owner of an animal will in many different circumstances be liable for injuries it causes to people and other animals and for damage to property. This responsibility often attaches, not only to the owner, but to the person who at the time has possession of the animal and, sometimes, to a person whose household includes a youngster who owns or possesses the animal. These are mainly matters of civil law with the sanction of an action in court, usually for damages for the injury or damage done.

Over the centuries a body of case law on the subject was created with sometimes complicated and unsatisfactory results. The Animals Act of 1971 was an attempt to rationalise this law, though not to change it except about animals escaping on to roads. Much of the law still rests on the precedents of legal cases. (A large body of law deals specially with dogs and this is contained in Chapter 4.)

A study of the subject, which can be quite involved, falls fairly conveniently into a number of sub-headings which will now be dealt with in turn.

Strict Liability

"Strict liability" is a legal term meaning that there is liability without proof that the person claimed against was negligent; if he was responsible for the animal and the animal caused the injury or damage, then, without more, that person is responsible for that injury or damage. This is a part of the law codified by the Animals Act 1971 and

---

[1] T.A. 1968, ss. 23, 34(2)(*b*).

itself falls into two parts: animals belonging to a dangerous species, and those which do not.

A dangerous species is a species[1] which is not commonly domesticated in the British Islands[2]; **and** whose fully grown animals normally have such characteristics that they are likely, unless restrained, to cause severe damage[3] or that any damage they may cause is likely to be severe.[4] Where any damage is caused by such an animal, any person who is a keeper[5] of the animal is liable for the damage except in the following cases[6]—

(1) Where the damage was due wholly to the fault of the person suffering it[7]; **or**

(2) If the person injured voluntarily accepted[8] the risk of injury[9]; **or**

(3) If the damage was caused by an animal kept on any premises or structure to a trespasser[10] there if it is proved—

    (a) **either** that the animal was not kept there for the protection of persons or property; **or**

    (b) if the animal was kept there for that purpose, that the keeping for the purpose was not unreasonable.[11]

It follows from (a) that a trespasser in a properly fenced field who is gored by a savage bull had no remedy.[12] What

---

[1] The word "species" includes sub-species and variety. (A.A. 1971, s. 11.)

[2] I.e., the United Kingdom, the Channel Islands, the Isle of Man, and the Republic of Ireland (IA 1978 ss. 5, 22(1), Sch 1, Sch. 2, para. 4(2)).

[3] "Damage" includes the death of, or injury to any person (including any disease and any impairment of physical or mental condition) (A.A. 1971 s. 11). The word will, of course, also have its ordinary meaning.

[4] A.A. 1971, s. 6(2).

[5] For the meaning of "keeper", see p. 65.

[6] A.A. 1971, s. 2(1).

[7] A.A. 1971, s. 5(1).

[8] A servant of a keeper of an animal who incurs a risk incidental to his employment is not to be treated as accepting that risk voluntarily. (A.A. 1971, s. 6(5).)

[9] A.A. 1971, s. 5(2).

[10] Briefly, a trespasser is a person on premises without the occupier's permission.

[11] A.A. 1971, s. 5(3).

[12] For new legislation about bulls in fields, see pp. 93–94.

is reasonable in case (*b*) will depend upon the circumstances; the keeping of a fierce dog in the access to a house which injures innocent visitors on lawful business would not be excusable;[1] but the keeping of an untamed Alsatian dog at loose at night in a scrapyard in East London to protect property is not unreasonable, although the court conceded that this decision might have been otherwise if Section 1 of the Guard Dogs Act 1975 (see pages 77 to 78) had been in force at the time.[2]

In the case of an animal not belonging to a dangerous species as defined, its keeper[3] is strictly liable, but with the same defences as have just been enumerated, for the damage[4] it causes if—

(1) the damage is of a kind which the animal, unless restrained, was likely to cause or which, if caused by the animal, was likely to be severe[5]; **and**

(2) the likelihood of the damage or of its being severe was due to characteristics of the animal not normally found in animals of the same species[6] or not normally so found except at particular times or in particular circumstances[7]; **and**

(3) those characteristics were known to the animal's keeper or were at any time known to a person who at that time had charge of the animal as the keeper's servant or, where the keeper is the head of a household, were known to another keeper of the animal who is a member of that household and under the age of 16.[8]

---

[1] *Sarch v. Blackburn* (1830) 4 C. & P. 297 at 300.

[2] *Cummings v. Grainger* (1976).

[3] For the meaning of "keeper", *see* p. 65.

[4] For the meaning of "damage", *see* note [3] on p. 7.

[5] A.A. 1971, s. 2(2)(*a*).

[6] The word "species" includes sub-species and variety. (A.A. 1971, s. 11.)

[7] A.A. 1971, s. 2(2)(*b*). The unpredictable nature of a horse is not to be regarded as a normal characteristic of horses (*Wallace* v. *Newton* (1982)). Nor is the propensity of a dog to attack people carrying bags to be regarded as a normal characteristic of dogs (*Kite* v. *Napp* (1982)).

[8] A.A. 1971, s. 2(2)(*c*).

The special provisions about guard dogs are discussed on pages 77 to 79.

Negligence

In addition to the strict liability cases just mentioned, the owner of a domestic and normally harmless animal, and the person having charge of it at the time, can be liable for injury or damage which it causes through his negligence. The word "negligence" has more than its ordinary meaning here; to succeed in a case of negligence the plaintiff must prove to the satisfaction of the court that the defendant had a duty to him to take care, that he failed in that duty and that the injury or damage resulted from that failure. Whether there is a duty in any particular case will depend mainly on case law, *e.g.* previously decided cases on similar situations. So far as animals are concerned, it is established that a person who brings an animal on to a highway has a duty to use all reasonable care to prevent it doing damage to other persons there. If he is driving animals along the highway he must have them under sufficient control.[1] These are admittedly imprecise tests; they cannot be otherwise. Each case depends on its own facts and on the precedents of case law.

Diseased Animals[2]

The owner or possessor of animals having an infectious or contagious disease is liable for the damage caused by their disease in the following cases:

(1) If, knowing them to be diseased, he allows them to mingle with the animals of another person.

(2) If, knowing them to be diseased and infectious to persons handling them, he employs a person to handle their carcases who is ignorant of their state, and that person becomes infected.

---

[1] *Halsbury's Laws of England*, 4th Ed., Vol. 2, para. 427.
[2] For the rules enacted by Parliament and the Ministry of Agriculture about animal diseases, *see* Chapter 9.

(3) If, knowing of their diseased state, he bails[1] the animals, knowing that the person to whom they are bailed probably will or may place them with other animals which are healthy, without warning that person of their diseased state.

(4) If he sells them with a warranty[2] that they are free from disease, whether he knows of their diseased state or not.

(5) If he is guilty of fraud or actual concealment about the disease in the sale.

(6) If, knowing them to be diseased and that they may be put in with healthy animals, he sells them at a public market or fair, or at a public auction; and possibly even if he sells them privately.[3]

Trespass by Animals Generally

In broad terms, an animal is said to trespass in the same way as a human trespasses, namely when it is on land where it has no right to be or, more precisely, where its owner has no right to put it; this includes an animal straying on to a highway as well as those straying from a highway on to private land.

For trespass to take place, it is enough if any part of the animal crosses the boundary of the properties in question, *e.g.*, the stretching of its neck over the boundary. But what is called trespass to the person or to goods (including horses or cattle), that is the touching of them by the animal, does not generally render the owner liable where there is no trespass to land.[4]

The rules of the law on the subject are concerned mainly with trespass of livestock. A cat[5] holds a unique position in

---

[1] "Bail" is a legal word meaning in this context, briefly, to deliver goods to another person for an agreed purpose, *e.g.*, to keep them safely or to do work on them.

[2] A warranty is an agreement collateral to the sale. *see also* pp. 24–25.

[3] *Halsbury's Laws of England*, 4th Ed., Vol. 2, para. 428.

[4] *Halsbury's Laws of England*, 4th Ed., Vol. 2, para. 429.

[5] *I.e.*, the ordinary domestic cat.

that its owner is not responsible for the consequences of its trespasses. Owners' liabilities for the trespasses of their dogs are governed by the particular rules which are examined on pages 64 to 67. Owners and keepers of cats and dogs which cause damage or injury when not trespassing may be liable under the strict liability rules or the law of negligence which have been considered on pages 6 to 9. Responsibilities for wild animals are dealt with in a concluding section on this topic. There remains some doubt about the position of a trespassing animal which is neither wild nor a dog, cat or livestock.[1] It appears that for animals in this residual category their owners will be liable for damage caused when they trespass which is in their nature ordinarily to commit;[2]

Trespass By Livestock on Private Land

Where livestock[1] belonging[3] to any person strays on to land in the ownership or occupation of another person, the first person is strictly liable[4] for the following damage and expenses unless he can establish any of the defences later considered—

(1) Damage done by the livestock to the land or to any property on it[5] which is in the ownership or possession of that other person.

(2) Expenses which are reasonably incurred by that other

---

[1] For this purpose "livestock" means cattle, horses, mules, hinnies (offspring of she-asses by stallions), sheep, pigs, goats and poultry, and deer not in a wild state. (A.A. 1971, s. 11.)

[2] *Halsbury's Laws of England*, 4th Ed., Vol. 2, para. 429, note 4.

[3] For this purpose livestock belongs to the person in whose possession it is. (A.A. 1971, s. 4(2).) For the meaning of "possession", *see* p. 65.

[4] For the meaning of strict liability, *see* p. 6.

[5] The words here used are wide enough, it is suggested, to cover the land itself and anything in, on or above it, and so embracing all growing things, buildings and objects placed, however temporarily, on the land, provided these are owned or possessed as described. The earlier definition of "damage" (in note [3] on p. 7) will not apply.

person[1] in keeping the livestock while it cannot be restored to the person to whom it belongs or while the occupier of the land is exercising his right to detain it,[2] and the expenses of finding out to whom the livestock belongs.[3]

There is no responsibility for straying livestock if—

(i) The damage is due wholly to the fault of the person suffering it, but he is not to be treated as at fault solely because he could have prevented the damage by fencing;[4] **or**

(ii) It is proved that the straying would not have occurred but for a breach of a duty to fence[5] imposed on another person who has an interest in the land in question. (This has the effect, for example, of a tenant being unable to claim for damage and expenses if his landlord had failed to honour the landlord's agreement with another person to fence as a result of which the animals had strayed on to the tenant's land); **or**

(iii) The livestock strayed from the highway and its presence there was a lawful use of the highway.[6] The highway need not adjoin the land; the stock may have wandered from the highway through other land. The only lawful use of the highway for live-stock (unless they have grazing rights on the verges) is to pass and repass on it.

In addition to his right to claim for damage and expenses, the occupier of land on to which livestock strays without

---

[1] Where that person is a local authority, it is proper for it to have reasonable standard charges if it would be impossible to keep exact and detailed records of each animal; an itemised bill in such circumstances is unnecessary (*Morris* v. *Blaenau Gwent District Council* (1982)).

[2] For this right of detention, *see* the text below.

[3] A.A. 1971, s. 4(1).

[4] "Fencing" includes the construction of any obstacle designed to prevent animals from straying. (A.A. 1971, s. 11.)

[5] A duty to fence against common land may arise by custom (*Egerton v. Harding and Another* (1974)).

[6] A.A. 1971, s 5(1), (5), (6).

being under the control of any person has the right to detain it unless ordered by a court to return it.[1] This right ceases—

(1) at the end of 48 hours unless beforehand the occupier gives notice of the detention to the officer in charge of a police station and to the person to whom the livestock belongs if the occupier knows who that person is; **or**

(2) if the person claiming the livestock offers to the occupier money sufficient to cover his proper claim for damage and expenses[2]; **or**

(3) if the occupier has no such claim, when the livestock is claimed by someone entitled to its possession.[3]

When the occupier has detained the livestock for at least 14 days he may sell it at market or public auction, unless court proceedings are then pending for the return of the livestock or for his claim for damage or expenses.[4] The occupier is entitled to the net proceeds[5] of sale. Any excess over his claim is to be paid to the person who would be entitled to possession of the livestock but for the sale.[6] If there is a shortfall, presumably, though the Act does not say so, the occupier may pursue his claim for that.

The occupier is liable for any damage caused to livestock detained by him by failure to treat it with reasonable care and supply it with adequate food and water.[7]

References in these matters to the occupier's claim do not include a claim arising before the particular straying as a result of which the stock was detained.[8]

---

[1] A court may so order on payment into court of a sum of money against the claim for which the stock is held.

[2] *I.e.*, a claim within the limitations described on pp. 11–12.

[3] A.A. 1971, s. 7(2), (3).

[4] A.A. 1971, s. 7(4).

[5] *I.e.*, after deducting sale costs and other costs "incurred in connection with" the sale.

[6] A.A. 1971, s. 7(5).

[7] A.A. 1971, s. 7(6).

[8] A.A. 1971, s. 7(7).

Trespass from the Highway

As we have seen,[1] there is no claim under strict liability for damage or expenses by a landowner or occupier for livestock straying on to his land, directly or indirectly, following their lawful presence on a highway. To succeed in a claim in these circumstances the person suffering loss must prove negligence by the person having charge of the livestock; in brief, he must show that reasonable control over the animals was not being exercised while they were being driven along the road. The law takes the view that it is a risk which a man takes who has property adjoining a road and, in the absence of negligence by the drover, the loss falls upon him if he does not take precautions by fencing or otherwise protecting his property. Though there is no legal decision on the point, it is suggested that an unreasonable delay in removing an animal that has strayed on to land from a road, though otherwise driven quite properly along it, could justify a claim for damage caused by the delay.[2]

Straying on the Highway

Until 1971,[3] unless there were special circumstances, owners of animals were not responsible for any injury or damage they caused by straying on to a highway. Now, owners of animals and those having control of them have a duty to take reasonable care to see that such injury or damage is not caused. This does not by itself oblige all owners to fence[4] but, for example, failure to fence where animals are kept near a busy road is likely to be treated as a breach of the duty.[5] However, no breach is caused when

---

[1] Page 12, item (iii).
[2] *Halsbury's Laws of England*, 4th Ed., Vol. 2, para. 433.
[3] 1st October 1971 when the Animals Act came into force.
[4] References to fencing in the Act include references to other obstacles designed to prevent animals from straying. (A.A. 1971, s. 11.)
[5] If a fence, though not 100% secure, is reasonably adequate to prevent the animal in question from escaping, it appears that the duty of care is fulfilled (*Smith v. Sudron and Coulson* (1981)).

a person, having the right to do so,[1] places animals on unfenced land which is common land,[2] or a town or village green,[3] or is in an area where fencing is not customary.[4]

The position is different, as has been shown on page 9, when animals are deliberately brought on to a highway.

If any horse,[5] or any cattle, sheep, goats or swine are found straying[6], or lying[7] on or at the side of any highway[8] (except such part of it as passes over any common or waste or unenclosed ground), the keeper[9] of the animals is liable to be prosecuted and fined. He may also be charged with the reasonable expenses of removing the animals to his premises or the common pound or other place provided, and with the proper charges of the pound-keeper.[10] Any person lawfully using the highway may remove the animals

---

[1] Persons having the right to put animals on the land described will include a person licensed to do so by another person having that right, provided the number of animals permitted for that other person is not exceeded. (*Davies v. Davies* (1974)).

[2] "Common land" means land subject to rights of common (which includes cattlegates or beastgates and rights of sole or several vesture or herbage or of sole or several pasture but not rights held for a term of years or from year to year) whether those rights are exercisable at all times or only during limited periods, and waste lands of a manor not subject to rights of common but does not include a town or village green or any land forming part of a highway. (A.A. 1971, s. 11; C.R.A. 1965, s. 22(1).)

[3] "Town or village green" means land which has been allotted by or under any Act for the exercise or recreation of the inhabitants of any locality or of which such inhabitants have a customary right to indulge in lawful sports or pastimes or on which they have indulged in such sports and pastimes as of right for not less than 20 years. (A.A. 1971, s. 11; C.R.A. 1965, s. 22(1).)

[4] A.A. 1971, s. 8.

[5] "Horse" includes pony, ass and mule. (H.A. 1980, s. 329 (1).)

[6] Animals are not "straying" if they are under the control of an attendant. (*Lawrence v. King* (1868).)

[7] The presence of a keeper by itself is not an excuse for "lying", but apparently animals on a journey may be allowed to rest for a reasonable time. (*Lawrence v. King* as above; *Horwood v. Goodall, etc.* (1872).)

[8] "Highway" means the whole or part of a highway other than a ferry or waterway, and includes a bridge over or a tunnel through which the highway passes; (H.A. s. 328 (1), (2)). Within this definition, a highway is, briefly, any road or other way over which the public has the right to pass to and fro.

[9] "Keeper" means the person in whose possession the animals are (H.A. 1980, s. 155 (11). As to "possession", see p. 65.

[10] H.A. 1980 s. 155(3).

to a pound[1] but if so must feed and water them.[2] Presumably,[3] such person might also remove them to their owner's premises.

These provisions do not apply in the case of a person having a right to pasture his animals on the side of a highway[4] but a keeper exercising this right must keep his animals from straying, except temporarily, or lying on the actual road.[5]

Except in the Greater London area, cattle[6] found at large in streets[7] without any person having charge of them may be impounded by any constable or resident in any common pound within the district or in such other place as the local authority may appoint for the purpose. They may be detained until the owner pays the authority a maximum penalty of £2 and the reasonable expenses of impounding and keeping them. The cattle may be sold if the money is not paid in three days, but seven days notice of the sale must first be given to the owner of the cattle or, if he is not known, by newspaper advertisement.[8]

Trespass by Wild Animals

A landowner is not liable for damage caused by wild animals from his land "trespassing" on and causing damage to another's land, unless he brings on to his land a greater quantity of wild animals than can reasonably and properly be kept on it. Mere failure to keep the existing stock of wild animals within reasonable limits is another matter, and

---

[1] *Halsbury's Laws of England*, 4th Ed., Vol. 2, para. 431, note 15.

[2] P.A.A. 1911, s. 7(1). He may be fined if he fails to do so. Food and water may be given to them by anyone if the animals are without them for 6 hours. In either case, the cost of food and water is chargeable to the animal's owner. (P.A.A. 1911, s. 11.)

[3] The law does not appear to cover the point.

[4] H.A. 1980, s. 155(5).

[5] *Halsbury's Laws of England*, 4th Ed., Vol. 2, para. 431.

[6] "Cattle" includes horses, asses, mules, sheep, goats and swine. (T.P.C.A. 1847, s. 3.)

[7] A. "street" means any street, road, square, court, alley, thoroughfare or public passage. (T.P.C.A. 1847, ss. 2, 3.)

[8] T.P.C.A. 1847, ss, 24, 25; P.H.A. 1875, s. 171; L.G.A. 1972, s. 180(2), Schedule 14, paras. 23, 26.

there would, for example, be no liability for a natural increase of rabbits on one person's land which caused damage to his neighbour's.[1]

If a man reclaims wild animals and puts them on his land, he is liable, if they trespass, for any damage caused by them which it is in their ordinary nature to commit. A question still open is for how long the owner of a reclaimed animal is liable after its escape; this may depend on whether, at the time of damage, the animal has fully reverted to its wild state.[2]

Animals and Vehicles on Roads

When a collision occurs on a public road between an animal and a vehicle and damage, injury or death is caused, the principles discussed on pages 9, 14 and 15 will be relevant in deciding where responsibility should lie. Breach of one of the duties there described will make the person in breach responsible. That is not to say that the driver of the vehicle involved has no duty of care in driving. Careless driving causing death or injury to an animal whose presence or behaviour on the road was blameless will make the driver liable. Often a measure of blame attaches to both sides in which case damages claimed will be reduced or apportioned.

The circumstances in which accidents of this kind may happen vary widely; the principles mentioned have to be applied to the facts of each case. A conclusion which emerges from what is said earlier on pages 14 to 15 is that a driver passing by unfenced land on which animals may be should be especially careful.

As a matter of criminal law, if owing to the presence of

---

[1] *Halsbury's Laws of England*, 4th Ed., Vol. 2, para 434. As to control of rabbits generally, *see* pp. 161–168.
[2] *Halsbury's Laws of England*, 4th Ed., Vol. 2, para. 430.

a motor vehicle[1] on a road[2] an accident occurs whereby personal injury is caused to an animal[3] (other than an animal in or on that motor vehicle or a trailer[4] drawn by it), the driver of the vehicle must stop.[5] If required to do so by any person having reasonable grounds for so requiring, the driver must give his name and address, the name and address of the vehicle's owner and the identification marks, i.e., the registration number, of the vehicle.[6] If he does not give his name and address,[7] he must report the accident at a police station or to a police constable as soon as reasonably practicable, and in any case within 24 hours of the accident.[8] Failure to comply with any of these requirements is an offence.[9]

The person in charge of any animal[10] which is carried by a vehicle[11] using a motorway shall so far as practicable secure that—

(a) the animal shall not be removed from or permitted to leave the vehicle while the vehicle is on the motorway **and**

(b) if it escapes from, or it is necessary for it to be removed from or permitted to leave, the vehicle,—

---

[1] "Motor vehicle" means a mechanically propelled vehicle intended or adapted for use on roads, but excludes: a mechanically propelled vehicle being an implement for cutting grass controlled by a pedestrian and not capable of being used or adapted for any other purpose; and any other mechanically propelled vehicle controlled by a pedestrian which may be specified by regulations made by the Secretary of State. (R.T.A. 1972, ss. 190(1), 193(1).)

[2] "Road" means any highway and any other road to which the public has access, and includes bridges over which a road passes. (R.T.A. 1972, s. 196(1).). As to "highway", see the brief non-statutory meaning in note 8 on p. 15.

[3] "Animal" means any horse, cattle, ass, mule, sheep, pig, goat or dog. (R.T.A. 1972, s. 25(3).)

[4] "Trailer" means a vehicle drawn by a motor vehicle. (R.T.A. 1972, s. 190(1).)

[5] A driver should stop for such time as in the circumstances will enable any person entitled to do so to require the information from the driver personally. (Lee v. Knapp (1966).)

[6] R.T.A. 1972, s. 25(1).

[7] This includes the case where nobody requires this information from the driver. (Peek v. Towle (1945).)

[8] R.T.A. 1972, s. 25(2).

[9] R.T.A. 1972, s. 25(4). No offence is committed by a driver who does not stop, being unaware that an accident has happened. (Harding v. Price (1948).)

[10] The word "animal" is not defined.

[11] The word "vehicle" is not defined but will include a trailer.

(i) it shall not go or remain on any part of the motorway other than a verge,[1] **and**

(ii) it shall whilst it is not on or in the vehicle be held on a lead or otherwise kept under proper control.[2]

But the person in charge of the animal need not comply with these requirements if so directed by the police or if such is indicated by a traffic sign.[3]

There still remains on the statute book a sizeable body of law regulating animal traffic on public roads and in other public places which has been inherited from the pre-motor age when horses were used for transport and farm animals were more commonly to be found on roads than they are now. It is not proposed here to deal in detail with these matters, which have only slight relevance in modern times, but rather to indicate those aspects on which legislation impinges so as to warn the reader of their existence.

Such aspects are: the driving, leading or riding of animals on footpaths at the sides of roads or their tethering which allows them to go on roads is generally not allowed; the turning loose, selling, cleaning, dressing, shoeing, bleeding, treating, exercising, breaking or slaughtering of animals on public roads or in other public places is forbidden; regulations exist about the marking, loading, construction and driving of horse-drawn vehicles, and about the leading or driving of animals through streets and their hiring there.

Nuisances

The keeping of any animals in such a position or in such circumstances as to cause a substantial discomfort or annoyance to the public in general or to a particular person constitutes, in law, the civil wrong of nuisance for which action may be taken in the courts. Examples from law cases include instances of a large number of pigs in premises adjoining a

---

[1] "Verge" means any part of a motorway which is not a carriageway or central reservation. (Motorways Traffic Regulations 1959 (S.I. 1959/1147), Art 3(1)(h).)
[2] 1959 Regulations, Art. 13.
[3] 1959 Regulations, Art. 15.

village street,[1] and cockerels crowing in the early morning.[2] The remedy is the award of damages or the granting of an injunction.[3]

In addition to the nuisances just described which derive from the common law, Parliament has created what are known as statutory nuisances. It is a statutory nuisance to keep any animal in such a place or manner as to be injurious, or likely to cause injury, to health, or to be a nuisance.[4] The proceedings which can be taken to remedy statutory nuisances may be summarised as follows.

The local authority,[5] if they are satisfied that a statutory nuisance exists, may serve an abatement notice on the person causing it requiring him to abate it.[6] If the notice is not complied with, the person served with it may be summoned before a magistrates' court who, if it is proved that the nuisance exists or is likely to recur on the same premises, will make a nuisance order requiring the abatement notice to be complied with[6] or prohibiting a recurrence of the nuisance or both. Fines may be imposed at the same time as a nuisance order is made, on conviction for contravening a nuisance order and for each day of contravention of an order after conviction. Non-compliance with a nuisance order entitles the local authority to abate the nuisance themselves and to recover their reasonable expenses from the person on whom the order was made. They may also recover their expenses incurred in court proceedings.[7]

---

[1] *Attorney-General v. Squire* (1906).

[2] *Leeman v. Montagu* (1936).

[3] An injunction is an order of the court forbidding the committing of a further nuisance, the penalty for non-compliance usually being imprisonment.

[4] P.H.A. 1936, ss. 92(1)(*b*), 343(1); L.G.A. 1963, s. 40. The meaning of "nuisance" in this context is imprecise. It appears to mean an activity affecting public health though not necessarily causing injury to health or annoyance to any particular person or injury to any particular property. (*Halsbury's Laws of England*, 4th Ed., Vol. 38, para. 403.)

[5] This is the district council outside London; in London it is the borough council, the Common Council of the City of London, or the Sub-Treasurer or Under-Treasurer in the Temples. (P.H.A. 1936, s. 1(1).)

[6] An abatement notice or a nuisance order may also require works to be done if necessary for the abatement.

[7] P.H.A. 1936, ss. 93–96.

Byelaws dealing with nuisances caused by animals are mentioned on pages 203 to 204 and 209.

CHAPTER 2

SALE AND AGISTMENT

A. SALE

Generally

In law domestic animals are treated as goods and chattels for sale purposes, and the ordinary law about sale of goods applies to them. Since there can be no absolute ownership of wild animals whilst alive,[1] they cannot be bought and sold.

The buying of an animal can be hazardous for no prudence can guard against all latent defects. A buyer can gain protection in law through requiring a condition or warranty of quality as part of the sale. Otherwise, the legal tag "*caveat emptor*" applies, that is, "let the buyer beware", and he must accept the animal as he finds it then and later and have no redress.

However, Acts of Parliament since 1893 have intervened to give buyers of goods (and therefore of domestic animals) some protection when there is no expressed condition or warranty on a sale. The position is complicated, and for a

---

[1] *See* p. 4.

full understanding of this protection the legislation[1] itself must be studied. Mainly and briefly, a buyer is entitled to expect: that his seller has the right to sell the animal; that the animal is reasonably fit for any particular purpose which he makes known to the seller (being one who is acting in the course of a business) showing that the buyer is relying on the seller's skill or judgment; and that the animal is not subject to any charge or incumbrance not known to the buyer.[2]

Since 1st February 1978 sellers' rights to exclude or restrict their liabilities on sales of goods by means of exemption clauses and guarantees have been limited.[3]

Notwithstanding these provisions, it is wise and usual for a buyer to protect himself by requiring an express warranty with the animal to cover any quality or virtue which he needs. He may equally well do this by making the matter in question a condition of his purchase. The difference is that if a condition is broken the buyer may repudiate the contract which means that he may return the animal and be entitled to have his money back; but a warranty is collateral to the main purpose of a sale and breach of it only entitles the buyer to sue the seller for the loss thereby suffered.[4]

A buyer should therefore carefully consider, not only what protection he needs, but also whether he wants it in the terms of a warranty or a condition. Obviously, either should be in writing and signed by the seller. In law both are effective if given orally, but then dispute may follow as to what was actually said and whether it was a warranty or a condition.

A statement by the seller that an animal is sound will on the face of it amount only to a warranty, but if he also undertakes to take back the animal if it proves not to be as stated, the warranty becomes a condition.[5]

---

[1] U.C.T.A. 1977 and S.G.A. 1979 are the principal Acts outside hire purchase legislation.
[2] S.G.A. 1979 ss 12(1)(2), 14(3).
[3] see U.C.T.A. 1977.
[4] S.G.A. 1979 s. 61(1).
[5] *Harling v. Eddy* [1951] 2 A.E.R. at 215.

Warranties

A warranty is not intended to guard against a defect which is obvious to the senses. This implies the use of ordinary care in examination of the animal by the buyer if he inspects it beforehand. If he does not inspect it, a warranty will cover patent defects.[1] Likewise, if the seller warrants the animal with the intention of preventing the buyer from examining it and discovering a patent defect, or if the seller uses any other artifice to conceal such a defect.[2] A person buying a horse, knowing it to be blind, cannot sue the seller on a general warranty of soundness.[3]

A person authorised by the owner as his agent to sell an animal is not necessarily authorised to give a warranty. It appears that, certainly in cases of selling horses,[4] a warranty given by an employee or agent of a horse-dealer will be effective against the horse-dealer, even though he expressly forbade the giving of a warranty or even if it was shown that it was not customary for horse-dealers to give warranties. But a dealer will not be bound by an unauthorised warranty given by his employee outside the negotiation of the sale; for example, by something said by the employee when delivering the animal after sale. On the other hand, in the case of a private sale, a warranty given by his employee or agent without authority will not bind the seller unless the sale is at a fair or other public market.

A buyer sending an employee with instructions to accept a horse with a warranty has been held by the Court not to be bound if the employee accepts it without a warranty, and the buyer could return the horse.[5]

No particular form of words is necessary to make a warranty; the word "warranty" need not be used. A warranty covers the defects warranted against, whether known to the warrantor or not, unless special words are

---

[1] *Drew v. E.* (1412) Y.B. 13 Hen. 4, fol. 1B.

[2] *Dorrington v. Edwards* (1621).

[3] *Margetson v. Wright* (1831) 7 Bing at 605.

[4] Though the principle stated is based upon cases concerning the selling of horses, it is suggested that it would be equally applicable to sales of other animals.

[5] *Halsbury's Laws of England*, 4th Ed., Vol. 2, para. 221.

used to limit it to defects within the seller's knowledge. To be effective the warranty must be given at the time of bargaining and sale and before the sale is completed.

If the word "warranty" is used, the warranty extends only to so much wording as is governed by that word. If the word is used alone without referring to any particular quality of the animal, it is taken to relate to its soundness only. The warranty may be limited in any way by the words used, and any quality may be warranted.

The fact that the price is a good or fair price for a sound animal is not a warranty of soundness. Statements of fact in an auctioneer's catalogue conferring additional value on the animal sold amount to warranties. Unless a warranty is so worded as to extend to the future, it relates only to facts as they are at the time of the sale.[1]

If at the time of sale an animal has any disease or defect which actually diminishes, or in its ordinary progress will diminish, its natural usefulness, it is not sound. The slightness of a disease, or the ease with which it is cured, may affect the amount which can be claimed for breach of warranty but does not affect the principle, unless so trifling as not to amount to unsoundness at all. A cough and temporary lameness have thus both been decided to be unsoundness.[2]

A breach of warranty does not affect the sale of the animal; ownership passes to the buyer notwithstanding. His remedy is to claim from, and if necessary sue in the courts, the seller for the amount of loss caused by the breach. The buyer should give notice to the seller of alleged breach of warranty as soon as possible, though this is not absolutely necessary.[3]

Return of Animal on Breach of Condition

If a buyer has reserved a right to return the animal within a specified time, he may return it at any time within that

---

[1] *Halsbury's Laws of England*, 4th Ed., Vol. 2, paras, 222, 224.
[2] The same, para. 223.
[3] The same, paras, 225, 226.

period and is not bound to do so the moment he discovers the defect; so that if any injury happens to the animal while in his possession and without his fault, he is not liable for it and may still return the animal within the period. If the animal under these circumstances becomes injured so that it cannot be returned within the specified time, the non-return of the buyer within that time will not bar a claim for breach of warranty.

If an animal is sold with a condition that it may be returned within a specified period in case of unsuitability or for any other reason, and it dies in that period without the buyer's fault, the loss falls on the seller.[1]

Selling Diseased Animals

In a sale of diseased animals without any warranty or condition being given by the seller the maxim *"caveat emptor"* applies, unless the seller was guilty of fraud, and the buyer suffers the loss even though the seller may be committing an offence.[2]

Sales by Old Clothes Dealers to Children

It is an offence punishable by a fine for a person who collects or deals in rags, old clothes or similar articles, or for anyone assisting him or acting on his behalf, to sell or deliver, gratuitously or not, to a child under 14 years of age any animal—

(a) in or from any shop or premises[3] used for or in connection with the business of a dealer in the articles described; **or**

(b) while engaged in collecting any such articles.[4]

B. AGISTMENT

A contract of agistment is a contract under which one man, the agister, takes another man's cattle, horses or other

---

[1] *Halsbury's Laws of England*, 4th Ed., Vol. 2, para. 227.
[2] The same, para, 219. For such an offence, *see* p. 175.
[3] "Premises" means lands as well as buildings. (P.H.A. 1936, s. 343(1).)
[4] P.H.A. 1936, s. 154; P.H.A. 1961, s. 42.

animals to graze on his land for reward, usually at a certain rate per week. It is implied that he will redeliver the animals to their owner on demand. The contract need not be in writing.

The agister is not an insurer of the beasts taken by him, but he must take reasonable and proper care of them and is liable for injury caused to them by negligence or neglect of such care. However, if the animals' owner is aware of the dangerous state of a field in which the animals are to be pastured, the agister will not be liable for injury thereby caused. If the animals are stolen, even without the agister's fault, he is expected to use reasonable diligence to recover them; otherwise he may be liable for their loss.

In the absence of special agreement, the agister has no right to keep the animals until paid (in law called "a lien"); his remedy is to sue their owner for the price of the grazing. He has, however, sufficient property in the animals to entitle him to take legal action against others who improperly take or interfere with the animals.[1]

---

[1] *Halsbury's Laws of England*, 4th Ed., Vol. 2, paras 214–216.

CHAPTER 3

IMPORT, EXPORT AND MOVEMENT OF ANIMALS

A. IMPORT

Generally

There is no general rule of law prohibiting the import of animals into this country. But Government Ministers[1] have wide powers under the Animal Health Act 1981 through orders which they can make to prohibit and regulate the import[2] of animals,[3] poultry and other things by which disease might be carried, by sea or air, into Great Britain[4] for the purpose of preventing the introduction or spreading of disease[5] into or within the country.[6] By means of these orders, or regulations as they are sometimes called, controls may be exercised over ships, boats, aircraft, hovercraft and vehicles of other descriptions, and over persons, animals, poultry and other things which have been or may have been in contact with imports. More particularly, the regulations may deal with: the points of entry to which landings are to be restricted; quarantine; seizure, detention and treatment on import; marking, testing and slaughter of animals, and compensation; movement of persons and animals; cleansing and disinfection of premises, places and vehicles; and rights of inspection.[7]

Inspectors[8] have extensive rights of entry to ships, boats,

---

[1] The functions of Ministers under AHA 1981 and under orders made under it or its predecessors are variously divided between the Minister of Agriculture and the Secretaries of State for Scotland and Wales. In this Chapter, for convenience, the expression "the Minister" is used to cover all situations.

[2] An animal is imported when it is brought to Great Britain from a country out of Great Britain. (A.H.A. 1981 s. 89(1)). See note [4] below for the meaning of "Great Britain".

[3] The expression "animal" in this context includes; (a) any kind of mammal except man; (b) any kind of four-footed beast which is not a mammal; and (c) fish, reptiles, crustaceans and other cold-blooded creatures not within (a) or (b). (AHA 1981 s. 10(4))

[4] "Great Britain" means England, Wales and Scotland, and excludes the Channel Islands and the Isle of Man.

[5] In this context the meaning of "disease" is unrestricted. (AHA 1981 s. 10(4)).

[6] A.H.A. 1981, s. 10(1)–(3).

[7] AHA 1981, ss. 10(2), (3), 90, Sch. 2.

[8] I.e., diseases of animals inspectors appointed by the Minister or local authority, the latter being county councils or, in London, borough councils and the Common Council of the City of London. (A.H.A. 1981, ss. 50 (1)(2), 89 (1)).

aircraft, hovercraft, vehicles, lands, buildings and other places.[1]

Other Acts of Parliament[2] give the Ministers or the Secretary of State for the Environment further powers to regulate or prohibit the import of animals. The application of all these powers to particular animals, or classes of them, are considered in the following Sections.

In addition to the foregoing controls which are specific to the import of animals, import licences are required for the import of goods generally into Great Britain[3]. Animals consigned from the Channel Islands are exempted[4]

Cattle, Sheep, Goats, all other Ruminating[5] Animals and Swine

The import of these kinds of animals is governed by the Importation of Animals Order 1977. It is illegal to land[6] or attempt to land them in Great Britain[3] without a licence from the Minister or except in accordance with the terms and conditions of such a licence.[7] The Minister may attach to it such conditions as he sees fit to prevent the introduction or spreading of disease[8] into or within Great Britain or to protect animals from unnecessary suffering on landing and during inland transit.[9] Every licence will designate the ports and airports at which the animals must be landed and, unless

---

[1] A.H.A. 1981, ss. 63 (5)(6), 90.

[2] D.I.A.A. 1932, D.N.H.A. 1949; E.S.A. 1976.

[3] "Great Britain" means England, Wales and Scotland, and excludes the Channel Islands and the Isle of Man.

[4] Import of Goods (Control) Order 1954 (S.I. 1954/23), Arts, 1, 2, 3. Some imports are covered by general or open general licences. Enquiries and applications for licences should be made to the Department of Trade, Import Licensing Branch, Charles House, 375 Kensington High Street, London W14 8QH.

[5] "Ruminating" means cud-chewing, and for the purpose of the provisions considered in this Section ruminating animals will include llamas, guanacos, alpacas, vicunas, Bactrian camels and Arabian camels. (Importation of Animals Order 1977 (S.I. 1977/944), Art. 2(1).)

[6] An animal is deemed to have been landed, if carried by sea, immediately it is put or otherwise arrives on land in Great Britain or, if carried by air, immediately the aircraft carrying it touches down in Great Britain. (1977 Order, Art. 2(3).)

[7] 1977 Order, Arts. 3(1), (2), 21(2).

[8] "Disease" means any disease of animals. (1977 Order, Art. 2(1).)

[9] 1977 Order, Art. 3(3).

re-exported within the terms of the licence, the premises to which they are to be moved after landing.[1]

An import licence may be general or specific.[2] The general licence will be used for the import of cattle, pigs, sheep and goats from Northern Ireland, the Republic of Ireland, the Channel Islands and the Isle of Man. It will be issued by publicising its provisions in such manner as the Minister thinks necessary to bring its terms to the attention of those likely to be affected by it.[3] The specific licence will be appropriate for importing high quality livestock from other countries and for small numbers of zoo animals. An application for it should be made to the Import of Livestock Section AH IB, Ministry of Agriculture, Fisheries and Food, Hook Rise South, Tolworth, Surbiton, Surrey, KT6 7NF, for imports into England and Wales, and to the Department of Agriculture and Fisheries for Scotland, Chesser House, 500 Gorgie Road, Edinburgh, EH11 3AW, for imports into Scotland.[4]

Either kind of licence may be revoked or varied by the Minister at any time.[5] This will be done, in the case of a general licence, by publication of a notice in the same way as the issue of the licence was published, or, in the case of a specific licence, by written notice to the person to whom it was issued.[6]

A licence is also needed for animals on board a vessel[7] which enters a harbour, even if the animals are not to be landed.[8]

After landing, imported animals must be moved to an

---

[1] 1977 Order, Arts. 3(5), 9(1).

[2] 1977 Order, Art. 3(3).

[3] 1977 Order, Art. 3(4).

[4] Enquiries about the 1977 Order and general licences should be made to the same addresses.

[5] But this will not prejudice anything lawfully done under a licence before the revocation or variation takes effect by publication or notice as described above. (1977 Order, Art. 3(6).)

[6] 1977 Order, Art. 3(6).

[7] "Vessel" includes hovercraft. (1977 Order, Art. 2(1).)

[8] 1977 Order, Art. 16.

approved reception centre[1] for resting or to approved quarantine premises[1] for the period specified in their import licence before they are allowed to go on to their final destination in Great Britain. Detention in quarantine depends on the disease risk involved in the animals' import. Detailed requirements are laid down about the action to be taken in case of injury, death or disease among imported animals and about their unloading and movement afterwards. Inspectors of the Ministry or local authority can require the cleansing and disinfection of vessels, aircraft, vehicles and containers which have brought the animals to Great Britain or which have become contaminated with animal matter. Where disease is found among imported animals, veterinary inspectors may require them to be slaughtered,[2] re-exported or detained subject to conditions. Similar powers are given to inspectors where there has been a breach of the 1977 Order or of the terms of the import licence. Where disease is found among animals at a reception centre or quarantine premises, veterinary inspectors can impose conditions on them and their use.

Wide default powers are given by the Order to enable the authorities to ensure that the requirements of the Order and of the different processes under it are properly carried out; the authorities can recover their reasonable expenses thus incurred.[3]

Cattle, Sheep and Pigs

The following provisions of the Imported Livestock Order of 1958[4] are designed to safeguard the Exchequer payments

---

[1] These premises are approved under licence from the Minister which may have conditions attached. The premises are subject to control by veterinary inspectors. (1977 Order, Arts. 10–11).

[2] The Minister is not liable to pay compensation in such cases and, moreover, may recover his reasonable expenses of slaughtering from the animals' owner. (1977 Order, Art. 19(1).)

[3] 1977 Order, Arts 4–19.

[4] S.I. 1958/558.

made under the Fatstock Guarantee Scheme for fatstock in the United Kingdom.

Unless authorised by the Minister, livestock (meaning the animals described in the heading above[1]) can only be brought into the United Kingdom[2] from the Channel Islands, the Isle of Man or the Republic of Ireland at one of the ports or by one of the land routes mentioned in the 1958 Order and, as regards the land routes, between the times mentioned. The ports in Great Britain are: Ayr, Birkenhead, Cardiff, Fishguard, Glasgow, Greenock, Heysham, Holyhead, Southampton and Stranraer. Those in Northern Ireland are: Belfast, Larne, Londonderry and Newry. The specified land routes are road and railway routes between the Republic of Ireland and Northern Ireland.[3]

Livestock so imported are not to be moved from the reception lair or port or point of entry until each has been examined and, where necessary, marked by or under the supervision of an authorised officer,[4] unless there is a special authorisation from the Minister.[5]

Other provisions in the 1958 Order deal with:—

(a) The ways in which imported livestock are to be marked. Registered pedigree livestock imported for breeding are exempt.[6]

(b) The forfeiture and seizure of livestock and their vehicles and containers when the stock is imported in contravention of the Order.[7]

(c) The powers of entry of authorised officers[4] on to land,

---

[1] In N. Ireland the term "livestock" includes also the carcases of pigs. (1958 Order, Art. 2(1).)

[2] *I.e.*, England, Wales, Scotland and N. Ireland.

[3] 1958 Order, Art. 3, and First Schedule.

[4] "Authorised officer" means any person authorised by the Minister and shall be deemed to include any constable or police officer, and in N. Ireland any member of the Royal Ulster Constabulary or a Special Constable on full-time police duty. (1958 Order, Art. 2(1).)

[5] 1958 Order, Art. 4.

[6] 1958 Order, Art. 6.

[7] 1958 Order, Arts. 7–15;

premises, vehicles and containers to check on illegally imported stock.[1]

(*d*) The exemption from the provisions of the Order of livestock brought into Northern Ireland from named places.[2]

Horses

Under the Importation of Equine Animals Order 1979 no equine animal[3] may be imported into Great Britain[4] from a place outside Great Britain except in accordance with a licence issued by the Minister; conditions may be attached to the licence.[5] There are two kinds of licence; a general licence which must be publicised to bring it to the attention of persons likely to be affected by it and a specific licence which is delivered to the licensee.[6]

A veterinary inspector, knowing or suspecting that an equine animal affected with disease has been landed in Great Britain, may by written notice served on its owner or the person in charge of it require him at his expense to detain or isolate it and take such other steps as the notice may specify, to subject it to tests, to export it or to slaughter it. In default, the inspector may carry out the notice's requirements.

The same procedure applies when an equine animal is

---

[1] 1958 Order, Art. 17(2), (3).

[2] 1958 Order, Art. 18, and Fourth Schedule. For regulations about certification and marking of sheep for the purpose of premium payments under E.E.C. arrangements, see the Sheep Variable Premium (Protection of Payments) (No. 2) Order 1980 (S.I. 1980/1811),

[3] The expression "equine animal" means a horse, ass, zebra or any cross-breed thereof (Importation of Equine Animals Order 1979 (S.I. 1979/1701), para 3).

[4] For meaning of "Great Britain", *see* note [3] on p. 30.

[5] Non-compliance with a condition is an offence which can be prosecuted.

[6] Applications for both kinds of licences should be made, in the case of landings in England or Wales, to the Import of Horses Section, Ministry of Agriculture, Fisheries and Food, Hook Rise South, Tolworth, Surbiton, Surrey KT6 7NF, or to the Department of Agriculture and Fisheries for Scotland, Chesser House, 500 Gorgie Road, Edinburgh, EH11 3AW, for landings in Scotland.

or has been landed contrary to the 1979 Order[1] or to the terms of any licence granted. No compensation is payable by the Minister for the slaughter of the animal under any of these provisions. The reasonable expenses of the inspector in taking the actions described are payable to the Minister by the owner or person in charge of the animal, who is also required to give "all reasonable assistance" to the inspector in taking those actions. Any contravention of the order or of a licence or notice is an offence.[2]

No docked[3] horse[4] coming from a place outside the United Kingdom[5] shall be landed from a ship, aircraft or hovercraft[6] unless permitted by Customs or licensed by the Minister[7] A Customs officer will not give permission unless satisfied that the horse will be exported from Great Britain as soon as practicable. The Minister will not grant a licence unless he is satisfied that the horse is to be used for breeding purposes.[8] It is an offence to land a docked horse illegally, or to make a false statement for the purpose of obtaining a permission or a licence.[9]

Hares

The landing in Great Britain of live hares from any country except the Channel Islands, the Isle of Man, Northern Ireland and the Republic of Ireland is prohibited unless authorised by licence of the Minister.[10] If this prohibi-

---

[1] A landing without a licence would be contrary to the Order.

[2] 1979 Order, paras 4–6, 7(1)(2), 9.

[3] 'Docked" means having had deliberately removed any bone or any part of a bone from the horse's tail. (D.N.H.A. 1949, s. 3.).

[4] "Horse" in this context includes stallion, gelding, colt, mare, filly, pony, mule and hinny (offspring of she-ass by stallion). (D.N.H.A. 1949, s. 3).

[5] *I.e.*, England, Wales, Scotland and Northern Ireland, excluding the Channel Islands and the Isle of Man.

[6] H.A. 1968, s. 3, Sch. para. 1(*e*).

[7] D.N.H.A. 1949, s. 2(1). Applications for licences should be sent in all cases to the Import of Livestock Section AH IIC at the Ministry's Tolworth address given in note 6 on p. 34.

[8] D.N.H.A. 1949, s. 2(2).

[9] D.N.H.A. 1949, s. 2(3), (4).

[10] Applications for licences should be sent to the addresses given in note [6] on p. 34.

tion is breached or a condition of a licence contravened, the Minister may by notice require the importer,[1] if the hares are not exported within the time given in the notice, to have them slaughtered. In default, a Ministry or local authority inspector may seize the hares and have them slaughtered. The importer must give the inspector all necessary facilities to do these things, and the inspector's expenses may be recovered from him.

A licence must accompany the hares throughout their movement and be produced on demand to such an inspector, a Customs officer or a police officer. The person in charge must allow a copy or extract of the licence to be taken, and, if required, give his name and address.

The master of every ship, aircraft and hovercraft[2] must before arrival in Great Britain inform the person in charge of live hares on board of these requirements.[3]

Destructive Animals

Under the Destructive Imported Animals Act 1932 the Minister may make orders prohibiting, either absolutely or except under licence, the import into and the keeping within Great Britain[4] of musk-rats (*fiber zibethicus*) or musquash (*ondetra zibethica*).[5] The Minister may make orders of the same effect applying to any animals of any non-indigenous mammalian species[6] if he is satisfied that by reason of their destructive habits it is desirable to prohibit or control their import or keeping in this country and to destroy any which may be at large.[7]

---

[1] "Importer" is defined to include any person who is in possession of a consignment of hares or is in any way entitled to their custody or control. (Hares (Control of Importation) Order 1965 (S.I. 1965/2040), Art. 2(1)).

[2] Hovercraft are included by virtue of the Hovercraft (Application of Enactments) Order 1972 (S.I. 1972/971), Art. 4, Sch. 1, Part B.

[3] Hares (Control of Importation) Order 1965.

[4] For meaning of "Great Britain", see note [3] on p. 30.

[5] D.I.A.A. 1932, s. 1(1).

[6] "Non-indigenous mammalian species" means a mammalian species which on 17th March 1932 was not established in a wild state in Great Britain or had only become so established during the preceding 50 years; but any species commonly kept in Great Britain on that date in a domesticated state is excluded from the definition. (D.I.A.A. 1932, s. 10(2).)

[7] D.I.A.A. 1932, s. 10(1).

The Minister may at his discretion grant licences authorising the importing and keeping of these kinds of animals[1] in accordance with the terms of the licences and regulations which he may make. Licences are renewable but may be revoked on failure to comply with those terms or if the holder is convicted of an offence under the 1932 Act.[2]

A person wishing to keep these kinds of animals[1] for exhibition, scientific research or other exceptional purposes may apply to the Minister to grant him a special licence (revocable at any time) authorising him to import and keep a limited number of the animals in the manner and upon the conditions described in the licence.[3]

A person commits an offence if—

(*a*) He imports, or attempts to import, these kinds of animals[1] at a time when their import is absolutely prohibited by order.

(*b*) He imports, or attempts to import, such animals without a covering licence at a time when their import is prohibited except under licence.

(*c*) Being the holder of a licence, he acts in contravention of any term of it or of the Minister's regulations.

(*d*) He obstructs an officer of, or a person authorised by or employed by or on behalf of, the Minister's department in the execution of his duties[4] under the 1932 Act.[5]

On conviction of an offence described at (*a*), (*b*) or (*c*) above, the court may order the animals concerned to be

---

[1] *I.e.*, any kind of animal in respect of which an order has been made as described above.

[2] D.I.A.A. 1932, s. 3.

[3] D.I.A.A. 1932, s. 8(1).

[4] Such duties will presumably include the seizure of animals described later in the text above.

[5] D.I.A.A. 1932, s. 6(1).

forfeited and destroyed.[1] A police officer and any person authorised by the Minister may seize animals when they have reason to believe that an offence under (*a*) or (*b*) above has been committed with respect to them. They may detain them until prosecution of the offence is completed or it is decided that a prosecution is unlikely.[2]

Under the order-making powers described on page 36 the import and keeping of musk-rats or musquash,[3] grey squirrels (*sciurus carolinensis*)[4] and rabbits other than the European rabbit (*oryctolagus cuniculus*)[5] are absolutely prohibited; *i.e* no licence can be granted. The import of mink and coypu, which was previously controlled by general licences issued by the Minister, is now governed by the Rabies (Importation, etc.) Order 1974.[6]

The provisions described above relate principally to the import of destructive animals. Other provisions (mainly about their keeping) will be found on pages 198 to 201.

Endangered Species

Following a convention on international trade in endangered species of wild fauna and flora in Washington in 1973, the Endangered Species (Import and Export) Act was passed in 1976.

Unless covered by a licence granted by the Secretary of State for the Environment,[7] the import or export of any live

---

[1] D.I.A.A. 1932, s. 6(1).

[2] D.I.A.A. 1932, s. 6(2).

[3] Musk-Rats (Prohibition of Importation and Keeping) Order 1933 (S.R. & O. 1933/106).

[4] Grey Squirrels (Prohibition of Importation and Keeping) Order 1937 (S.R. & O. 1937/478).

[5] Non-indigenous Rabbits (Prohibition of Importation and Keeping) Order 1954 (S.I. 1954/927).

[6] For the provisions of this Order, *see* pp. 42–44 and 220–221. Coypus are included in the list on p. 221 because they belong to the Order "*Rodentia*".

[7] So far as England and Wales are concerned, applications for licences should be addressed to the Wildlife Licensing Section, Room 310, Tollgate House, Houlton Street, Bristol BS2 9DJ. For an imported animal, an import licence is sometimes also required. Enquiries should be made of the Ministry of Agriculture at the address in note [6] on p. 34.

or dead animal[1] described in the Act is prohibited.[2] Such animals are mostly described by exception; in those cases the Act applies to all animals **except** those kinds which are listed. The list, so far as it relates to mammals, is given in Appendix A to this book. Birds, reptiles, amphibians, fish, insects, molluscs and plants are also listed in the Act as well as parts and products of them. The lists may be altered by the Secretary of State from time to time.[3]

A licence may be: general or specific; may be issued to all persons, to persons of a class or to a particular person; may be modified or revoked at any time and, subject to that, will be in force for such period as may be stated on it.[4] The Secretary of State must take scientific advice before deciding whether to issue a licence,[5] and he may charge a fee for it.[6] It appears that there is no right of appeal against a refusal to grant a licence.

It is an offence for a person to make a false statement or representation or to furnish a false document or information for the purpose of obtaining a licence, whether for himself or someone else, and a licence granted subsequently to these offences is made void.[7] Power is given to Customs to require any person possessing or having control of any live or dead animal[8] in course of being imported or exported, or which has been imported, to furnish proof that the import or export is or was not unlawful. If such proof is not furnished

---

[1] The only limitation on the meaning of "animal" is that it is not to include man. The words "dead animal" include the body of an animal which is frozen, dried or preserved by chemicals or which, though not complete (whether because eviscerated or because the whole of its inside has been removed and the animal stuffed, or for any other reason) is substantially complete and externally substantially resembles the complete body of the animal. (E.S.A. 1976, s. 12(1), (2).)

[2] E.S.A. 1976, s. 1(1), (2).

[3] E.S.A. 1976 ss. 3, 11.

[4] E.S.A. 1976 s. 1(4).

[5] E.S.A. 1976 s. 1(3), (3A)

[6] E.S.A. 1976 ss. 1(5), 11.

[7] E.S.A. 1976 s. 1(6), (7).

[8] Note that this power is not restricted to animals for which a licence is required. Thus, for example, an importer may have to prove that an imported animal is of a kind which does not need a licence.

to the satisfaction of Customs, the animal may be forfeited.[1]

The two principal offences under the 1976 Act are as next described, and the exceptions and defences which apply follow those descriptions.

A person who sells, offers or exposes for sale,[2] has in his possession[3] or transports for the purpose of sale, or displays to the public[4] a live or dead animal whose import was not in accordance with any required licence will commit an offence.[5]

The second offence has been newly created.[6] This occurs if a person sells, offers or exposes for sale,[2] or has in his possession[3] or transports for the purpose of sale—

(1) a live or dead mammal of any of the kinds listed in Appendix B[7] or an egg or other immature stage of such an animal or

(2) any part of, or anything which is derived from, or which is made wholly or partly from, anything referred to at (1) above.[8]

But the provisions relating to this last offence do not apply to—

(a) anything falling within the first offence, or

---

[1] E.S.A. 1976 s. 1(8). Customs' expenses consequent on forfeiture may be recovered from the importer or intending exporter of the animal or from anyone possessing or having control of it when it was seized (E.S.A. 1976 s. 1(9)).

[2] Any reference to sale includes references to hire, barter and exchange (E.S.A. 1976 s. 4(6)).

[3] For some notes on the meaning of "possession", see p. 65.

[4] An animal is deemed to be displayed to the public if it is displayed to the public generally or any section of it, and (in either case) whether in return for money or otherwise (E.S.A. 1976 s. 4(7)).

[5] E.S.A. 1976 s. 4(1). This offence applies in the same terms to many derivatives from endangered species which are listed in Sch. 3 to the Act.

[6] By WCA 1981 s. 15, Sch. 10, para. 3(2).

[7] Appendix B is derived from E.S.A. 1976 , Sch. 4, but does not include the birds, fish, reptiles, amphibians and molluscs listed in that Schedule. The Schedule may be modified from time to time by the Secretary of State (E.S.A. 1976 s. 3).

[8] E.S.A. 1976 s. 4(1A).

(*b*) anything which—

> (i) has been imported before 30th October 1981,[1] or
>
> (ii) is a part of, or derives from, or is made wholly or partly from, anything which has been imported before that date.

The defences available for both offences are:–

(A) That the act in question was done under and in accordance with the terms of a licence issued by the Secretary of State.[2]

(B) That the defendant proves to the satisfaction of the court—

> (i) that at the time when the animal or article which is the subject of the offence charged first came into his possession he made such enquiries (if any) as in the circumstances were reasonable to ascertain whether it was properly imported;
>
> **and**
>
> (ii) that, at the time the alleged offence was committed, he had no reason to believe that it was improperly imported.[3]

As a means[4] of showing to the court that he had made the enquiries needed under paragraph (i), a person prosecuted may produce to the court a certificate furnished and signed by his supplier, or a person authorised by him, stating that—

> (i) the supplier made enquiries at the time the animal came into his possession to ascertain whether it was properly imported; **and**
>
> (ii) the supplier had no reason to believe at the time he

---

[1] E.S.A. 1976 s. 4(1A). The date is the date on which the Wildlife and Countryside Act 1981 was passed.

[2] E.S.A. 1976 s. 4(1B). The provisions about licences mentioned on p. 39 will apply to this licence.

[3] E.S.A. 1976 s. 4(2).

[4] This does not exclude other means of demonstrating compliance with para. (i).

relinquished possession of the animal to the accused that the animal was at that time improperly imported.[1]

To assist in discovering the illegal import of animals, the Secretary of State may make orders prohibiting and regulating the import of live animals by certain means.[2]

Where a licence has been applied for or issued for a live animal, the Secretary of State may give "a direction" relating to the animal. This enables him to require the animal to be taken to premises nominated by him immediately after it completes its detention in quarantine or leaves other premises connected with its import, whichever is the later.[3] The animal must be kept at the nominated premises until the Secretary of State requires or permits it to be moved to other nominated premises or until he revokes his direction.[4] A number of offences is created for doing things contrary to these arrangements.[5]

The Secretary of State must take scientific advice before nominating premises in a direction, and must not nominate them unless in his opinion the animal may suitably be kept there. A person authorised by him in writing may at any reasonable time enter[6] nominated premises for one or both of the following purposes: to enable the Secretary of State to decide whether the premises remain suitable for the animal; to check whether the animal is being kept there.[7]

Restrictions to Prevent the Introduction of Rabies

For the purpose of preventing the introduction of rabies into Great Britain[8] the Minister made an order in 1974[9]

---

[1] E.S.A. 1976 s. 4(3). A supplier furnishing a false certificate is guilty of an offence. (E.S.A. 1976 s. 4(4).)

[2] E.S.A. 1976 ss. 5, 11. No such orders have yet been made.

[3] E.S.A. 1976, s. 6(1), (2), (4), (5).

[4] E.S.A. 1976, s. 6(2).

[5] E.S.A. 1976, s. 6(3).

[6] Wilful obstruction of entry is an offence. (E.S.A. 1976, s. 7(4).)

[7] E.S.A. 1976, s. 7(1)–(3).

[8] For meaning of "Great Britain", see note [3] on p. 30.

[9] The Rabies (Importation of Dogs, Cats and Other Mammals) Order 1974 (S.I. 1974/2211). There is a maximum fine of £1000 for contravention of the order (A.H.A. 1981 s. 75(2)(3); Rabies Virus Order 1979).

which controls the landing in this country of any animal belonging to the eleven orders of mammals which are listed in Parts I and II of Appendix C at the end of this book. The order prohibits the landing of those animals in Great Britain except under the authority of, and in accordance with the conditions of, a licence previously granted by the Minister.[1] However, licences are not needed for animals coming from Northern Ireland, the Irish Republic, the Channel Islands and the Isle of Man if they have not been outside the British Isles in the preceding six months. Nor is a licence necessary for an animal which is landed at a British port or airport for the purpose of re-export from the same port or airport within 48 hours, although in this case the animal is subjected to stringent controls on its movement, detention and isolation.

Other than in exceptional circumstances,[2] animals may only be licensed to be landed at the following ports and airports:

Ports	Airports
Dover, Eastern Docks	Birmingham
Harwich, Navyard Wharf	Edinburgh
Hull	Gatwick
Liverpool	Glasgow
International Hoverport,	Heathrow
Ramsgate (Pegwell Bay)	Leeds
Southampton	Manchester
	Prestwick

The animals must be moved as soon as practicable after landing to authorised quarantine premises.[3] All kinds of animals, except vampire bats, are quarantined for six

---

[1] The addresses to which applications for licences are to be sent are, depending on whether quarantine is to be in England or Wales, or in Scotland, those given in note [6] on p. 34, referring, in the former case, to the Import of Dogs and Cats Section.

[2] In exceptional circumstances the Minister may license an animal to be landed at another port or airport. Also, if the ship or aircraft is diverted in the interest of safety, or in other exceptional circumstances, the animal may be landed at a port or airport different from that for which it is licensed if the prior written authority of a Ministry inspector is given.

[3] *I.e.*, premises approved under licence from the Minister.

months. Offspring born in quarantine may be released 15 days after they have been weaned if both the dam and the offspring are certified to be healthy. Vampire bats and their progeny born here are quarantined for life. The expenses of maintaining animals in quarantine must be borne by their owners.[1]

During quarantine every dog and cat[2] must at its owner's expense be vaccinated against rabies. But if the Minister is satisfied that it has been brought to Great Britain for scientific research and vaccination might interfere with that, he may excuse vaccination.

The 1974 Order contains detailed provisions for the movement of animals during quarantine, the licensing of carrying agents[3] and of quarantine premises, and the control of animals which are on board a vessel in a British port. The Minister also has power to deal with certain animals[4] which come into contact with animals from abroad.

If an animal is landed illegally, or if there is a breach of the terms of licence, the animal may be destroyed by a Ministry or local authority inspector and the expenses of so doing recovered from its owner. Alternatively, the inspector may require the animal to be re-exported or detained in quarantine, also at the owner's expense. In addition, any person[5] contravening the Order may be prosecuted.

B.   EXPORT

Generally

As with the importing of animals, there is no general rule of law prohibiting the export of animals from this country.

---

[1] An authorised carrying agent, being in charge of an animal on landing, may also be liable for their expenses. (*City of London Corporation v. British Caledonian Airways* (1980).

[2] These are domestic dogs and cats only. (1974 Order, Art. 2(1).)

[3] The movement of an animal from quarantine for urgent veterinary treatment which is not available there can only be done by a carrying agent approved by the Minister.

[4] These animals are all those animals which are listed at Appendix C at the end of this book.

[5] Note that liability to prosecution is not restricted to owners of the animals.

However, the Minister is given certain powers over exports and related matters. He may provide facilities for the examination of animals[1] intended for export, and may provide or approve export quarantine stations for the reception, isolation and examination of such animals.[2] No compensation is payable for any animal intended for export which is slaughtered in an export quarantine station because it is diseased, suspected of disease[3] or having been exposed to infection.[4]

In the interests of animal or human health the Minister may make orders regulating the export from Great Britain[5] to a state which is a member of the European Communities of animals[1] or their carcases. In particular, he may prohibit exports without a prescribed certificate or licence, and provide for the circumstances in which and the conditions on which a certificate or licence may be obtained.[6]

An ordinary export licence must be obtained from the Department of Trade[7] for the export of any animal, except in the following cases:—

(a) Live animals of the bovine species, live swine and live sheep exported from Great Britain,[5] or from Northern Ireland to the Republic of Ireland.

(b) Any animals exported from the United Kingdom[8] to the Channel Islands.[9]

---

[1] For the meaning of "animals," see note 3 on p. 29.

[2] A.H.A. 1981, s. 12(1). Approval of, and movement of animals into and out of, export quarantine stations is regulated by the Export Quarantine Stations (Regulation) Order 1973 (S.I. 1973/824).

[3] In this context "disease" means cattle plague, pleuro-pneumonia, foot-and-mouth disease, sheep-pox, sheep scabs, or swine fever; by Ministerial order further animal diseases may be added to this list. (A.H.A. 1981, s. 88(1)(2)).

[4] A.H.A. 1981, ss. 3. 12(2), 89(1).

[5] For the meaning of "Great Britain", see note 3 on p. 30.

[6] A.H.A. 1981, s. 11.

[7] Some exports are covered by open general export licences. Enquiries and applications for licences should be sent to the Department of Trade, Export House, 50 Ludgate Hill, London E.C.4.

[8] "United Kingdom" means Great Britain and N. Ireland.

[9] Export of Goods (Control) Order 1978 (S.I. 1978/796), Art. 3(1)(b),(i).

Many foreign countries to which animals are exported from Great Britain require as a condition of issuing an import licence that the health of the animals shall be certified, usually by a Ministry vet, just before export.

Cattle,[1] Goats, Sheep and Swine

These animals may not be exported from Great Britain[2] to any place outside the United Kingdom,[3] the Channel Islands and the Isle of Man except under and in accordance with the terms of a Ministerial licence.[4] If export involves moving the animals across a frontier, they are to be rested for at least 10 consecutive hours in approved premises.[5] Detailed and lengthy requirements about the condition of these premises and the treatment of the animals while in them are laid down. Further provisions deal with loading, the inspection of animals for fitness to travel, and the banning of travel in adverse weather.[6] Exemption from all these requirements, except those relating to fitness to travel, manner of loading and the banning of travel in adverse weather, may be obtained by further Ministerial licence in the cases of:—

(a) pedigree animals intended for breeding;

(b) animals intended for breeding which are capable of imparting commercially valuable characteristics to their progeny;

(c) companion animals;

---

[1] "Cattle" means bulls, cows, steers, heifers and calves; and "calves" means cattle under the age of 6 months (Export of Animals (Protection) Order 1981 (S.I. 1981/1051), Art. 2(1)).

[2] For the meaning of "Great Britain", see note [3] on p. 30.

[3] That is, Great Britain and Northern Ireland.

[4] 1981 Order as above, Art. 3(1). Applications for licences are to be made as follows:

(a) For export to the EEC only; from England or Wales, to the local Animal Health Office of the Ministry of Agriculture;

(b) For export to non-EEC countries: from England, to the Ministry of Agriculture, Fisheries & Food, Animal Health IIB, Government Offices, Hook Rise South, Surbition, Surrey KT6 7NF; from Wales, to the Welsh Office Agriculture Department 2, Cathays Park 2, Cardiff CF1 3NQ.

[5] That is, approved by the Minister.

[6] 1981 Order, as above, Arts. 2(1), 4–6, Sch.

(*d*) animals intended for exhibition or other special purposes.[1]

Horses

The expression "horse" includes ass and mule.[2] It also includes a pony, and the provisions in this Section, except those immediately following dealing with examination and certification,[3] apply equally to ponies.[4] Other provisions restricted to ponies as defined are to be found in the next Section.

Except in the cases dealt with below, it is unlawful to ship, or attempt to ship, any horse in any vessel or aircraft from any port or aerodrome in Great Britain[5] to any port or aerodrome outside the United Kingdom,[6] the Channel Islands and the Isle of Man unless immediately before shipment the horse has been examined by a veterinary inspector appointed by the Minister of Agriculture and certified by the inspector to comply with the following conditions:[7]

(*a*) That it is capable of being conveyed to its landing place and disembarked without cruelty; **and**

(*b*) That it is capable of being worked without suffering; **and**

(*c*) That, if it is a heavy draft horse, vanner,[8] mule, jennet,[9] or ass, it is in the inspector's opinion not more than 8 years old and of not less than the following values—

---

[1] 1981 Order, as above, Arts. 10–13.
[2] A.H.A. 1981 s. 89(1).
[3] A.H.A. 1981 s. 40(1).
[4] For the distinction between ponies and other horses, *see* note [5] on p. 50.
[5] For the meaning of "Great Britain", *see* note [3] on p. 30.
[6] "United Kingdom" means Great Britain and N. Ireland.
[7] Exemption from these requirements may be granted by Ministerial order.
[8] A vanner is thought to be a horse suitable for pulling a van such as a milk float.
[9] A jennet is a small Spanish horse.

    (i) A heavy draft horse £715
    (ii) A vanner, mule or jennet £495
    (iii) An ass ... ... £220[1]

However, the inspector's certificate is not required to cover condition (a) above if he is satisfied that—

(1) it is intended to use the horse as a performing animal; **or**

(2) the horse is registered in the stud book of a society for the encouragement of horse breeding recognised by the Minister, and is intended to be used for breeding or exhibition; **or**

(3) the horse is a foal at foot accompanying such a horse as is described in (2) above.[2]

The inspector's certificate must be delivered at the time of shipment to the master of the vessel or the pilot of the aircraft on which the animal is shipped. He must produce it on demand to any constable[3] or to an inspector or other officer of the Minister or local authority, and allow them to take copies or extracts.[4]

If the inspector finds the horse to be in such a physical condition that it is cruel to keep it alive or to be permanently incapable of being worked without suffering, he may have it slaughtered. No compensation is payable to the owner.[5]

The inspector may, for identification, mark a horse certified by him as laid down by Ministerial order.[6] It is an offence for anyone else to mark a horse with a view to evading the certification process.[7]

If any horse shipped between the ports described in the second paragraph of this Section has a limb broken or is

---

[1] A.H.A. 1981, s. 40(2)(3). These values are increased from time to time by Ministerial order.

[2] A.H.A. 1981, s. 40(4).

[3] See note [5] on p. 162.

[4] A.H.A. 1981, s. 48.

[5] A.H.A. 1981, s. 44.

[6] A.H.A. 1981, s. 45(1). The relevant order is the Animals (Miscellaneous Provisions) Order 1938 (S.R.&O., No. 197), Art. 1(2).

[7] A.H.A. 1981 s. 45(2).

otherwise seriously injured while on board so as to be incapable of being disembarked without cruelty, the master of the vessel must have it slaughtered at once. Both the owner and master of a vessel exporting horses must see that it is provided with a proper slaughtering instrument.[1]

The provisions of the last paragraph and of the earlier paragraphs concerning inspectors' examinations and certificates do not apply in the case of shipment of any thoroughbred horse certified in writing by a steward or the secretary of the Jockey Club—

(a) to have arrived in Great Britain not more than one month before the date of shipment for the purpose of being run in a race; **or**

(b) to be shipped for the purpose of being run in a race; **or**

(c) to be shipped in order to be used for breeding purposes.[2]

The Jockey Club certificate must be delivered, produced, etc., in the same way as an inspector's certificate—see page 48.[3]

Examination and certification by a veterinary inspector are not needed for—

(i) any horse over 14½ hands in height shipped to any port or aerodrome which is in the Irish Republic or which is not in Europe and any foal travelling with its dam if the dam is such a horse so shipped; **or**

(ii) any horse of such a height which the Minister is satisfied is intended for exhibition, breeding, racing, jumping, riding or polo; **or**

(iii) a foal travelling with its dam if the dam is such a horse as is referred to in item (ii) above.

A permit is required before shipment in cases (ii) and (iii)

---

[1] A.H.A. 1981, s. 46. The instrument must be of a type approved by the Minister, and must, if required, be produced by the master to an inspector.

[2] A.H.A. 1981, s. 47.

[3] A.H.A. 1981, s. 48.

above. Permits must be applied for on the prescribed form at least seven days before shipment.[1] The applicant must supply such information and evidence as the Minister requires to satisfy himself that the circumstances fall within cases (ii) or (iii). Similar requirements for the delivery of the permit and its production apply as in the case of an inspector's certificate—see page 48; a Customs officer can also demand to see it. A master of a vessel or a captain of an aircraft shipping a horse without having a permit commits an offence.[2]

Inspectors of the Minister or local authority may enter any vessel or aircraft to see whether the foregoing provisions are being complied with. Persons contravening the provisions commit an offence, as does the master of a vessel or the pilot of an aircraft who permits a horse to be shipped contrary to the provisions.[3]

The conditions on board ship under which horses may be transported by sea are referred to on page 59.

Ponies[4]

The provisions for horses in the last Section, except those on pages 47 to 48, dealing with examination and certification, apply equally to ponies. The following regulations apply only to ponies.

It is an offence to ship, or attempt to ship, any pony in any vessel or aircraft from any port or aerodrome in Great Britain[5] to any port or aerodrome outside the United Kingdom,[6] the Channel Islands and the Isle of Man unless—

---

[1] Application is to Section AH IIB at the Ministry of Agriculture, Fisheries and Food, Hook Rise South, Tolworth, Surbiton, Surrey KT6 7NF who may at their discretion allow less than 7 days.

[2] Export of Horses (Excepted Cases) Order 1969 (S.I. 1969/1742), Arts. 3, 4.

[3] A.H.A. 1981, ss. 49(1), (3), 89(1).

[4] In this context "pony" means any horse not more than 147 cms. (14½ hands) in height but excludes a foal travelling with its dam if the dam is over 147 cms. (A.H.A. 1981, s. 89(1)).

[5] For the meaning of "Great Britain", see note 3 on p. 30.

[6] "United Kingdom" means Great Britain and N. Ireland.

(1) The Minister is satisfied that the pony is intended for breeding, riding or exhibition, *and*—

    (i) is of not less value than £300;[1] *or*

    (ii) in the case of a pony not more than 122 cms. high, other than a pony of the Shetland breed not more than 107 cms. high, is of not less value than £220;[1] *or*

    (iii) in the case of such a pony of the Shetland breed, is of not less value than £145;[1]

and

(2) immediately before shipment the pony has been individually inspected by a veterinary inspector[2] and has been certified by him to be capable of being conveyed to the port or aerodrome to which it is to be shipped, and disembarked there, without unnecessary suffering.[3]

But the inspector shall not certify a pony to be capable of being so conveyed and disembarked if, being a mare, it is in his opinion heavy in foal, showing fullness of udder, or too old to travel, or being a foal, it is in his opinion too young to travel.[4]

In connection with the requirements in (1) above, the owner or other person intending to ship the pony must supply to the Minister seven days[5] before the intended date of shipment such evidence as the Minister may require about the purpose for which the pony is intended to be used after export and its value. If the Minister considers the evidence to be satisfactory, he will issue a certificate to that effect.[6] The certificate must be produced before shipment to the

---

[1] These values are increased from time to time by Ministerial order. (A.H.A. 1981 s. 41(1)(a)(iv)).

[2] That is, an inspector appointed by the Minister of Agriculture. (A.H.A. 1981 s. 89, (1)).

[3] A.H.A. 1981, s. 41 (1).

[4] A.H.A. 1981, s. 41(2).

[5] The Minister may at his discretion allow less than 7 days.

[6] Export of Horses (Protection) Order 1969 (S.I. 1969/1784), Art. 13.

master of the vessel or the pilot of the aircraft, who in turn must produce it on demand to a police officer or any officer of the Minister or the local authority or to a Customs officer.[1]

It is an offence for the master of a vessel or the pilot of an aircraft to permit a pony to be shipped unless he has been given a certificate that it has been properly rested[2] or a licence from the Minister that by reason of special circumstances it does not require resting.[3]

It is an offence to ship, or attempt to ship, a registered pony[4] in any vessel or aircraft from any port or aerodrome in Great Britain[5] to any port or aerodrome outside the United Kingdom,[6] the Channel Islands and the Isle of Man unless there has first been obtained from the secretary of a society in whose stud book the pony is registered a certificate (called an export certificate) that the pony is registered with that society. The certificate is to be delivered and produced in the same way as has been described for an inspector's certificate on page 48.[7]

Detailed requirements[8] have been made dealing with the care of ponies prior to export; the main points covered are listed on page 46. The conditions required on board ship for the transport of ponies by sea are referred to on page 59.

---

[1] 1969 Order, cited above, Art. 14(1).

[2] Resting for at least 10 hours before shipment is normally compulsory.

[3] 1969 Order, cited above, Arts. 3, 11, 14 (2).

[4] "A registered pony" means a pony registered in the Arab Horse Society Stud Book, the National Pony Society Book, the British Palomino Society Stud Book, or the British Spotted Horse and Pony Society Stud Book, or in the stud book of any of the following native breed societies, namely, English Connemara, Dales, Dartmoor, Exmoor, Fell, Highland, New Forest, Shetland and Welsh. (A.H.A. 1981, s. 42).

[5] For the meaning of "Great Britain", see note [3] on p. 30.

[6] "United Kingdom", means Great Britain and N. Ireland.

[7] A.H.A. 1981, ss. 42, 48.

[8] These are contained in the 1969 Order cited above.

Endangered Species

The export of endangered species of animals is prohibited unless covered by a licence granted by the Secretary of State.[1] These species are all mammals except those listed in Appendix A to this book. The licence and associated matters are discussed on pages 38 to 40.

C. MOVEMENT OF ANIMALS

Introduction

The movement of animals is regulated by the Animal Health Act 1981 and by many ministerial regulations made under powers given in that Act and its predecessors. The Act itself only deals directly with the obligation of railways to provide food and water to animals travelling on them. The regulations broadly fall into two groups. There are those concerned with diseases of animals, either when disease is suspected or has occurred, of which instances are given on pages 172 to 175 and 177, or those designed to make sure that records of movements are kept to enable animals to be traced in the event of disease; these are dealt with in the next Section which is followed by some notes on the provisions governing the movement and sale of pigs. The second group of regulations is aimed at securing decent conditions, the supply of food and water and protection from unnecessary suffering whilst animals are travelling by road, rail, sea or air. Each mode of transport is dealt with in turn.

Movement Records

With the exceptions listed below, any person who moves, or permits to be moved, certain animals[2] to or from any premises[3] shall enter particulars of the movement in a form

---

[1] E.S.A. 1976, s. 1(1), (2).

[2] These are sheep, goats, pigs, bulls, cows, oxen, heifers and calves. (Movement of Animals (Records) Order 1960 (S.I. 1960/105), Art, 2(1).)

[3] "Premises" includes land with or without buildings on it and any market, saleyard, fairground, place of exhibition or lair; and includes all premises that adjoin each other and are in the same occupation. (1960 Order, Arts, 2(1), 3(4).)

of record.[1] Entries must be made in ink or indelible pencil within 36 hours after movement.[2] They must be kept for 3 years in the case of bovine animals—bulls, cows, oxen, heifers and calves—and for one year in the case of sheep, goats and pigs. Entries must be produced at all reasonable times on demand to any inspector of the Minister or county council who may take copies.[3]

Records need not be kept—

(1) when animals are moved between "different parts of the premises". This appears to mean "different parts of the same premises"; *see* note [3] on page 53;

(2) when animals are moved for feeding, watering or milking or returned afterwards within 24 hours;

(3) when the movement of a pig is entered in a register by a pig dealer under the Swine Fever Order of 1938;[4]

(4) when an imported animal is moved from its landing port or airport to approved premises for detention in quarantine or for its reception and resting and its subsequent movement from such premises under licence;[5]

---

[1] 1960 Order, Art. 3(1). A form of record is set out in the Schedule to the Order which provides for the following particulars: name and address of the person keeping the record; date of movement; breed, age, sex and ear mark or tag mark number in the case of each bovine animal or only the quantities of each in the case of sheep, goats or pigs; premises from which or to which moved; and name and address of the person delivering or taking delivery. But the particulars required for bovine animals need not be recorded when moved direct to a slaughterhouse, fatstock market or certification centre if the quantity of animals is recorded as "cattle". The definition of "slaughterhouse" is given in note [1] on p. 55.

The form mentioned or a form "to the like effect" must be used. The local authority may supply the forms. (1960 Order, Arts, 3(1), 4(3); Movement of Animals (Records) Amendment Order 1961 (S.I. 1961/1493), Art. 2(1)(*b*) and Schedule.) A suitable Record Book is obtainable from the publishers of this book—Cat. No. DA 200.

[2] 1960 Order, Art. 4(1).

[3] 1960 Order, Arts 2(1), 4(2).

[4] Now revoked and replaced by the Swine Fever Order 1963 (S.I. 1963/286).

[5] The approval of the premises and the issue of the licence mentioned in this case are done under the provisions of the Importation of Animals Order 1977, Arts. 10(1) and 11(5). The Order is discussed on pp. 30–32.

(5) by any person acting as—

    (i) a market authority; or

    (ii) an auctioneer at any saleyard, market, fairground or other premises; or

    (iii) a person responsible for holding any exhibition of animals; or

    (iv) a person having the control or management of a slaughterhouse[1] in the case of animals in relation to which his interest (or, if employed, the interest of his employer) has not at any time extended beyond the provision of slaughterhouse facilities;

(6) by the British Railways Board or any person carrying on the business of transporting goods by rail, road, air or water whilst moving animals in the course of that business on behalf of other persons.[2]

Records must also be kept by a person selling pigs at an auction market; *see* page 56.

Movement and Sale of Pigs

The Movement and Sale of Pigs Order 1975[3] contains 15 pages of detailed restrictions, requirements and forms. Briefly, the main provisions of the Order are:

(1) Pigs must not be moved off premises within 21 days of the movement of **any** pigs on to those premises. But this does not apply to any premises which are a market, fairground, saleyard or licensed collecting centre, artificial insemination centre, performance testing station, exhibition, show or approved premises for the detention or reception and resting

---

[1] "Slaughterhouse" means a place for slaughtering animals the flesh of which is intended for sale for human consumption and includes any place available in connection with such a place for the confinement of animals whilst awaiting slaughter. (Movement of Animals (Records) Amendment Order 1961, Art. 2(1)(*a*).)

[2] 1960 Order, Art. 3(2), (3).

[3] S.I. 1975/203.

of imported animals. Particular pig movements are also exempted from the prohibition.[1]

(2) The movement of pigs from all premises must be licensed[2] with the exception of certain named movements. If moved from premises where waste food is kept or from a slaughter market, the pigs will only be licensed for movement to a slaughterhouse.

(3) Before the movement to a slaughterhouse or slaughter market pigs must be marked on the back with a red cross as described.

(4) Road vehicles must be cleansed and disinfected with an approved disinfectant before and after use for moving pigs, and restrictions are placed upon the circumstances in which pigs can be moved in a road vehicle with other categories of pigs or with other things.

(5) A sale of pigs anywhere must be licensed[3] and certain requirements met, though sales may be held during or at the end of an exhibition or show without a licence but within limitations.

(6) A person selling pigs, by auction or privately, at an auction market must make and keep for a year records of the names and addresses of their vendors and purchasers and the numbers of the pens in which each lot was held.

---

[1] These are, very briefly, the following movements: between premises occupied by the same person; to a market for immediate slaughter; to a slaughterhouse; to a vessel or aircraft for, or to detention before, export; from an exhibition, show, performance testing station or artificial insemination centre; and from an approved source for breeding. Some of these movements are only exempt if certain conditions are met.

[2] Most licences are obtainable from diseases of animals inspectors of the local authority.

[3] Licences are obtainable from diseases of animals inspectors of the local authority for the area in which the sale is held.

Movement by Road and Rail

The British Railways Board and other railway operators[1] must provide food and water, or either of them, to the Minister's satisfaction for animals[2] carried by them at such railway stations as the Minister directs,[3] and must supply food and water on the request of the consignor or the person in charge of the animals.[4] Each of these persons is guilty of an offence if, as the result of a request not being made, an animal remains without water for 24 consecutive hours. The Minister may by order[5] reduce this period to not less than 12 hours, either generally or for particular kinds of animals.[6]

The Railways Board or other railway operator may charge for food or water supplied of such amounts as the Minister may by order approve.[7] These charges shall be a debt due from the consignor and consignee of the animals to the railway, and may be recovered in court from either. Also, the railway has a lien[8] on the animals for which charges are made and on any other animal at any time consigned by or to the same consignor or consignee to be carried by the same railway.[9]

The Transit of Animals (Road and Rail) Order 1975[10] applies to cattle,[11] sheep, swine, goats and horses.[12] In 27

---

[1] Specifically, these are: (i) the British Transport Docks Board; (ii) the British Waterways Board; (iii) the London Transport Executive; (iv) wholly owned subsidiaries of the preceding organisations; (v) every railway company, which includes a person working a railway under lease or otherwise. (A.H.A. 1981, s. 38(2)).

[2] "Animals" means cattle, sheep, goats, all other ruminating animals and swine; and "cattle" means bulls, cows, steers, heifers and calves. These meanings may be extended by Ministerial order (A.H.A. 1981, ss. 87 (1)–(3). 89 (1).)

[3] No such directions have been given by the Minister.

[4] A.H.A. 1981, s. 38(2), Sch. 4, para. 1.

[5] No such order has yet been made.

[6] A.H.A. 1981, s. 38(2), Sch. 4, paras. 2, 3.

[7] The Minister has not given any such approval.

[8] Briefly, a lien is a legal right belonging to a person who has done work or supplied services to keep the object of that work or those services until he is paid for them.

[9] A.H.A. 1981, s. 38(2), Sch. 4, paras 4–6.

[10] S.I. 1975/1024.

[11] "Cattle" is defined to mean bulls, cows, steers, heifers and calves. "Calves" means cattle under the age of 6 months. (1975 Order, Art. 2(1).)

[12] "Horse" includes pony, ass, mule and hinny (offspring of she-ass by stallion). (1975 Order, Art. 2(1).)

pages it lays down detailed requirements for the construction and maintenance of vehicles[1] and receptacles[2] used for transporting animals, and contains measures to safeguard the animals' welfare during loading, unloading and carriage. The Order also deals with such matters as the carriage of unfit animals, disinfection and the keeping of records.[3]

The Transit of Animals (General) Order 1973[4] applies to a variety of creatures[5] but not to those animals covered by the 1975 Order. The 1973 Order deals with: protection from injury and unnecessary suffering during loading, unloading and carriage; feeding, watering and general care during carriage; procedures for unfit and pregnant animals and for those injured during carriage; requirements for animals carried in receptacles; and overcrowding, safety and separation.

Movement by Sea

The Transit of Animals Order 1927[6] and the Animals (Sea-Transport) Order 1930[7] apply to all cattle, sheep, goats, all other ruminating animals, and swine carried on any vessel to or from a port in Great Britain.[8] They deal with: the parts of the vessel to be used; specifications for pens, fittings and receptacles; the spaces to be provided; overcrowding; passageways; ventilation; light; food and water; securing of cattle; separation of mixed consignments; construction of approaches, gangways and other apparatus; attendants; drainage; water for fire-fighting and washing down; submission of plans of accommodation to the Minister; handling of animals during embarkation and disembarkation; provision of an approved killing instrument; protec-

---

[1] This term includes railway rolling stock. (1975 Order, Art. 2(1).)
[2] These are crates, boxes or other rigid containers used for carrying animals. (1975 Order, Art. 2(1).)
[3] Record of carriage of animals by road—Shaw's form Cat. No. DA 95.
[4] S.I. 1973/1377.
[5] These are all mammals, except man, and any kind of four-footed beast which is not a mammal, and all fish, reptiles, crustaceans, and other cold-blooded creatures of any species, and poultry. (1973 Order, Art 3(1).)
[6] S.R. & O. 1927/289.
[7] S.R. & O. 1930/923.
[8] For the meaning of "Great Britain", see note [3] on p. 30.

tion for shorn sheep; requirement to keep cattle pens in reserve; annual inspection of vessels by a Ministry inspector; prevention of carriage of animals in unfavourable weather; provision of food and water at shipping and unshipping places; procedure when landed animal is diseased; cleansing and disinfection of vessels, gangways and other apparatus; disposal of fodder and litter; procedures for dealing with injured or dying animals; records of casualties; and carriage of unfit or pregnant animals.

The Minister has power to exempt a vessel from any of these provisions if he is satisfied that it is not practicable or reasonable to require full compliance.[1]

The Horses (Sea-Transport) Order 1952[2] applies to horses[3] carried on vessels to or from a port in Great Britain.[4] Its provisions follow the same pattern as that used in the 1927 and 1930 Orders mentioned above. Additionally, it puts restrictions on carrying horses in open barges to or from a vessel and requires a horse insufficiently protected against the weather by its natural coat to have a rug provided.

The Transit of Animals (General) Order 1973[5] applies to the transport by sea of those kinds of animals[6] which are not covered by the 1927, 1930 or 1952 Orders mentioned in the last three paragraphs. It affects any vessel (including a hovercraft) carrying animals to or from a port[7] in Great

---

[1] The 1927 Order applies only to vessels carrying animals between ports in G.B. or between such ports and ports in Ireland, the Channel Islands or the Isle of Man. The 1930 Order applies to all other journeys to or from a port in G.B. The listed topics dealt with in the text are drawn from both Orders but are not necessarily covered by each of them, and a topic may be dealt with differently in each Order.

[2] S.I. 1952/1291.

[3] "Horse" is defined in the Order (Art 2(1)) to include ass, mule and jennet (small Spanish horse).

[4] Two provisions in the Order apply only to vessels leaving a port in G.B.

[5] For the provisions of this Order, see p. 58.

[6] For the meaning of "animals" in this context, see note [5] on p. 58.

[7] "Port" is defined as any place in G.B. at which animals are loaded into or unloaded out of a vessel, or at which a vessel calls while carrying animals. (Transit of Animals (General) Order 1973, Art. 3(1).)

Britain, whether or not the animals are loaded or unloaded at such a port.[1]

Movement by Air

The Transit of Animals (General) Order 1973, which has just been mentioned, is the only order regulating the transport of animals by air. It applies to animals[2] carried on any aircraft to or from an airport[3] in Great Britain, whether or not the animals are loaded or unloaded at such an airport.[4]

---

[1] 1973 Order, Art 3(1), (3).

[2] For the meaning of "animals" in this context, *see* note [5] on p. 58.

[3] "Airport" is defined as any place in G.B. at which animals are loaded into or unloaded out of an aircraft, or at which an aircraft lands while carrying animals. (1973 Order, Art 3(1).)

[4] 1973 Order, Art. 3(3).

PET ANIMALS

Introduction

This Chapter brings together the law which particularly affects pet animals in a number of ways. Most of it relates to dogs who by their popularity and nature have generated more legislation than the other kinds of pets.

Necessarily other Chapters contain law which also affects pets. In particular, these are: Chapter 6 on **dangerous wild animals**, which are sometimes kept as pets; the powers to deal with **rabies** on pages 42 to 44 and 177 to 180 in Chapters 3 and 9; and the passages in Chapter 8 covering **abandonment** of animals (page 119), **experiments** on dogs and cats (page 125), **operations** on animals (pages 126–129), and **killing or injuring** animals (pages 163–165).

Matters relating especially to horses (and allied kinds of animals) may be found on other pages as follows: importing (34–35), exporting (47–52), transport by sea (59), riding stables (81–85), breeding (85–91), docking and nicking (120–121) and public performances (184).

Dog Licences

Except in the cases mentioned below, anyone who keeps a dog over 6 months old must take out an annual licence. The licence will cover one or more dogs and costs 37½p for each dog. It is in force from the day and hour when it is taken out and expires at the end of the 12 months beginning with the first day of the month in which it is taken out.[1] It is obtainable from Post Offices transacting money order business.[2]

A licence is not needed for:—

(1) A hound under the age of 12 months which has never been entered in or used with a pack of hounds where the owner or master of hounds has taken out proper licences for all the hounds entered in any pack kept by him.[3]

(2) A dog kept and used solely by a blind person for his guidance.[4]

(3) A dog kept and used solely for the purpose of tending sheep or cattle[5] on a farm, or by a shepherd in the exercise of his calling or occupation.[6]

A person in whose custody, charge or possession or in whose house or premises, a dog is found or seen is deemed to be the person who keeps the dog unless he can prove to

---

[1] D.L.A. 1959, ss. 1(1), 2(1), 9(1). Government Ministers may by order alter these provisions about annual payment of the fee, its amount, the duration of the licence or the minimum age of the dog. (L.G.A. 1966, ss. 35(2), 36(1), Schedule 3, Part II, para. 29.).

[2] Licences may also be issued by district and London borough councils and by the Common Council of the City of London. (L.G.A. 1972, s. 213(1), (4).)

[3] D.L.A. 1959, s. 2(2).

[4] D.L.A. 1959, s. 3.

[5] There is no definition of "cattle" in the Dog Licences Act. In D.A. 1953, s. 3(1) it is defined to mean bulls, cows, oxen, heifers and calves; in A.H.A. 1981, s. 89(1) the definition is the same, except that "steers" is substituted for "oxen".

[6] D.L.A. 1959, s. 4(1).

the contrary; and the owner or master of hounds is deemed to be the person who keeps them.[1]

It is an offence to keep a dog (unless exempted as mentioned above) without a licence, or to keep more dogs than licensed for, or to fail to produce a licence for inspection to an authorised officer of the local council or a police constable within a reasonable time.[2] If prosecuted, it is for the accused to prove that the dog was under age,[3] or to establish one of the other exemptions above. He cannot escape conviction by taking out a licence after he has been caught.[4] And he may be convicted a second time in the same year for the same dog.[5] But the exceptional use of a dog exempted under items (2) or (3) above for another purpose will not lose the exemption by which a licence is not needed[6].

If a person is convicted of an offence of cruelty to a dog under the Protection of Animals Act 1911,[7] the court may order him to be disqualified from keeping a dog and from holding or obtaining a dog licence for as long as the court thinks necessary.[8] He may appeal to the Crown Court against the order which may be suspended by the court making it until the appeal is heard.[9] If the disqualified person has a licence, it is suspended and of no effect as long as the disqualification continues.[10] He commits an offence if he keeps a dog or applies for or obtains a licence while disqualified.[11]

Six months after disqualification he may apply to the court for its removal. The court may refuse or grant the application, and in deciding they will have regard to the

---

[1] D.L.A. 1959, s. 12(2).
[2] D.L.A. 1959, ss. 12(1), 13(1).
[3] D.L.A. 1959, s. 12(3).
[4] *Campbell v. Strangeways* (1877).
[5] *Flack v. Church* (1917).
[6] *Egan v. Floyde* (1910).
[7] For cruelty offences under this Act, *see* pp. 119–132.
[8] D.L.A. 1959, ss. 12(2), 16(7); P.A.A. 1933, s. 3.
[9] P.A.A. 1933, s. 1(2).
[10] P.A.A. 1933, s. 1(3); D.L.A. 1959, s. 9(1), proviso.
[11] P.A.A. 1933, s. 1(4).

applicant's character, his conduct since disqualification, the nature of his offence of cruelty, and any other circumstances. If this application is refused, 3 months must elapse before he can apply again.[1]

As well as needing a dog licence, anyone who uses a dog for taking, killing or pursuing game,[2] woodcock, snipe, rabbits or deer must take out a game licence.[3] But this is not needed for pursuing and killing hares by coursing with greyhounds or by hunting them with beagles or other hounds, nor for pursuing and killing deer by hunting with hounds.[4]

Trespassing by Dogs

If a dog of its own accord enters land without permission but does no more, its owner is not liable under civil law for trespass. But the owner is so liable if he deliberately sends a dog on to someone else's land in pursuit of game,[5] although he himself did not enter the land,[6] or if he allows a dog to roam at large knowing it to be addicted to destroying game.[7]

Except as noted below, where a trespassing dog causes damage by killing or injuring[8] livestock,[9] a keeper of the dog is liable for the damage.[10] A number of aspects of this liability needs examination.

---

[1] P.A.A. 1933, s. 2.

[2] "Game" means hares, pheasants, partridges, grouse, heath or moor game and black game. (G.A. 1831, s. 2.).

[3] G.L.A. 1860, s. 4 For game licences generally, see pp. 102–107.

[4] G.L.A. 1860, s. 5, Exceptions 3 and 4.

[5] Possibly he is also liable if the dog is so sent for a different purpose and causes damage.

[6] R. v. Pratt (1855).

[7] Read v. Edwards (1864).

[8] Injury can include indirect injury, e.g., dog barking at foals which injured themselves (Campbell v. Wilkinson (1909)), and poultry ceasing laying as a result of shock (Ives v. Brewer (1951)).

[9] "Livestock" means cattle, horses, asses, mules, hinnies (offspring of she-ass by stallion), sheep, pigs, goats and deer not in a wild state; the domestic varieties of fowls, turkeys, ducks, geese, guinea-fowls, pigeons, peacocks and quails, and while in captivity only, pheasants, partridges and grouse. (A.A. 1971, s. 11.)

[10] A.A. 1971, s. 3. For the circumstances in which the dog may justifiably be killed or injured to protect livestock, see pp. 71–72.

In the cases listed below no liability arises; but otherwise it matters not what active or passive role is played by the keeper of the dog. It is enough that he is its keeper and that the dog does the damage. There is no liability—

(1) if the damage to livestock is due wholly to the fault of the person whose livestock it is[1]; **or**

(2) if the livestock was killed or injured on land on to which it had strayed **and—**

    (*a*) either the dog belonged to the occupier of that land, **or**

    (*b*) its presence on that land was authorised by him.[2]

The meaning of "keeper" is described at some length. A person is a keeper of a dog if he either owns it, or has it in his possession, or is the head of a household[3] of which a member under 16 years old owns the animal or possesses it. Such a person remains the keeper of the dog until someone else fulfilling these qualifications succeeds him as keeper.[4] But a person who takes possession of a dog to prevent it causing damage or to restore it to its owner does not, just because of that possession, become its keeper.[5]

A few words on the meaning in law of "possession" and "possessing" may be helpful at this point. The words must be construed in a popular and not a narrow sense; a person would be regarded as having possession of a dog, not only when he or she is actually with it and controlling it, but also when the dog is in some place, *e.g.*, a building or a vehicle, over which the person has control. If, however, the person does not realise that the dog is, or may be, in that place, the person cannot be said to be in possession of it.[6]

---

[1] A.A. 1971, s. 5(1).

[2] A.A. 1971, s. 5(4).

[3] Presumably, and despite modern trends, in the common case of a household with husband, wife and children the husband is assumed to be its head. But proof of the fact could be difficult, and establishing the identity of the head in many households of different composition more so.

[4] A.A. 1971, s. 6(3).

[5] A.A. 1971, s. 6(4). But he should nevertheless take reasonable care of the dog; otherwise, if the dog causes damage or injury, he may be liable under the laws of negligence or nuisance.

[6] *Lockyer v. Gibb* (1966); *Warner v. Metropolitan Police Commissioner* (1968).

Where damage is caused by two or more dogs acting together, the law regards each dog as causing the whole of the damage, and consequently the owner of each will be responsible for the whole damage.[1]

If a dog worries livestock[2] on agricultural land,[3] its owner, and, if it is in the charge of anyone else, that person also, is guilty of an offence.[4] The phrase "worrying livestock" is defined as meaning:

(a) attacking livestock; **or**

(b) chasing it[5] in such a way as may be reasonably expected to cause it injury[6] or suffering or, in the case of females, abortion or loss or diminution in their produce; **or**

(c) being at large (i.e., not on a lead or otherwise under-close control) in a field or enclosure in which there are sheep[7].

But (c) does **not** apply to the following dogs:

(i) a dog owned by, or in the charge of, the occupier of the field or enclosure, or the owner of the sheep, or a person authorised[8] by either of those persons;

(ii) a police dog;

(iii) a guide dog;

(iv) a trained sheep dog;

(v) a working gun dog;

---

[1] *Arneil v. Paterson* (1931). *I.e.* the keeper of any one of the dogs can be sued for the whole cost of the damage.

[2] "Livestock" here means bulls, cows, oxen, heifers, calves, sheep, goats, swine, horses, asses, mules, domestic fowls, turkeys, geese and ducks. (D.A. 1953, s. 3(1).)

[3] "Agricultural land" means land used as arable, meadow or grazing land or for the purpose of poultry or pig farming, market gardens, allotments, nursery grounds or orchards. (D.A. 1953, s. 3(1).) This can include a cricket field on which sheep are grazing. (*Williams v. Richards* (1970).)

[4] D.A. 1953, s. 1(1) *I.e.* he can be prosecuted and fined, as opposed to being sued on a claim for damages as earlier described.

[5] Actual pursuit need not be proved; it is enough for the dog to run among the livestock so as to alarm them. (*Stephen v. Milne* (1960).)

[6] As to injury, *see* note [8] on p. 64.

[7] D.A. 1953, s. 1(2).

[8] The authorisation is not required to be in writing.

(vi) a pack of hounds.[1]

But there will be no offence—

(1) by the owner if he proves[2] that at the time in question the dog was in the charge of some other person whom he reasonably believed to be a fit and proper person to be in charge of it;[3] **or**

(2) if at the material time the livestock were trespassing on the land in question and the dog was owned by, or in the charge of, the occupier of that land or a person authorised[4] by him, except in a case where the authorised person[5] causes the dog to attack the livestock.[6]

If a police officer reasonably believes that a dog found on land has been worrying livestock[7] there, and the land appears to him to be agricultural land,[8] and no person is present who admits to being the owner of the dog or in charge of it, then the officer may, in order to find out the owner, seize and keep the dog until the owner has claimed it and paid all the expenses of its detention.[9]

For the purpose of preventing the worrying of cattle,[10] a local authority[11] may make regulations requiring that dogs generally or any class of dogs shall, during all or any of the hours between sunset and sunrise, be kept under control as

---

[1] D.A. 1953, s. 1(2A).

[2] It is enough for the owner to satisfy the court of the probability of existence of the facts in defence (1). (*R. v. Carr-Briant* (1943).)

[3] D.A. 1953, s. 1(4).

[4] The authorisation is not required to be in writing.

[5] The Act is phrased so as to refer at this point only to the authorised person though it seems odd that the occupier of the land should not be coupled with him.

[6] D.A. 1953, s. 1(3).

[7] For the definition of "livestock", "see note [2] on p. 66.

[8] For the definition of "agricultural land", see note [3] on p. 66.

[9] D.A. 1953, s. 2(2). The dog is then treated as though seized as a stray (D.A. 1953, s. 2(3)), for which *see* pp. 69–70.

[10] "Cattle" includes horses, mules, asses, sheep, goats and swine. (Control of Dogs Order 1930 (S.R. & O. 1930/399), Art. 2(2).)

[11] This is the county council, or, in London the borough council or the Common Council of the City of London or, in Scotland, the regional or islands council (A.H.A. 1981, s. 50 (1)–(3)).

described in the regulations.[1] It is an offence without lawful authority or excuse to break the regulations, or to aid, abet, counsel or procure a breach of them.[2]

Dangerous Dogs

If it appears to a magistrates' court that a dog is dangerous and not kept under proper control,[3] they may order it to be kept by the owner[4] under proper control or to be destroyed. The penalty for non-compliance is a daily sum not exceeding £1,[5] but notice of the penalty must be given to the owner.[6]

Where a dog is proved to have injured cattle or poultry or chased sheep, it may be dealt with as a dangerous dog.[7] "Dangerous" includes dangerous to animals,[8] and a dog may be dangerous though not ferocious.[9] An order may be made though the owner did not know that the dog was dangerous.[10]

An order to destroy a dog may be made without giving the owner the option of keeping it under proper control.[11] If the owner does not comply with a control order, court proceedings must be started again when the court can make a destruction order.[12] An appeal can be made to the Crown Court against a destruction order[13] but not apparently against a control order.

---

[1] Control of Dogs Order 1930, Art. 2(1).

[2] 1930 Order, Art. 6; A.H.A. 1981, s. 73(a).

[3] The need for proper control is not limited to public places but extends to places where the dog is on the owners' private property to which other people have a right of access. (*Philp v. Wright* (1940).)

[4] It is thought that "owner" has its ordinary meaning here and not any extended meaning as is given to the keeper of a dog in another context.

[5] D.A. 1871, s. 2.

[6] *Haldane v. Allen* (1956).

[7] D.A. 1906, s 1(4);

[8] *Williams v. Richards* (1907). Though a dog which killed two tame white rabbits in a neighbour's garden was held to be not dangerous, it being in the nature of dogs to wound and kill little animals (*Sansom v. Chief Constable of Kent* (1981)).

[9] This seems to be a matter of degree; a dog with a propensity only to bite small children, postmen or any other class of persons will be dangerous but could not be described as ferocious. (*Keddle v. Payn* (1964)).

[10] *Parker v. Walsh* (1885).

[11] *Pickering v. Marsh* (1874).

[12] *Rhodes v. Heritage* (1951).

[13] D.A.A. 1938, s. 1(1); C.A. 1971, s. 56(2), Schedule 9, Part I.

Ferocious Dogs

Except in the Greater London area, it is an offence for a person in any street,[1] to the obstruction, annoyance or danger of the residents or passengers, to "suffer to be at large"[2] any unmuzzled ferocious[3] dog, or to set on or urge any dog or other animal to attack, worry or put in fear any person or animal.[4] Similar offences are created for the Metropolitan Police District.[5]

Stray Dogs

A police officer may seize any dog found in a highway or place of public resort[6] which he has reason to believe is a stray dog, and detain it until the owner has claimed it and paid all expenses incurred in its detention.[7] If the dog wears a collar with an address, or the owner is known, the police must serve on the person whose address is given or the owner (as the case may be) written notice that the dog has been seized and is liable to be sold or destroyed if not claimed within 7 clear days after service of the notice.[8] The dog must be properly fed and maintained during detention by the person having charge of it.[9]

After 7 days,[10] and if the owner has not claimed the dog and paid all expenses, the dog may be sold, or destroyed in a manner so as to cause as little pain as possible, but not given or sold for purposes of vivisection.[11]

---

[1] The word "street" extends to and includes any road, square, court, alley, thoroughfare or public passage. (T.P.C.A. 1847, s. 3.).

[2] A dog on a lead is not "at large". (*Ross v. Evans* (1959).)

[3] For comment on the distinction between "ferocious" and "dangerous", *see* note [9] on p. 68.

[4] T.P.C.A. 1847, s. 28; P.H.A. 1875, s. 171; L.G.A. 1972, s. 180. Schedule 14, paras. 23, 26.

[5] M.P.A. 1839, s. 54, para. 2.

[6] A "place of public resort" has been said to mean a place to which the public goes as a matter of fact, as distinct from a matter of right (*Kitson v. Ashe* (1899)) notwithstanding that a charge is made for admission (*Glynn v. Simmonds* (1952)).

[7] D.A. 1906, s. 3(1).

[8] D.A. 1906, s. 3(2).

[9] D.A. 1906, s. 3(8).

[10] That is, 7 days after the original detention of the dog or, if a notice has been served, 7 days after service of it.

[11] D.A. 1906, s. 3(4), (5).

The police must keep a register of dogs seized and record particulars. It is open to public inspection at all reasonable times for a fee of 5p.[1]

Anyone who finds or keeps a stray dog must at once either return it to its owner or take it to the nearest police station, telling the police where it was found.[2] If the finder wants to keep the dog, he may, after taking it to the police station, take it away with him after giving his name and address. The police will give him a certificate of particulars of the dog, of its finding and of the finder, and he must keep the dog for at least one month.[3] At the same time the police serve a 7-day notice in the same way as if they had found the dog (assuming they know the owner or have an address for the dog). If the owner claims it within the 7 days, he is entitled to it; otherwise the finder is entitled to keep it.[4]

If the finder does not want to keep the dog, the police detain it as if it was a stray seized by them.[5] The finder may be fined for not complying with the foregoing requirements.[6]

Dog Collars

Every dog while in a highway or place of public resort[7] must wear a collar with the name and address of its owner inscribed on it or on a plate or badge attached to it. But a collar is not needed for—

(1) a pack of hounds; or

(2) any dog while being used for sporting purposes, for the capture or destruction of vermin, or for the driving or tending of cattle or sheep.[8]

If this requirement is not complied with, the dog may be

---

[1] D.A. 1906, s. 3(6), (7).
[2] D.A. 1906, s. 4(1).
[3] D.A. 1906, s. 4(2)(a).
[4] *Halsbury's Laws of England*, 4th Ed., Vol. 2, para. 377, footnote 2.
[5] D.A. 1906, s. 4(2)(b).
[6] D.A. 1906, s. 4(3).
[7] For the meaning of "a place of public resort", *see* note [6] on p. 69.
[8] Control of Dogs Order 1930 (S.R. & O. 1930/399), Art. 1.

seized by the police and treated by them as a stray.[1] Its
owner, any person in charge of it and any person allowing
the dog to be in the places described are each guilty of an
offence unless they had lawful authority or excuse.[2]

Killing or Injuring Dogs

Without legal justification it is a civil wrong[3] to kill or
injure another person's dog.[4] A notice that trespassing dogs
will be shot is no defence.[5] Legal justification can arise in
three ways.

To protect livestock,[6] a person is entitled to kill or injure
another's dog if—

(1) the livestock or the land on which it is belongs to
him[7] or to any person under whose express or implied
authority he is acting[8]; **and**

(2) in a case where the livestock was killed or injured on
land on to which it had strayed, **either** the dog
belonged to the occupier of that land **or** its presence
there was authorised by him[9]; **and**

(3) **either** the dog is worrying[10] or about to worry livestock
and there are no other reasonable means of ending
or preventing the worrying[11]; **or**

(4) the dog has been worrying livestock, has not left the
vicinity, is not under the control of any person, and

---

[1] 1930 Order, Art. 4. For stray dogs, see pp. 69–70.
[2] 1930 Order, Arts. 5 and 6; I.A. 1978, s. 17(2)(b); A.H.A. 1981 s. 73(a).
[3] I.e., the dog's owner may sue for damages.
[4] Vere v. Earl Cawdor (1809). As to when it is a crime, see pp. 122–124.
[5] Corner v. Champneys (1814) cited in 2 March at 584.
[6] For the meaning of "livestock" see note [2] on p. 66.
[7] For this purpose the livestock belongs to the person who owns it or has it in
his possession, and land belongs to the person who occupies it. (A.A. 1971, s.
9(5).)
[8] A.A. 1971, s. 9(2)(a).
[9] A.A. 1971, ss. 5(4), 9(2)(b).
[10] There is no definition of "worrying" in the Animals Act 1971 which contains
these provisions. For the definition in another Act, which is suggested as a guide,
see p. 66.
[11] A.A. 1971, s. 9(3)(a)

there are no practicable means of ascertaining to
whom it belongs[1]; **and**

(5) within 48 hours of the killing or injuring the person
doing it gave notice[2] of it to the officer in charge of
a police station.[3]

A dog attacking a human being may be shot in self-
defence,[4] and presumably by one person when it is attacking
another. Whether shooting is justified when the dog is
running away after an attack is uncertain in the present state
of the law.[5]

The third justification arises when a dog attacks domestic
animals which are not livestock if—

(a) at the material time the dog was actually attacking
the animals **or**, if left at large, would renew the attack
so that the animals would be left in real and imminent
danger unless renewal was prevented; **and**

(b) **either** there was in fact no practicable means other
than shooting of stopping the present attack or such
renewal, **or** that, having regard to all the circumstances in which he found himself, the shooter acted
reasonably in regarding the shooting as necessary.[6]

It is doubtful whether there is a defence to a civil claim
for killing or injuring another's dog because it is attacking
wild animals (except game) on one's land or property. The
position in relation to the protection of game is discussed
on page 116.

A man must not so use his land as to tempt other people's
dogs to destruction; thus, if he sets traps baited with strong
smelling meat so near his neighbour's yard, or so near a

---

[1] A.A. 1971, s. 9(3)(b). A belief on reasonable grounds that either condition
(3) or (4) was satisfied is enough. (A.A. 1971, S. 9(4).)

[2] Written notice is not stipulated, but will be advisable in case of later proceedings. A copy of the notice should be receipted by the police officer and endorsed
by him with the time and date of receipt.

[3] A.A. 1971, s. 9(1)(b).

[4] *Morris v. Nugent* (1836).

[5] *Halsbury's Laws of England* 4th Ed., Vol. 2, para. 379.

[6] *Cresswell v. Sirl* (1947).

highway where dogs may lawfully pass, that dogs are irresistibly drawn to the traps, he may be sued for damages by the owner of any dog caught.[1]

Boarding Kennels

Boarding kennels for cats and dogs must be licensed by the local council.[2] For this purpose the keeping of such kennels is defined as the carrying on at any premises (including a private dwelling) of a business of providing accommodation for other people's cats and dogs.[3] But if the accommodation is provided in connection with a business of which the proviison of such accommodation is not the main activity, a licence is unnecessary.[4] Nor is a licence necessary if cats or dogs are kept on premises pursuant to a requirement under the diseases of animals legislation.[5]

In deciding whether to grant a licence the council, as well as being able to withhold it for other reasons, must pay regard particularly to the need to secure that the animals will be suitably accommodated, fed, exercised and protected from disease and fire, and that a proper register of animals is kept with their dates of arrival and departure and their owners' names and addresses. A licence will contain conditions to these ends.[6]

A fee for the licence will be charged; there is no maximum.[7] It covers the year in which it was granted or the next following year.[8] A person aggrieved by the refusal of

---

[1] *Townsend v. Wathen* (1808). He would probably also be liable to prosecution under C.D.A. 1971, s. 3, for possessing articles with intent to damage or destroy, or under P.A.A. 1911, s. 1(1)(*a*), for which *see* pp. 131–132.

[2] A.B.E.A. 1963, s. 1(1), (2). This is the district council, the London borough council or the Common Council of the City of London in whose area the kennels are. (A.B.E.A. 1963, s. 5(2).) Application form: Shaw's form Cat. No. AB 2.

[3] A.B.E.A. 1963, s. 5(1), (2).

[4] A.B.E.A. 1963, s. 5(1), proviso (*a*). *E.g.* a vet who provides board as a sideline to his practice.

[5] A.B.E.A. 1963, s. 5(1), proviso (*b*). Examples of such a requirement appear in Chapter 9.

[6] A.B.E.A. 1963, s. 1(3).

[7] A.B.E.A. 1963, s. 1(2).

[8] A.B.E.A. 1963, s. 1(5), (6). *I.e.* the licence runs, at the applicant's choice, from the day it is granted to the end of the current year, or from the beginning of the next year to the end of that year.

a licence or by any of its conditions may appeal to a magistrates' court who will adjudicate.[1]

The council may authorise in writing any of its officers or any vet to inspect licensed kennels and they have powers of entry and inspection at all reasonable times on producing their authority.[2] It is an offence wilfully[3] to obstruct or delay the exercise of these powers,[4] or to keep kennels without a licence, or to fail to comply with a condition of a licence.[5] On convicting a person of an offence under the regulating Act[6] or other named Acts,[7] the court may cancel his licence and may, whether he has a licence or not, disqualify him from keeping kennels for as long as it thinks fit.[8] Such a person cannot therefore be granted a licence while disqualified; nor may anyone else while disqualified from keeping a pet shop,[9] from keeping a dog[10] or from having the custody of animals.[11]

When the licence holder dies, the licence is treated as having been granted to his personal representatives to remain in force for 3 months after the death. The council may extend and re-extend the 3 months if satisfied that that is necessary for winding up the deceased's estate and that no other circumstances make it undesirable.[12]

---

[1] A.B.E.A. 1963, s. 1(4).
[2] A.B.E.A. 1963, s. 2(1).
[3] This means deliberately and intentionally, and not by accident or inadvertence. (*R.v. Senior* [1899] 1 Q.B. 283, at pp. 290–291).
[4] A.B.E.A. 1963, s. 2(2).
[5] A.B.E.A. 1963, s. 1(8). ·
[6] *I.e.*, the Animal Boarding Establishments Act 1963.
[7] These are: the Protection of Animals Act 1911 (for which *see* pp. 119–133); the Protection of Animals (Scotland) Act 1912; and the Pet Animals Act 1951 (for which *see* pp. 75–77).
[8] A.B.E.A. 1963, s. 3(3). There is a right of appeal to the Crown Court against an order for cancellation or disqualification; the magistrates may suspend the order pending the appeal. (A.B.E.A. 1963, s. 3(4).)
[9] *See* p. 76.
[10] *See* pp. 63–64.
[11] A.B.E.A. 1963, s. 1(2). For cases where a person may be disqualified from having the custody of animals, *see* p. 133.
[12] A.B.E.A. 1963. s. 1(7).

Dog Breeding

Dog breeding kennels must also be licensed by the local council.[1] For this purpose the keeping of such kennels is defined as the carrying on at premises of any nature (including a private dwelling) of a business of breeding dogs with a view to their being sold in the course of such business, whether by their keeper or any other person,[2] and the kennels are defined as any premises (including a private dwelling) where more than two bitches are kept for the purpose of breeding for sale.[3]

The rules for this kind of licensing are almost identical to those applying to the licensing of boarding kennels.[4] The significant differences are:—

(1) In addition to the cases in which a person may be disqualified from holding a licence or may have it cancelled which are mentioned on page 74, a person may have this action taken against him for an offence under the regulating Act[5] itself.[6]

(2) The licence fee is £2 or such reasonable sum as the council may fix.[7]

(3) A register of animals need not be kept.

Pet Shops

A person keeping a pet shop must be licensed by the local council.[8] The regulating rules are similar to those for boarding kennels and dog breeding kennels. The keeping of a pet shop is defined to mean the carrying on at premises

---

[1] For the identity of the local council, *see* note [2] on p. 73. Shaw's form Cat. No. DB2 for form of application for licence.
[2] B.D.A. 1973, s. 5(1).
[3] B.D.A. 1973, s. 5(2).
[4] *See* pp. 73–74.
[5] The Breeding of Dogs Act 1973.
[6] B.D.A. 1973, s. 3(3).
[7] B.D.A. 1973, s. 1(2).
[8] P.A.A. 1951, s. 1(1). For the identity of the local council, *see* note [2] on p. 73. Shaw's form Cat. No. PA 22 for form of application for licence.

of any nature (including a private dwelling) of a business of selling animals[1] as pets[2] and includes the keeping of animals[1] in any such premises with a view to their being sold in the course of such a business, whether by their keeper or any other person.[3] This definition is qualified in two ways. First, a person is not treated as keeping a pet shop only because he keeps or sells pedigree animals[4] bred by him or the offspring of an animal kept by him as a pet. The second qualification arises where a person carries on a business of selling animals as pets in conjunction with a business of breeding pedigree animals, and the local council are satisfied that the animals so sold by him (in so far as they are not pedigree animals bred by him) are animals which were acquired by him with a view to being used, if suitable, for breeding or show purposes but have later been found by him not to be suitable or required for such use. In that situation the council may direct that the person shall not be treated as keeping a pet shop by reason only of his carrying on a business of selling animals as pets.[5]

The conditions which can attach to a licence include one that mammals will not be sold at too early an age,[6] but there will be no condition about keeping a register.[7] A person is disqualified from having a licence and may have any licence held cancelled for offences under the regulating Act[8] or the Protection of Animals Acts.[9] The fee, the right of appeal,

---

[1] "Animal" includes any description of vertebrate. (P.A.A. 1951, s. 7(3).)

[2] The phrase "selling animals as pets" is itself defined; for cats and dogs, as including selling wholly or mainly for domestic purposes; and, for all animals, as including selling for ornamental purposes. (P.A.A. 1951, s. 7(2).)

[3] P.A.A. 1951, s. 7(1). A person keeping animals on premises for short periods (48 hours in this particular case) for the purpose of exporting them nevertheless keeps a pet shop within the definition, even though the public did not go to the premises to buy animals. (*Chalmers v. Diwell* (1975).)

[4] A pedigree animal means an animal of any description which is by its breeding eligible for registration with a recognised club or society keeping a register of animals of that description; (P.A.A. 1951, s. 7(3).)

[5] P.A.A. 1951, s. 7(1), provisoes.

[6] No specific ages are given, the intention being presumably that young mammals (but not other animals) are not to be separated too early from their mothers, the ages depending on the species.

[7] P.A.A. 1951, s. 1(3).

[8] *I.e.*, the Pet Animals Act 1951.

[9] P.A.A. 1951, s. 5(3). For these Acts, *see* pp. 119–133.

the duration of the licence, the powers of inspection and the creation of offences are the same as those for boarding kennels.[1]

Additional offences are created for: carrying on a business of selling animals[2] as pets[3] in any part of a street or public place[4]; selling an animal as a pet[3] to a person whom the seller has reasonable cause to believe to be under the age of 12.[5]

Guard Dogs

Although perhaps guard dogs may not be regarded as pet animals, it is convenient to consider in this Chapter the law which affects them.

Following a number of accidents in which dogs guarding property savaged people, the Guard Dogs Act was passed in 1975 and is partly in force. For the purposes of the Act a guard dog is defined as a dog which is being used to protect premises,[6] or property kept on the premises, or a person guarding the premises or such property.[7]

It is an offence to use, or permit the use of, a guard dog at any premises unless a person (called "the handler") who is capable of controlling the dog is present on the premises, and the dog is under the control of the handler at all times while it is being used as a guard dog, except while it is

---

[1] P.A.A. 1951, ss. 1(2), (4)–(7), 4, 5(4). For boarding kennels, see pp. 73–74.
[2] For the meaning of "animal", see note [1] on p. 76.
[3] For the meaning of "selling animals as pets", see note [2] on p. 76.
[4] P.A.A. 1951, s. 2.
[5] P.A.A. 1951, s. 3.
[6] "Premises" means land (other than agricultural land and land within the curtilage of a dwelling house) and buildings, including parts of buildings other than dwelling houses. (G.D.A. 1975, s. 7.). "Agricultural land" means land used as arable, meadow or grazing land, or for the purpose of poultry farming, pig farming, market gardens, allotments, nursery grounds or orchards (G.D.A. 1975, s. 7; D.A. 1953, s. 3(1)). A "curtilage" is briefly, the garden and more immediate surrounds of a house.
[7] G.D.A. 1975, s. 7.

secured so that it is not at liberty to roam the premises.[1] The handler's duty to control the dog is only relaxed if another handler has control of it or if it is secured so that it cannot roam.[2] A guard dog is not to be used at all unless a notice warning of its presence is clearly shown at each entrance to the premises.[3]

The following provisions of the Act are **not yet operative**.

It will be an offence for a person to keep a dog at guard dog kennels unless he holds a licence for the kennels.[4] "Guard dog kennels" are defined as a place where a person in the course of business keeps a dog which (notwithstanding that it is used for other purposes) is used as a guard dog elsewhere, other than a dog which is used as a guard dog only at premises belonging to its owner.[5] It will also be an offence for anyone to use, or permit the use of, a guard dog at premises if he knows, or has reasonable cause to suspect, that the dog (when not being used as a guard dog) is kept at unlicensed kennels.[6]

Licences will be obtained from local councils[7] by completing a form and paying a fee. They will be issued subject to conditions,[8] and will come into force on the date given on them; they will last for 12 months unless cancelled by a court order. This cancellation can be ordered if the holder of the licence is convicted of an offence against the 1975 Act or against a number of other Acts,[9] but the cancellation

---

[1] G.D.A. 1975, s. 1(1). It has been ruled that these requirements are met if the handler is on the premises with the dog under his control or if, in his absence, the dog is secured as described in the text. (*Hobson v. Gledhill* (1977).)

[2] G.D.A. 1975, s. 1(2).

[3] G.D.A. 1975, s. 1(3).

[4] G.D.A. 1975, s. 2(1).

[5] G.D.A. 1975, s. 7.

[6] G.D.A. 1975, s. 2(2).

[7] G.D.A. 1975, s. 7. For the identity of local councils, see note 2 on p. 73.

[8] The conditions will be those (if any) which the Government lays down and any others which the district council may choose to add. (G.D.A. 1975, ss. 3(2), 7.)

[9] These are:— the Protection of Animals Act 1911 (*see* pp. 119–133); the Protection of Animals (Scotland) Act 1912; the Pet Animals Act 1951 (*see* pp. 75–77); the Animal Boarding Establishments Act 1963 (*see* pp. 73–74); and the Breeding of Dogs Act 1973 (*see* p. 75).

can be suspended pending an appeal.[1]

An applicant for a licence or the holder of one, as the case may be, will be able to appeal to a magistrates' court against the following decisions of the local council:—

(a) A refusal to grant a licence.

(b) The conditions attached to it, unless they are conditions laid down by the Government.

(c) A refusal to vary the conditions on the request of the licence holder.

(d) A revocation of the licence.[2]

When hearing an appeal the court may give directions to the local council about the licence or its conditions[3] which must be obeyed.[4]

Control of Dogs on Roads[5]

A local authority[6] may by order designate particular roads the effect of which is that it becomes an offence for a person to cause or permit a dog to be on a designated road without it being held on a lead.[7] This is not to apply to dogs proved to be kept for driving or tending sheep or cattle in the course of a trade or business, or proved to be at the material time in use under proper control for sporting purposes. The local authority may put other limitations or exceptions in an order.[8]

Proposals for making these orders must be publicised in

---

[1] G.D.A. 1975, s. 3(1)–(5).

[2] G.D.A. 1975, s. 4(1). Government regulations are to be made about revoking licences, varying conditions and a number of other ancillary matters. (G.D.A. 1975, s. 6).

[3] In effect, these directions will be the court's decision on the appeal which is to be carried out by the council, e.g. to remove a condition appealed against.

[4] G.D.A. 1975, s. 4(2).

[5] As to dogs fouling footpaths on roads, see p. 203.

[6] Orders are made by county councils, the Common Council of the City of London, and London borough councils. (R.T.A. 1972, s. 31(7).)

[7] R.T.A. 1972, s. 31(1), (2).

[8] R.T.A. 1972, s. 31(3).

the local press to give the public an opportunity to comment
and object, and a public inquiry may be held.[1]

---

[1] R.T.A. 1972, s. 31(5), and regulations made thereunder.

CHAPTER 5

HORSES AND FARM ANIMALS

Riding Stables

With (as usual) exceptions, it is illegal to keep riding stables[1] without a licence from the local authority.[2] The keeping of stables[3] is defined to mean the carrying on of a business of keeping horses[4] for **either or both** of the following purposes:

(a) the purpose of the horses being let out on hire for riding;

(b) the purpose of their being used in providing, in return for payment, instruction in riding.

But excluded from the definition, and therefore not needing a licence, is the carrying on of such a business—

(i) where the premises[5] where the horses employed for the purpose of the business are kept are occupied by or under the management of the Secretary of State for Defence, *i.e.*, military establishments; or

---

[1] Somewhat pretentiously called in the regulating Acts "riding establishments".
[2] R.E.A. 1964, s. 1(1);
[3] A person is deemed to keep the stables at the premises (which includes land) where the horses employed for the purposes of the business concerned are kept. (R.E.A. 1964, s. 6(3), (4).)
[4] "Horse" includes any mare, gelding, pony, foal, colt, filly or stallion, and also any ass, mule or jennet (small Spanish horse). (R.E.A. 1964, s. 6(4).)
[5] "Premises" includes land. (R.E.A. 1964, s. 6(4).)

(ii) solely for police purposes; or

(iii) by the Zoological Society of London; or

(iv) by the Royal Zoological Society of Scotland.[1]

Also excluded are universities providing approved courses for veterinary students.[2]

The rules about licensing of riding stables are similar to those for dog breeding kennels, pet shops, and boarding kennels which were examined in the last Chapter, but they are more detailed and provide also for provisional licences to be issued. Application must be made to the district council.[3] A number of pre-conditions must be fulfilled before a licence can be granted; these are:—

(1) The applicant must be at least 18 years old or an incorporated body.

(2) The applicant must not be disqualified from keeping riding stables[4] or from keeping a dog,[5] a pet shop[6] or boarding kennels,[7] or from having the custody of animals.[8]

(3) The payment of the fee required by the district council.

(4) The riding stables must be in the area of the district council.[9]

(5) The stables must have been inspected[10] by a vet whose report must contain sufficient particulars to enable the council to decide whether they are suitable and

---

[1] R.E.A. 1964, s. 6(1).
[2] R.E.A. 1964, s. 6(2).
[3] Or, if the stables are in London, to the Common Council of the City of London or to a London borough council, as the case may be. (R.E.A. 1964, s. 6(4)), Form of Application for Licence—Shaw's form Cat. No. RE 12.
[4] See p. 85.
[5] See p. 63.
[6] See p. 76.
[7] See p. 74.
[8] See p. 133.
[9] R.E.A. 1964, s. 1(2).
[10] The inspection must be made not earlier than a year before the application is received.

must describe their condition and the condition of any horses or thing found there.[1]

(6) In deciding whether to grant a licence the council must have regard to whether the applicant appears to be suitable and qualified to hold the licence by—

(a) experience in the management of horses; or

(b) being the holder of an approved certificate[2]; or

(c) employing in the management of the stables a person qualified as in (a) or (b).

(7) Before granting a licence the council must also consider in particular the need to secure that a number of other matters will be in order. These (in brief) concern; health, shoeing and suitability of the horses; suitability of their accommodation; adequacy of their food and water supply, shelter, bedding material, exercising, grooming and resting; precautions against disease and provision of first aid equipment and medicines; fire precautions; adequacy of accommodation for forage, bedding, stable equipment and saddlery.[3]

Even if all the foregoing matters are satisfactory, the council nevertheless have a discretion to refuse a licence on any other grounds.[3] If a licence is issued; it will be subject to compulsory conditions dealing with, briefly: unfit horses not to be returned to work unless covered by a vet's certificate; supervision or hiring of horses by responsible persons; stables not to be left in charge of anyone under 16; licence holder to be insured against his liability for injury to other persons; licence holder to keep a register of horses under four years old. These conditions apply whether or not they

---

[1] R.E.A. 1964, s. 1(3).

[2] "Approved certificate" means: Assistant Instructor's Certificate of, or Instructor's Certificate and Fellowship of, the British Horse Society; or Fellowship of the Institute of the Horse; or any other certificate approved by order of the Secretary of State. (R.E.A. 1964, s. 6(4).) No such order has yet been made.

[3] R.E.A. 1964, s. 1(4).

are written into the licence.[1] The council may add further conditions, particularly conditions dealing with the matters mentioned in item (7) above.[2]

The provisions dealing with the duration of a licence, the right of appeal against its refusal or its conditions (except the compulsory conditions which are not appealable) and the continuation of the licence after the holder's death are the same as those for boarding kennels already mentioned in Chapter 4.[3]

If the council are not satisfied that they would be justified in granting an ordinary licence, they may grant a provisional licence for a period of three months.[4] This may be extended for a further three months if applied for before the first period expires; but stables cannot be licensed in this way for more than six months in any year.[5] There is no right of appeal against refusal of a provisional licence. Otherwise the provisions relating to a full licence apply equally to a provisional licence.[6]

Officers of any district council and vets, if authorised in both cases in writing by a district council, may enter and inspect premises which are licensed, for which a licence has been sought or which are suspected of being used as riding stables. They may be required to produce their authorisations; obstruction of them is an offence.[7]

A number of other offences related to riding stables is created. These are, briefly: keeping unlicensed stables, except of course when a licence is not required[8]; breach of a condition of a licence by a licence holder; using a horse when that is likely to cause it suffering; supplying defective equipment for use with a horse which is likely to cause it suffering or an accident to its rider; failing to provide cura-

---

[1] R.E.A. 1964, s. 1(4A).
[2] R.E.A. 1964, s. 1(2), (4), (4A).
[3] R.E.A. 1964, s. 1(5), (6), (8). *See* pp. 73–74.
[4] R.E.A. 1970, s. 1(1).
[5] R.E.A. 1970, s. 1(2).
[6] R.E.A. 1970, s. 1(3).
[7] R.E.A. 1964, s. 2(1), (2), (4).
[8] *See* pp. 81–82.

tive care for a horse; knowingly permitting a person disqualified from keeping stables to control or manage stables; concealing a horse with intent to avoid its inspection; using a horse under four years old or a mare heavy with foal or within three months after foaling; and giving false information to obtain a licence.[1]

On conviction of any of these offences, or of offences under other named Acts dealing with animals,[2] the magistrates' court may cancel the offender's licence and may, whether or not he holds a licence, disqualify him from keeping riding stables for such time as the court thinks fit.[3] The operation of the court's orders for cancellation or disqualification may be suspended while an appeal[4] is made.[5]

Horse Breeding

With the exceptions mentioned below, it is not lawful for a person to keep[6] a stallion which has reached the age of five years[7] unless he holds a licence or permit for it from the appropriate Government Minister.[8] This does not apply to a thoroughbred stallion, which is defined as one entered or eligible for entry in the General Stud Book, or to a stallion which is a pony of one of six breeds prescribed in regulations[9]; but these exceptions do not allow the person

---

[1] R.E.A. 1964, ss. 1(9), 3.

[2] These Acts are: the Protection of Animals Act 1911 (*see* generally Section B of Chapter 8); the corresponding Protection of Animals (Scotland) Act 1912; the Pet Animals Act 1951 (*see* pp. 75–77); and the Animal Boarding Establishments Act 1963 (*see* pp. 73–74).

[3] R.E.A. 1964, s. 4(3).

[4] Appeal lies, presumably, to the Crown Court.

[5] R.E.A. 1964, s. 4(4).

[6] A person is deemed to keep a stallion if he owns it or has the control of it. (H.B.A. 1958, s. 1(4).)

[7] The Act says that a stallion shall be treated as reaching the age of one year on the 1st January following the year in which it is foaled. (H.B.A. 1958, s. 16(2).) It follows that it becomes five years old four years later.

[8] H.B.A. 1958, ss. 1(1), 16(1), 17(2); Horse Breeding Rules 1948 (S.I. 1948/ 2677), Rule 3.

[9] H.B.A. 1958, ss. 1(2), 16(1), 17(2); Horse Breeding Rules 1948, Rule 4., First Schedule. The pony breeds are: Dartmoor, Exmoor, Fell, New Forest, Shetland and Welsh Mountain. They are only exempted while they are within their respective districts (*see* the Rules for details), except the Shetland pony which is exempt anywhere in Great Britain.

who keeps[1] a stallion at least five years old to travel it for use for breeding purposes, or to exhibit it on any premises not in his occupation with a view to its use for breeding purposes, or to permit it to be so travelled or exhibited, unless he has a licence from the Minister.[2]

To keep a stallion without a licence or permit (unless excepted as above), or to travel or exhibit it, or to permit either, without a licence is a finable offence. But it is a defence to prove that at the time in question application had been properly made[3] for a licence or permit and—

(a) the Minister had not given notice of his decision on the application; **or**

(b) a licence had been refused or revoked **and**—

(i) **either** the time for applying for a referee's inspection and examination[4] had not expired;

or

(ii) an application under (i) above had been properly made[5] and the Minister had not told the applicant his decision about confirmation of the refusal or revocation.[6]

An application to licence a stallion must be made between 1st July and 30th September inclusive in the year before it is treated as reaching the age of five years[7]; if it is imported, application must be made within two months before the date of import; if, being five years old, it ceases to be a pony of a prescribed breed,[8] application must be made before that happens.[9] The application must be made to the Ministry of

---

[1] A person is deemed to keep a stallion if he owns it or has the control of it. (H.B.A. 1958, s. 1(4).)

[2] H.B.A. 1958, s. 1(2). Horse Breeding Rules 1948, Rule 3.

[3] *I.e.*, in the manner described in the text following.

[4] For a referee's inspection and examination, *see* p. 89.

[5] *I.e.*, in the manner described in the text following.

[6] H.B.A. 1958, s. 1(3).

[7] As to reckoning of age, *see* note [7] on p. 85.

[8] For the meaning of "prescribed breed", *see* p. 85.

[9] Horse Breeding Rules 1948, Rule 6(1)(b), (c) and (e). The Minister may extend the time for making the application. (H.B.A. 1958, s. 2(1).)

Agriculture, Fisheries and Food (Section AH IIC), Tolworth Tower, Surbiton, Surrey KT6 7DX. on a particular form with payment of a fee of £60.[1] The owner or other person having the control of the stallion must provide all reasonable facilities for its inspection and examination by a person authorised by the Minister.[2]

The Minister will grant a licence if these conditions are met but may refuse if it appears to him that the stallion—

(a) is permanently affected with any contagious or infectious disease; or

(b) is permanently affected with any other disease or defect of a type laid down by regulations[3] as making the stallion unsuitable for breeding; or

(c) has proved to be inadequately prolific; or

(d) is calculated, if used for breeding purposes, to injure the breed of horses by reason of its defective or inferior conformation or physique.[4]

A licence for a stallion continues in force until—

(1) it is revoked by the Minister; or

(2) it ceases to be in force because the requirements about change of ownership or letting are not complied with[5]; or

(3) the stallion dies or is castrated; or

(4) the stallion has been outside Great Britain[6] for a

---

[1] Horse Breeding Rules 1948, Rules 5(1), 13(1), (2). The fee may be returned if the applicant withdraws his application for an inspection of the stallion. (Regulations quoted in note [1] on p. 90).

[2] Horse Breeding Rules 1948, Rule 7; H.B.A. 1958, s. 7(2).

[3] The diseases and defects so laid down are: cataract, roaring, whistling, ring bone (high or low), side bone, bone spavin, navicular disease, shivering, stringhalt, and defective genital organs. (Horse Breeding Rules 1948, Rule 9).

[4] H.B.A. 1958, s. 2(1), (3). Notice of refusal will be served on the applicant for the licence. (H.B.A. 1958, s. 6(2)(a). See, further, note [6] on p. 88.

[5] See pp. 90–91 for these requirements.

[6] I.e. England, Scotland and Wales.

continuous period of 14 days or such longer consecutive period[1] as the Minister may allow.[2]

A licence may be revoked by the Minister for the same reasons as he is entitled to refuse to grant it in the first place (*see* items (*a*) to (*d*) above), except that under item (*d*) the licence shall not be revoked on the ground only of the stallion being affected in its wind if it is at least nine years old and the licence has been in force for two years.[3] On pain of being fined, the owner of a stallion whose licence has ceased to be in force must return it at once to the Minister.[4]

If in the Minister's view a stallion which is licensed or about to be licensed is temporarily affected by a disease or defect[5] rendering it unsuitable for use, or use in a particular way, for breeding purposes, he may, by serving a notice,[6] make it a condition of the licence that the stallion shall not, for the period given in the notice or until further notice, be used, or be used in that way, for breeding purposes.[7]

In a number of cases the Minister may, instead of issuing a licence, grant a permit to keep a stallion. This is the situation when—

(*a*) the Minister has refused, or has power to refuse,[8] a

---

[1] The period of absence outside G.B. is calculated from the time it is put on board a ship or plane on departure to the time it is landed in G.B. on its return. (H.B.A. 1958, s. 2(2).)

[2] H.B.A. 1958, s. 2(2).

[3] H.B.A. 1958, s. 2(3): Horse Breeding Rules 1948, Rule 11. Notice of revocation will be served, it appears, on the person stated in the licence to be the stallion's owner. (H.B.A. 1958, s. 6(2)(*b*).) For manner of service of notice, *see* note [6] below.

[4] H.B.A. 1958, s. 2(4). Any certified copy of the licence held (which may be requested without further charge when the licence is issued) must also be returned.

[5] If permanently affected, the Minister is entitled to refuse the licence altogether; *see* items (*a*) and (*b*) on p. 87.

[6] The notice must be in writing and served on the owner of the stallion or, if the licence has only been applied for, on the applicant. It must be delivered or sent to the address given on the licence or in the application or to a change of address notified by the licence holder. (Horse Breeding Rules 1948, Rules 10, 14(*c*) and (*d*).) The kind of post to be used, if sending it in that way, is not specified.

[7] H.B.A. 1958, s. 4(1). Contravention of the condition is an offence.

[8] For the power of refusal, *see* p. 87.

licence for a stallion which is not a thoroughbred or a pony of a prescribed breed[1]; or

(b) he has revoked or proposes to revoke[2] a licence for such a stallion as is described as (a) above; **and in either case—**

(c) he considers it expedient to authorise the stallion to be kept entire.[3]

The rules governing an application for a permit are similar to those for a licence.[4] The rules for its duration[5] are also the same, except that in addition a permit can be given for a limited duration.[6] The Minister may refuse to grant a permit on any grounds which appear to him sufficient, and may grant it subject to conditions breach of which is an offence. He may revoke it for breach of a condition of the permit or of another permit granted to the same person. When it ceases to be in force it must be returned to the Minister.[7]

The owner of a stallion has a right of appeal against the Minister's refusal to grant a licence or his revocation of a licence; he may also appeal against a notice by the Minister restricting the animal's use for breeding.[8] There can be no appeal on the Minister's decision on a permit.

The manner of the appeal is for the owner to apply to the Ministry of Agriculture at the address given on page 87 on a particular form, within 28 days of notification by the Minister of the fact which entitles him to appeal, for the stallion to be examined by a referee or referees.[9] A fee

---

[1] For the meanings of "thoroughbred" and "prescribed breed", see p. 85.

[2] For revocation, see p. 88.

[3] I.e., not castrated.

[4] H.B.A. 1958 s. 3(1). See pp. 86–87; the fee is also £60 except that no further charge is made if a fee has been paid for a refused licence. (Horse Breeding Rules 1948, Rule 13(1).)

[5] See pp. 87–88.

[6] H.B.A. 1958, s. 3(2).

[7] H.B.A. 1958, s. 3(3)–(6).

[8] For such a notice, see p. 88.

[9] The Minister appoints a panel of registered vets for this purpose after consulting horse breeding societies. No referee chosen must have been previously employed to examine the stallion. (H.B.A. 1958, s. 5(2), (3).)

of £70 should be remitted.[1] The Ministry arrange for the examination, and the report of the referee or referees is considered by the Minister who notifies the owner whether he has altered his original decision.[2]

If a stallion at least five years old[3] has no licence or permit, then, unless it is a thoroughbred or a pony of a prescribed breed,[4] the Minister may by notice[5] require the stallion to be slaughtered or castrated within the time stipulated in the notice.[6] If the person receiving the notice is not the owner, he must at once inform the owner of it and in default is liable to the owner for any loss suffered by the default.[7] Failure to comply with a notice renders the recipient liable to a fine of up to £3 for each day of non-compliance.[8] It also entitles the Minister to arrange for the stallion to be slaughtered or castrated and recover the cost from the recipient of the notice.[9]

If, while a licence or permit is in force, the ownership of a stallion changes or it is let for more than six months, the document can be transferred to the new owner[10] by applying to the Minister. Unless transferred in this way, the document ceases to be in force from one month after change of ownership.[11] Notice of change of ownership or letting must

---

[1] It will be returned if the Minister does not confirm his original decision, and may be returned if the owner withdraws his application for an examination. (Horse Breeding (Amendment) Regulations 1975 (S.I. 1975/1777), Art. 3.) The Minister pays the referee's charges. (H.B.A. 1958, s. 5(5), (6).)
[2] H.B.A. 1958, s. 5(1), (4); Horse Breeding Rules 1948, Rules 12, 13(1). The Minister's decision on the appeal is final, subject to certain legal processes which may be available. He is not obliged to follow any recommendation in the report.
[3] For the calculation of the animal's, age, see note [7] on p. 85.
[4] For the meanings of "thoroughbred" and "prescribed breed", see p. 85.
[5] For the service of the notice, see note [6] on p. 88.
[6] H.B.A. 1958, ss. 1(2)(b), 6(1).
[7] H.B.A. 1958, s. 6(3).
[8] H.B.A. 1958, s. 6(5). Moving the animal after notice without the Minister's permission, except to have it slaughtered or castrated, is also an offence. (H.B.A. 1958, s. 6(6).)
[9] H.B.A. 1958, s. 6(7).
[10] "Owner" means the person to whom for the time being the stallion belongs whether absolutely or as lessee. (H.B.A. 1958, s. 16(1).)
[11] H.B.A. 1958, s. 8(1).

anyhow be given at once to the Minister; this is also the case if the animal dies or is castrated.[1]

The regulating Act, *i.e.*, the Horse Breeding Act 1958, contains a number of other supplementary provisions dealing with: inspection and marking of stallions by Ministry officers and their powers of entry to premises[2]; production of licences and permits, and penalties for their forgery or fraudulent use[3]; provisions for evidence in proceedings[4]; and the application of the Act to stallions on commons and in the New Forest.[5]

Cattle and Sheep Breeding

Formerly, legislation controlled the breeding of both cattle and sheep. This ceased to have effect, in the case of cattle in October 1976, and in the case of sheep in July 1981.

Feeding Untreated Food to Animals

It is unlawful to feed, or cause to permit to be fed, to any livestock[6] or poultry waste food[7] or other feeding stuffs for them which have been in contact with unprocessed[8] waste food, unless the waste food or feeding stuffs have first been processed[8] by licensed plant and equipment. Likewise, processed waste food which has been in contact with unpro-

---

[1] H.B.A. 1958, ss. 8(2), 9.
[2] H.B.A. 1958, s. 7.
[3] H.B.A. 1958, ss. 10, 11.
[4] H.B.A. 1958, s. 12.
[5] H.B.A. 1958, s. 15.
[6] "Livestock" means cattle, sheep, pigs and goats. (Diseases of Animals (Waste Food) Order 1973 (S.I. 1973/1936), Art. 2(1).)
[7] "Waste food" means: (*a*) any meat, bones, blood, offal or other part of the carcase of any livestock or of any poultry, or product derived therefrom or hatchery waste or eggs or egg shells; or (*b*) any broken or waste foodstuffs (including table or kitchen refuse, scraps or waste) which contain or have been in contact with any meat, bones, blood, offal or with any other part of the carcase of any livestock or of any poultry; but does not include meal manufactured from protein originating from livestock or poultry. (1973 Order, Art. 2(1).)
[8] "Processed" means all the waste food being kept at boiling point at least for one hour or more, or treated by another process authorised by the Minister; and "unprocessed" is interpreted accordingly. (1973 Order, Art 2(1).

cessed waste food must not be so fed until it has been processed again. No one is allowed to have untreated waste food for feeding to livestock or poultry unless he holds a licence for processing it, but a person may have waste food from his own household and may feed it to his livestock and poultry after processing.[1]

In no circumstances must imported waste food, or other waste food which has been in contact with it, be fed to any animal[2], poultry or other bird.[3]

Other restrictions imposed on waste food deal with: its movement only to licensed premises; preventing unprocessed waste food coming into contact with animals and animal feeds; and precautions when transporting unprocessed waste food by road.[4]

Licences to process and handle waste food are issued by the Ministry of Agriculture.[5]

No person shall feed, or cause or permit to be fed, to animals[6] or buy for the purpose of feeding to them—

(a) any milk,[7] unless it has been pasteurised or boiled; or

(b) any whey, cheese washings or other liquid containing or derived from milk, unless either the liquid has been boiled or the milk which it contains or from which it is derived has been pasteurised or boiled

if in either case the milk originates from premises in a controlled area.[8] There is nothing to prevent milk or other

---

[1] 1973 Order, Art. 3.
[2] "Animal" means any kind of mammal except man, and any kind of four-footed beast which is not a mammal. (1973 Order, Art. 2(1).)
[3] 1973 Order, Art, 4.
[4] 1973 Order, Arts, 5, 6, 9.
[5] 1973 Order, Arts, 7, 8.
[6] "Animals" means cattle, sheep, goats and all other ruminating animals and swine. (Diseases of Animals (Milk Treatment) Order 1967 (S.I. 1967/1714), Art. 2(1)).
[7] "Milk" includes separated or skimmed milk. (1967 Order, Art. 2(1).)
[8] As to controlled areas, see pp. 173–174.

liquids being fed to animals on the farm from which the milk originated.[1]

Bulls on Public Paths

A new rule about keeping bulls on public paths was brought into force on 30th November 1981. This provides that it will be a finable offence for the occupier of a field or enclosure which is crossed by a public path to permit a bull to be at large in it.[2] But this is not to apply to any bull—

(a) whose age does not exceed 10 months; **or**

(b) which is not of a recognised dairy breed[3] **and** is at large in any field or enclosure in which cows or heifers are also at large.[4]

The public paths to which this provision applies are ways over which the public have the following rights of way—

(i) on foot only, exclusive of a footpath at the side of a public road;

(ii) only on foot and a right of way on horseback[5] or leading a horse,[5] with or without the right to drive animals along the way;

(iii) for vehicular and all other kinds of traffic, but which are used by the public mainly as in (i) or (ii) above.[6]

Formerly, in many areas, district council byelaws were in

---

[1] 1967 Order Art. 3.

[2] WCA 1981 s. 59(1).

[3] "A recognised dairy breed" means one of the following breeds: Ayrshire, British Friesian, British Holstein, Dairy Shorthorn, Guernsey, Jersey and Kerry (WCA 1981 s. 59(4)). The Secretary of State may by order add any breed to, or remove any breed from, this list (WCA 1981 s. 59(5)).

[4] WCA 1981 s. 59(2).

[5] "Horse" includes a pony, ass and mule, and "horseback" is to be interpreted accordingly (WCA 1981 s. 66(1)).

[6] WCA 1981 ss. 59(1), 66(1). Public paths have been surveyed and the different categories are marked on maps which have been deposited at one or more places in each district council area for free inspection at all reasonable hours. (WCA 1981 s. 57(5)). These maps are to a major extent conclusive as to the status and particulars of the paths contained in them. (WCA 1981 s. 56).

force which prohibited bulls from being at large in fields crossed by public paths. Such byelaws are now superseded by the new provisions.[1]

---

[1] WCA 1981 s. 59(3).

CHAPTER 6

DANGEROUS WILD ANIMALS

The Dangerous Wild Animals Act was passed in 1976 to regulate the keeping of certain kinds of dangerous wild animals. The fundamental provision of the Act is to prohibit, with exceptions, the keeping of named animals except in accordance with a licence granted by the local authority.[1] A number of the ingredients of this provision needs to be examined in turn.

The exceptions to the prohibition are: a zoological garden[2]; a circus[3]; premises licensed as a pet shop[4]; and a place registered under the Cruelty to Animals Act 1876 for performing experiments.[5]

The Act is at pains to define the meaning of "keeping" in relation to the named animals. A person is a keeper of an animal if he has it in his possession[6]; for those times when an animal cannot be said to be in the possession of anybody it is treated as being in the possession of the person who last had it in his possession.[7] But a person is not to be

---

[1] D.W.A. 1976, s. 1(1). Contravention is an offence punishable by fine. (D.W.A. 1976, ss. 2(5), 6(1).)

[2] "Zoological garden" means any place, other than a circus or deer-park, where wild animals not living in their natural surroundings are kept for the purpose of being regularly exhibited to members of the public for gain; and in this definition "deer-park" means any enclosure where deer of a species indigenous to or feral (*i.e.* wild) in the United Kingdom are kept. (D.W.A. 1976, s. 7(4).)

[3] "Circus" includes any place where animals are kept or introduced wholly or mainly for the purpose of performing tricks or manoeuvres. (D.W.A. 1976, s. 7(4)). An enclosure in a high street, to which a lioness was taken from a zoo for exhibition purposes, is not a circus within the definition (*Hemming v. Graham–Jones* (1980)).

[4] For licensing of pet shops, *see* pp. 75–77.

[5] D.W.A. 1976, s. 5.

[6] For some notes on the meaning of "possession", *see* p. 65.

[7] D.W.A. 1976, s. 7(1).

treated as the keeper of an animal **only** because he has it in his possession for the purpose of: preventing it from causing damage[1]; restoring it to its owner; it undergoing veterinary treatment; or it being transported on behalf of another person.[2]

The animals to which the Act applies are listed in its Schedule which is reproduced in Appendix D at the end of this book. It may be varied by regulations made by the Secretary of State.[3]

Licences to keep dangerous wild animals are granted by district councils.[4] They are not permitted to grant a licence unless several conditions are met. In the first place, an application for a licence must—

(a) specify the species of animal and the number of animals of each species proposed to be kept[5];

(b) specify the premises[6] where any animal concerned will normally be held which must be within the council's area;

(c) be made by a person who is neither under 18 years old nor disqualified from keeping any dangerous wild animal[7]; and

(d) be accompanied by such fee as the council may stipulate.[8]

In the second place, a licence is not to be granted unless the council is satisfied that—

---

[1] "Damage" includes the death of, or injury to, any person. (D.W.A. 1976, s. 7(4).)

[2] D.W.A. 1976, s. 7(2).

[3] D.W.A. 1976, ss. 7(4), 8.

[4] D.W.A. 1976, ss. 1(1), 7(4). In London the licensing authority is the Common Council of the City of London or, elsewhere, a London borough council. Application for Licence, Shaw's form Cat. No. DWA 1.

[5] "Kept" is to be interpreted in accordance with the definition of "keeper", (D.W.A. 1976, s. 7(3))—*see* above.

[6] "Premises" can include any place. (D.W.A. 1976, s. 7(4).)

[7] For disqualification, *see* p. 99.

[8] D.W.A. 1976, s. 1(2). The fee should be sufficient to meet the direct and indirect costs which the council may incur as a result of the application.

(1) it is not contrary to the public interest on the grounds of safety, nuisance or otherwise to grant it;

(2) the applicant for the licence is a suitable person to hold it;

(3) the animal's accommodation will be escape-proof and suitable as regards construction, size, temperature, lighting, ventilation, drainage, cleanliness and the number of animals to be accommodated;

(4) the animal will be protected in case of fire or other emergency;

(5) all reasonable precautions will be taken to prevent and control the spread of infectious diseases; and

(6) the animal can take adequate exercise within its accommodation.[1]

Two further conditions must be fulfilled before a licence can be granted. Unless in the council's opinion the circumstances are exceptional, the application must be made by a person who both owns and possesses,[2] or proposes both to own and possess, any animal concerned.[3] Secondly, the council must consider a report by a vet[4] on the premises where any animal will normally be held and cannot issue a licence unless, viewed in the light of that report, they consider the premises suitable.[5]

Even if all these pre-requisites are met, the grant or refusal of a licence is, subject to the right of appeal mentioned later, entirely within the council's discretion. If a licence is issued, it must include conditions about a number of matters detailed in the Act (including insurance against liability for damage[6] caused by the animal) to which the

---

[1] D.W.A. 1976, s. 1(3).
[2] For some notes on the meaning of "possession", see p. 65.
[3] D.W.A. 1976, s. 1(4).
[4] The vet's fee will be part of the cost of the licence to be charged to the applicant; see note [8] on p. 96. For costs of inspection of premises, see p. 99.
[5] D.W.A. 1976, s. 1(5).
[6] "Damage" includes the death of, or injury to, any person. (D.W.A. 1976, s. 7(4).)

council may add their own conditions.[1] With some limitations, the council may at any time vary or revoke the conditions, or add new conditions; unless a variation or new condition is requested by the licence-holder, he must be given reasonable time to comply with it.[2]

Contravention of or non-compliance with a condition is an offence. In addition to the licence-holder, the offence may be committed by any other person who is entitled to keep any animal under the authority of the licence and who was primarily responsible for the contravention or non-compliance. Neither may be convicted if he proves that he took all reasonable precautions to avoid committing the offence.[3]

At the choice of the applicant, the licence will last from the day it is granted to the end of the current calendar year or from the beginning of the next year to the end of that year.[4] Unless previously cancelled,[5] the licence then expires, but if a further licence is applied for beforehand it continues in force pending the grant or refusal of the application. A new licence will run from the expiry date of the previous licence.[6] Personal representatives of a deceased licence-holder have the benefit of the licence for 28 days from death; if they apply for a new one within that time, the original licence continues in force until the application is determined.[7]

There is a right of appeal to a magistrates' court[8] against—

(a) the council's refusal to grant a licence;

(b) a condition of the licence whether imposed when it was granted or later;

(c) the variation or revocation of a condition.[9]

---

[1] D.W.A. 1976, s. 1(6), (7).
[2] D.W.A. 1976, s. 1(9), (10).
[3] D.W.A. 1976, s. 2(6), (7)
[4] D.W.A. 1976, s. 2(2).
[5] See p. 99.
[6] D.W.A. 1976, s. 2(3).
[7] D.W.A. 1976, s. 2(4).
[8] In Scotland, to the sheriff. (D.W.A. 1976, s. 2(8).)
[9] D.W.A. 1976, s. 2(1).

Powers of entry to and inspection of premises connected with a licence are given to vets and others with written authorisation from the council.[1] To obstruct or delay them is an offence.[2] The reasonable costs of the inspection may be charged to the applicant for the licence or, if it has been issued, to the licensee.[3]

If a dangerous wild animal is kept[4] without a licence, or a condition of a licence is contravened or not complied with, the council in whose area the animal is may seize it and keep it or destroy or otherwise dispose of it. No compensation is payable.[5] The council's costs are recoverable in the first case from the animal's keeper and, in the second case, from the licence-holder.[6]

In addition to fining a person for an offence against the Act, the court may cancel his licence and, whether he is a licence-holder or not, disqualify him from keeping[4] any dangerous wild animal to which the Act applies for such period as the court thinks fit. These sanctions can also be imposed for convictions for offences against certain other Acts[7] relating to animals. The court's order of cancellation or disqualification may be suspended pending an appeal.[8]

In concluding this Chapter, the point is made that there is no exception to or mitigation of the 1976 Act's requirements when only few very young animals of the kind described are kept. For example, a newly born tiger requires a licence as much as a cage of adult tigers.

---

[1] D.W.A. 1976, s. 3(1).

[2] D.W.A. 1976, s; 3(4).

[3] D.W.A. 1976, s. 3(3).

[4] "Kept" and "keeping" must be interpreted in accordance with the definition of "keeper" given on pp. 95–96. (D.W.A. 1976, s. 7(3).).

[5] D.W.A. 1976, s. 4(1).

[6] D.W.A. 1976, s. 4(2), (3).

[7] These Acts are: the Protection of Animals Acts 1911 to 1964 (*see* pp. 119–133); the Protection of Animals (Scotland) Acts 1912 to 1964; the Pet Animals Act 1951 (*see* pp. 75–77); the Animal Boarding Establishments Act 1963 (*see* pp. 73–74); the Riding Establishments Acts 1964 and 1970 (*see* pp. 81–85); and the Breeding of Dogs Act 1973 (*see* p. 75).

[8] D.W.A. 1976, s. 6. The appeal lies, presumably, to the Crown Court.

CHAPTER 7

ANIMALS AS GAME

Introduction

In the Acts of Parliament dealing with game there are different definitions of the word or no definition at all. So far as four-legged animals are concerned, only hares, rabbits and deer are involved, but not all the in same way. The differences will appear when the relevant Acts are considered.

Where an animal is thus treated as game, a dead or tame animal of that kind is, when appropriate in the context, likewise treated.[1]

The Game Acts, when regulating dealings with game, generally use the words "take or kill". "Taking" has been interpreted to mean catching, as in a snare, with a view to keeping or killing,[2] and this word will be used in this Chapter to mean both killing and taking.

---

[1] *Cook v. Trevener* (1911).
[2] *R. v. Glover* (1814); *Watkins v. Price* (1877).

Prohibited Times for Taking Game

Close Seasons

There is no close season, *i.e.* period of the year in which game must not be taken, for rabbits or hares.[1] The only close seasons for deer are for certain species, and it is an offence to take them out of season, but with certain exceptions; these matters are considered on pages 136 to 138.

Sunday and Christmas Day

It is an offence to take hares on Sunday or Christmas Day or then to use any dog, gun, net, or other engine[2] or instrument for that purpose.[3] (In defining the meaning of game in this context the Act says that the word **includes** hares and particular game birds, and it is a matter for speculation whether, since deer are sometimes regarded as game, they may be included also.) It matters not that the net "or other engine or instrument" was set on another day; the person doing so is regarded by the law as using it on the prohibited days if it was then in position.[4]

At Night

It is an offence unlawfully[5] to take hares or rabbits at night[6] on any open or enclosed land, including any public road, highway or path or the sides of them and the openings, outlets or gates from any open or enclosed land leading on to any public road, highway or path.[7]

Other provisions about shooting hares and rabbits at night

---

[1] But occupiers of certain lands may not take hares and rabbits under the Ground Game Acts during certain periods of the year; *see* p. 109.

[2] The word "engine" includes a snare. (*Allen v. Thompson* (1870) L.R. 5 Q.B. 336 at 339.) *See also* note [5] on p. 116.

[3] G.A. 1831, s. 3. The use of one dog, gun, etc. by two or more people acting together may constitute an offence by each. (*R. v. Littlechild* (1871).)

[4] *Allen v. Thompson*, as above.

[5] Though mainly directed at common poachers, this offence may be committed by others not having the right to take the animals and, possibly, by someone unlawfully acting because he has no game licence.

[6] This is from one hour after sunset to one hour before sunrise. (N.P.A. 1828, s. 12).

[7] NPA 1828, s. 1; N.P.A. 1844, s. 1.

are described on pages 109 to 110 and 111. The offence of killing or taking deer at night is considered on page 138.

Game Licences

With the exceptions mentioned later,[1] a person must hold a game licence before he can take game. This obligation is created by two Acts of Parliament.[2] Because their wording is different and their combined scope is wide, it is worthwhile to set down the exact words used so far as they describe the acts which require a licence to be held:

(1) To take or kill any game or use any dog, gun, net or other engine[3] or instrument for the purpose of searching for or killing or taking game.[4]

(2) To take, kill or pursue, or aid or assist in any manner in the taking, killing or pursuing by any means whatever, or use any dog, gun, net or other engine[3] for the purpose of taking, killing or pursuing game.[5]

So far as four-legged animals are concerned, hares only are mentioned in the definition of "game" in (1), and "game" (undefined) and rabbits and deer in (2); though it may be argued that deer also are included in (1) and hares in (2).[6] It will be seen that the scope of the words used in (2) is generally wider than in (1), but the latter brings in searching for game.

Some examples taken from decided cases help to show the wide scope of these requirements. To walk about unlicensed with a dog or gun where there is game or to point a gun at game is evidence of the commission of an offence.[7]

---

[1] *See* pp. 103–105.
[2] G.A. 1831 and G.L.A. 1860.
[3] *See* note [2] on p. 101.
[4] G.A. 1831, s. 23.
[5] G.L.A. 1860, s. 4.
[6] In case (1) because the word "include" is used in defining game and the list of birds and animals in the definition is not therefore exhaustive and may include deer which are often regarded as game. In case (2) because the word "game" is not defined and hares are generally treated as game.
[7] *R. v. Davis* (1795).

If an unlicensed person kills game by accident and takes it away, he has committed an offence.[1] So a motorist knocking over a hare, who picks it up, puts it in the car and drives on, is guilty if he has no game licence. To take game out of a trap in which it has been accidentally caught with a view to killing or keeping it is an act which requires a licence.[2] It is up to anybody caught with game in his possession to prove that he acquired it innocently, *i.e.*, in circumstances in which a licence was not needed.[3]

The same act may constitute an offence under both Acts of Parliament and subject the offender to the separate penalties[4] which they provide.[5]

A game licence is not needed in the following cases—

(1) The taking of deer[6] in any enclosed lands by the owner or occupier, or by his direction or permission.[7] A court decision usefully illustrates two points on this exception; the court considered that the meaning of "enclosed lands" included "lands used for farming and enclosed by normal agricultural hedges" in contrast with "moorland where there are no enclosures and where the deer can run free"; secondly, the court made it clear that a game licence is not needed when a deer is shot on enclosed land with the owner's permission though the deer runs on and drops on land where the killer does not have that permission.[8]

(2) The taking of rabbits by the proprietor of any warren or of any enclosed ground whatever, or by the tenant of lands,[9] either by himself or by his direction or permission.[10]

---

[1] *Molton v. Cheeseley* (1788).
[2] *Watkins v. Price* (1877).
[3] *Hemming v. Halsey* (1823).
[4] £24 (G.A. 1831, s. 23) and £50 (G.L.A. 1860, s. 4).
[5] *Clark v. Westaway* (1927).
[6] For the protection of deer generally, *see* pp. 136–141.
[7] G.L.A. 1860, s. 5, Exception 5.
[8] *Jemmison v. Priddle* (1972).
[9] *I.e.*, any lands, whether enclosed or not.
[10] G.L.A. 1860, s. 5, Exception 2.

(3) Shooting by the Royal Family and Her Majesty's gamekeepers.[1]

(4) A person aiding or assisting in the taking of game in the company or presence of, and for the use of, another person who has a game licence in his own right, who is taking some active part in the sport with his own dog or gun and who is not acting "by virtue of any deputation or appointment".[2] The effect of this is to exempt beaters, loaders and other assistants from the necessity of being licensed; but such unlicensed beaters, etc., must not assist a gamekeeper since he holds his position by "deputation or appointment". Moreover, they apparently must not use or lend the use of any dog of their own, even to a licensed person who is by virtue of his licence then and there taking game. A loader may carry his employer's gun and thus aid in killing game, but he must not carry a gun of his own, and he must not fire his own or his employer's gun.[3]

(5) The actual occupier of any enclosed lands,[4] or the owner thereof who has the right of killing hares on those lands, or a person authorised by either of them, may kill hares on those lands without a game licence, but not at night.[5] Any authority so given must be in writing stating the names of the persons involved, a description of the lands in question, and be signed and witnessed by the person giving it.[6]

(6) A person required by a Government Minister to kill certain animals and birds as pests need not hold a game licence for that purpose.[7]

---

[1] G.L.A. 1860, s. 5, Exemptions 1 and 2.
[2] G.L.A. 1860, s. 5, Exemption 3.
[3] *Ex parte Sylvester* (1829).
[4] For an interpretation of "enclosed lands", *see* p. 103.
[5] H.A. 1848, ss. 1, 5; "night" lasts from one hour after sunset to one hour before sunrise. (H.A. 1848, s. 7.).
[6] H.A. 1848, s. 1, and Schedule.
[7] A.A. 1947, ss. 98, 100(4). For further details of the requirement, *see* pp. 186–188.

(7) An occupier of land, and certain persons who may be authorised by him in writing[1] may kill hares and rabbits on that land without a licence.[2]

(8) Persons pursuing and killing hares, whether by coursing[3] with greyhounds or by hunting with beagles or other hounds, or pursuing and killing deer by hunting with hounds.[4]

Game licences are obtained at any Post Office at which money order business is transacted. The licence must show the amount of duty charged and the proper christian names and surname and place of residence of the person to whom it is issued. It will be dated on the day when it is actually issued[5] and will show the time of issue. It will be in force from that day[6] and time so that an offence committed on that day but before the time of issue is not condoned.[7] It continues in force until the end of the day on which it is stated to expire,[8] but becomes null and void immediately its holder is convicted of trespassing in the daytime in search of game in England, Wales, or Scotland.[9] It is not transferable.

Game licences are issued for different periods and at different prices as follows:—

To be taken out after July and before November and to expire on 31st July following ... £6

To be taken out after July and before November and to expire on 31st October in the same year £4

To be taken out after October and to expire on 31st July following £4

---

[1] As to who these persons may be, *see* pp. 108–109.
[2] G.G.A. 1880, ss. 4, 8.
[3] Coursing is not confined to organised coursing. (*Dolby v. Halmshaw* (1936).
[4] G.L.A. 1860, s. 5, Exceptions 3 and 4.
[5] G.L.A. 1860, s. 16.
[6] G.L.A. 1860, s. 16.
[7] G.L.A. 1860, s. 4. *Campbell v. Strangeways* (1877).
[8] G.L.A. 1860, s. 16.
[9] G.A. 1831, s. 30; G.(S.)A. 1832; G.L.A. 1860, s. 11.

| Any continuous period of 14 days (known as an occasional licence) ... ... | £2 |
| A gamekeeper's licence ... ... | £4[1] |

A gamekeeper's licence is an annual licence expiring on 31st July and obtained by his employer. It excuses the game-keeper from having an ordinary game licence but lasts only while he is employed as gamekeeper and is limited to use on land on which the employer has a right to take game. On a change of gamekeeper during the currency of the licence it may be endorsed by the issuing authority in favour of the new employee without further charge so as to operate in his favour for the remainder of the period of the licence.[2]

The holder of a £6 game licence is entitled to sell game, but only to a licensed gamedealer.[3] Otherwise it is an offence for anyone to sell, or offer for sale (but not to give away), hares to anyone else, except by:—

(1) A licensed gamedealer[4];

(2) An innkeeper selling game for consumption in his own house provided he obtains it from a licensed gamedealer[5]

(3) A person directed in writing by a J.P. to sell game seized as having been unlawfully taken[6]; and

(4) An occupier of land selling ground game taken on land in his occupation by him or persons authorised[7] by him.[8]

A gamekeeper's licence only entitles him to sell hares on

---

[1] G.L.A. 1860, s. 2; C.I.R.A. 1883, ss. 4, 5; Fees for Game and Other Licences (Variation) Order 1968 (S.I. 1968/120). The Government may from time to time alter these fees. (L.G.A. 1966, s. 35(2), and Sch. 3, Part II.)
[2] G.L.A. 1860, ss. 2, 7, 8, 9.
[3] G.A. 1831, ss. 17, 25; G.L.A. 1860, s. 13.
[4] G.A. 1831, s. 25.
[5] G.A. 1831, s. 26.
[6] G.L.A. 1960, ss. 3(4), 4(4).
[7] As to who these persons may be, *see* pp. 108–109.
[8] G.G.A. 1880, s. 4; This listing produces the rather curious result that others entitled to take hares, *e.g.*, non-occupying owners with reserved shooting rights and shooting tenants, cannot legally sell them unless, holding a £6 game licence, he sells them to a licensed gamedealer.

the account and with the written authority of his employer. None of these restrictions applies to the sale of deer or rabbits.[1]

Hares, unless imported,[2] must not be sold or exposed for sale during the months of March to July inclusive.[3]

Ground Game

By the Ground Game Act of 1880 an occupier of land was given the right to take hares and rabbits (called "ground game" in the Act) on the land which he occupies, whether or not any other person has that right. The right is incidental to and inseparable from his occupation so that he cannot be divested of it in any way. Any agreement, condition or arrangement which purports to divest or alienate this right, or which gives him any advantage in return for him forbearing to exercise it, or which imposes any disadvantage on him in consequence of his exercising it, is void and of no effect.[4]

This means that the occupier has the right to take ground game concurrently with any other person who has that right because, for example, he is the owner or the shooting tenant. The right was given to allow farming tenants without shooting rights to protect their crops. Under other legislation they may claim from their landlords compensation for crop damage caused by deer and certain birds[5]; there is no right to compensation for damage done by hares and rabbits.

The occupier's rights under the Act are not to affect in any way his ability to acquire and exercise sporting rights in the normal way. So, if gaming rights are not reserved to his landlord under the tenancy agreement and are vested in the occupier, he may take ground game without the restrictions which the Act imposes on the statutory right and which are considered later.[6] If, having only a statutory right, he

[1] G.A. 1831, ss. 2, 25; G.L.A. 1860, s. 13. But see p. 144 as to the sale of venison.
[2] For the import of live hares, *see* p. 35–36.
[3] H.P.A. 1892, ss. 2, 3.
[4] G.G.A 1880, ss. 1, 3, 7, 8.
[5] *See* pp. 114–115.
[6] G.G.A. 1880, s. 2. For these restrictions, *see* pp. 109–110.

takes game other than hares and rabbits, or gives permission to another to do so, without in either case the authority of the person having the right to that game, he may be prosecuted.[1]

Clearly, an occupying owner, tenant or sub-tenant of land is an occupier for the purpose of the Act. A person having a right of common is not.[2] Nor, says the Act, shall a person be deemed to be an occupier "by reason of an occupation for the purpose of grazing or pasturage of sheep, cattle or horses for not more than nine months".[2]

This leaves in doubt the position of a grazier having other kinds of animals, or having grazing rights for more than nine months.

In addition to the occupier, one other person may be authorised by him in writing[3] to shoot ground game[4]; more than one may be so authorised to take them otherwise than by shooting.[5] If a person acts on a verbal permission only, he is strictly a trespasser.[6] The only persons who can be authorised in writing are—

(1) One or more members of the occupier's household[7] resident[8] on the land in his occupation; and

---

[1] G.A. 1831, s. 12.

[2] G.G.A. 1880, s. 1, proviso (2).

[3] No particular form is necessary but sensibly it should clearly show the date, the particulars of the person to whom it is given and the situation and extent of the land in question, and be signed by the occupier. It should also indicate whether or not authority to shoot is included.

[4] Where there are joint occupiers, each is at liberty to exercise the right to take ground game (*Morrison v. Anderson* (1913)) but if they authorise other persons, they must presumably do so jointly.

[5] G.G.A. 1880, s. 1, proviso (1)(*a*) and (*b*).

[6] Richardson v. Maitland (1897).

[7] The household will include household servants living and boarding at the occupier's house but presumably not those living in other houses on the land. (*re Drax, Savile v. Yeatman* (1887); *Ogle v. Morgan* (1852).)

[8] Residence is a question of fact in each case. A person invited to stay for a week and shoot rabbits was held in a Scottish case to satisfy the condition. (*Stuart v. Murray* (1884).) It is not necessary that the occupier should reside there himself. (*R. v. North Curry (Inhabitants)* (1825).)

(2) One or more people in the occupier's ordinary service[1] on such land; and

(3) Any one other person *bona fide* employed by the occupier for reward[2] in the taking and destruction of ground game.[3]

An authorised person must produce his written authority, if asked to do so, to any person having a concurrent right to take ground game on the land or to any person authorised by the latter in writing to make the demand. In default, the authorised person's right to ground game ceases.[4]

In the case of moorlands and unenclosed non-arable lands, except detached portions of either which are less than 25 acres in extent and adjoin arable lands, the occupier's right to take ground game is suspended from 1st April to 31st August inclusive, and he must not use firearms between 1st September and 10th December inclusive.[5] But a valid agreement may be made between the occupier on the one hand and the owner or shooting tenant on the other hand for the joint exercise by them between the last two dates of the right to take ground game or for its exercise for their joint benefit.[6]

The occupier, or one authorised person[7], may use firearms to kill ground game on the occupier's land at night.[8] But, before either may do so, the occupier must have the written

---

[1] "Ordinary service" presumably means regular service so that casual labour taken on for a week or two, as for harvest, would be excluded. Moreover, servants who, however regularly employed, do not find their customary work *on the land* would also be excluded.

[2] The fact of, for example, a rabbit catcher being allowed to keep all or some of the rabbits taken would probably be sufficient evidence of such employment for reward (*Bruce v. Prosser* (1898)) but a similar gift to a friend asked to come and shoot would hardly be so.

[3] G.G.A. 1880, s. 1, proviso (1)(*b*).

[4] G.G.A. 1880, s. 1, proviso(1)(*c*).

[5] G.G.A. 1880, s. 1, proviso (3); G.G.A. 1906, s. 2.

[6] G.G.A. 1906, s. 3.

[7] *I.e.*, one of the persons mentioned in items (1) to (3) in the text above who has been authorised by the occupier. It seems that this person should be that one of those persons who has been previously authorised to shoot generally—see p. 108.

[8] "Night" extends from the end of the first hour after sunset to the beginning of the last hour before sunrise.

authority of the other person, or one of the other persons, entitled to kill and take ground game on the land.[1] Any other shooting of ground game at night by the occupier or an authorised person is an offence.[2]

In Greater London poison must not be used at any time for killing ground game.[3]

Owners' and Tenants' Rights to Game

The rights of owners and tenants to take game will vary according to their status and the kinds of relationships created between them; these relationships usually, but not always, depend on a lease or tenancy agreement made between them and particularly on the terms of the document.

The description given in the document to the animals which may be taken by landlord or tenant will be important. Use of the words "game" or "gaming rights" will provoke some uncertainty in the absence, as we have seen,[4] of a standard definition of "game". A probable interpretation would be that the word means, so far as four-legged animals are concerned, deer, hares and rabbits since only these three come within the definitions used in Acts of Parliament. The common use of the words "shooting rights" or "sporting rights" is perhaps more satisfactory; they have been interpreted to mean the right to kill all things which are usually the object of sport.[5] Though not watertight, this interpretation will generally cover the kinds of animals in which landlords and tenants have particular interests.

In all the different situations the rights of the occupier, whether he be owner or any kind of tenant, to take hares and rabbits remain constant and, as described earlier,[6] cannot be altered by leases or written or verbal agreements.

The most straightforward situation is that of the owner-

---

[1] *E.g.*, the landlord to whom the sporting rights are reserved.

[2] G.G.A. 1880, s. 6; WCA 1981, s. 12, Sch. 7, para. 1.

[3] G.G.A. 1880, s. 6. As to the use of poisons generally, see pp. 122–24.

[4] On p. 100.

[5] Jeffryes v. Evans (1865); *Moore v. Earl of Plymouth* (1817) 7 Taunt. 614 at 627.

[6] On p. 107.

occupier who has not let the sporting rights. He may take game whenever and however he pleases, though of course he must obey the laws about game licences,[1] protected animals,[2] prohibited times,[3] and cruelty to animals.[4]

If the owner does not occupy his land but lets it to a tenant, sporting rights may or may not be reserved[5] to the owner. When they are not reserved they pass in every case with possession of the land to that tenant.[6] (A contrary principle obtains in Scotland where the right to game is considered to be a right personal to the owner of the land[7]). The tenant cannot however shoot hares or rabbits at night which he could do if the rights had been expressly granted to him by the owner.[8] The tenant may grant his rights to a shooting tenant. If the grant includes the right to ground game (hares and rabbits), the effect is that both have that right concurrently.[9]

Sporting rights may be reserved to the owner in the lease or tenancy agreement or by a separate contract or simply by verbal agreement. The terms used may prohibit the owner from letting the rights; if not prohibited, they may be let. A reservation of "exclusive rights" has the effect of giving the owner all rights, except over hares and rabbits the taking of which he shares with the occupier.[10] The reservation is defended by the law making it an offence for the tenant to take game, except hares and rabbits if he is an occupier, or to permit anyone else to do so.[11]

The tenant may claim damages from the shooting tenant for injury caused to his crops by the land being overstocked

---

[1] *See*, pp. 102–106.

[2] See, generally, Chapter 8.

[3] See pp. 101–102.

[4] See, generally, pp. 119–133.

[5] A reservation of rights to the owner is made by words in the lease or tenancy agreement showing those rights as belonging to him, *i.e.*, reserved out of the tenancy.

[6] *Pochin v. Smith* (1887); *Anderson v. Vicary* (1900).

[7] *Saunders v. Pitfield* (1888).

[8] *See* the cases mentioned in footnote [6] and [7] above.

[9] *Morgan v. Jackson* (1895).

[10] G.G.A. 1880, s. 3; *Stanton v. Brown* (1900). And *see* p. 107.

[11] G.A. 1831, s. 12.

with game[1] if this is due to that tenant's extraordinary non-natural or unreasonable action.[2] Within certain limitations, he may also claim compensation from his landlord for damage to crops by game.[3]

Where sporting rights are thus reserved, the owner, or any person to whom he may grant them, may exercise the rights to the same extent as, and precisely as if he was, the occupier of the land, subject to the tenant's rights to take ground game and to the possible claims by the tenant just mentioned.

The farming tenant is entitled to use the land and destroy gorse and underwood in the ordinary way[4] or to carry out any reasonable and normal operations which might be deemed advisable for the purpose of dealing with the land to the best advantage,[5] but he must not designedly drive game away.[6] On the other hand, the owner, or his tenant of shooting rights, must not trample fields of standing crops at a time when it is not usual or reasonable to do so; and if the owner or that tenant causes game to increase to an unreasonable extent, the tenant of the land can recover damages for the injury to his crops.[7] The owner is however entitled to be reimbursed by the shooting tenant for such damages[8] but not if the grant of rights to the latter does not enable him (the shooting tenant) to shoot on the part of the land adversely affected.[9]

The last type of situation which needs consideration is when there is a shooting tenant, *i.e.*, a person who, usually by lease or tenancy agreement, is granted sporting rights but no other rights over land. He may have these rights from: (*a*) the owner-occupier; or (*b*) an owner who has let his land but reserved the rights; or (*c*) an occupying tenant

---

[1] *Farrer v. Nelson* (1885).
[2] *Seligman v. Docker* (1948).
[3] *See* pp. 114–115.
[4] *Jeffryes v. Evans* (1865).
[5] *Peech v. Best* [1931] 1 K.B. 1 at p. 18.
[6] *Jeffryes v. Evans*, as above.
[7] *Hilton v. Green* (1862).
[8] A.H.A. 1948, s. 14.
[9] *Cornewall v. Dawson* (1871).

where the rights have not been reserved. In all these cases the shooting tenant may have either the right to shoot the game or general shooting and sporting rights.[1] Subject to this, in cases (*a*) and (*b*) he takes precisely those rights which the owner himself would have had, but in case (*a*) the owner keeps his right to take ground game.[2] An owner-occupier or a tenant who infringes his shooting tenant's rights by pursuing or taking game commits an offence for which he may be prosecuted,[3] but a non-occupying owner who does so is merely liable to a civil claim for breach of contract. A person who has been granted exclusive sporting rights has a right of action in the courts against anyone whose acts interfere with his enjoyment of them.[4]

Unless there is something to the contrary in the agreement which grants the sporting rights, the grantor of those rights is not prevented from using the land in the ordinary and accustomed way but having regard to its character at the date of the grant.[5] Thus, in the case of farming land, he cannot be prevented from altering the course of husbandry,[6] cutting down timber or underwood, or doing any other act falling within the ordinary course of estate management.[7] But any act done with the intention of injuring the rights granted[8] or which makes a substantial change in the character of the land can be the subject of court action if it substantially injures the rights granted.[9]

Where an accident, such as fire, threatens damage to his shooting rights, the shooting tenant is entitled to adopt such means for the preservation of his rights as are reasonably necessary.[10]

---

[1] For comments on these terms, *see* p. 110.

[2] Halsbury's Laws of England, 4th Ed., Vol. 2, para. 249. Though not so stated in Halsbury, it seems that in case (c) also the occupying tenant must retain his rights to ground game; *see* p. 107.

[3] G.A. 1831, s. 12.

[4] *Fitzgerald v. Firbank* (1897); *Nicholls v. Ely Sugar Beet Factory* (1931).

[5] *Peech v. Best* [1931] 1 K.B. 1 at 18.

[6] *Jeffryes v. Evans* (1865).

[7] *Gearns v. Baker* (1875).

[8] *Jeffryes v. Evans* and *Gearns v. Baker*, as above; *Bird v. Great Eastern Railway Co.* (1865).

[9] *Dick v. Norton* (1916).

[10] *Cope. v. Sharpe* (No. 2) (1912). For protection against dogs, *see* p. 116.

The right to take game is a form of property and may therefore be sold, leased or, if already held under a lease, sub-let to a third person. Constraints on this arise when the person wanting to dispose of the right holds it by virtue of an agreement which prevents him from doing so or restricts him in doing it. For example, the lease of sporting rights to a shooting tenant may stipulate that he is not to sub-let or assign, or that he is only to do so with the grantor's consent.

Though verbal agreements are occasionally effective, transactions in sporting rights should always be recorded in writing to eliminate doubts about their effect. The law sometimes requires the written document to be sealed by the parties.[1] This and the uncertainties which may arise as appearing from the preceding pages make it generally worthwhile to take legal advice, certainly if the rights involved are substantial.[2]

Compensation for Damage to Crops

If the occupier of land is a tenant of an agricultural holding[3] and has suffered damage from game,[4] he is entitled to compensation from his landlord if the damage exceeds twelve pence per hectare of the area over which the damage extends. It matters not that the game has come from a neighbouring owner's land and during the close season.[5] The right to compensation cannot be avoided by an agreement to the contrary between the landlord and tenant.[6]

The following conditions must be met to obtain compensation:—

(1) The tenant must not have written permission to kill the game.

---

[1] L.P.A. 1925, ss. 52(1), 205(1)(ix).
[2] On these matters generally, see *Halsbury's Laws of England*, 4th Ed., Vol. 2, para. 429.
[3] Briefly, "agricultural holding" means land used for agriculture for the purposes of a trade or business which is comprised in a tenancy agreement (AHA 1948, s. 1.).
[4] In this context "game" means, so far as four-legged animals are concerned, deer only. (A.H.A. 1948, s. 14(4).)
[5] *Thomson v. Earl of Galloway* (1919).
[6] A.H.A. 1948, s. 65(1).

(2) The right to take game must not belong to the tenant, nor to anyone claiming under him[1] other than the landlord.

(3) The tenant must give written notice[2] to the landlord[3] within one month after the tenant first became, or ought reasonably to have become, aware of the occurrence of the damage.

(4) The landlord must be given reasonable opportunity to inspect the damage, and, in the case of a growing crop, before it is begun to be reaped, raised or consumed, and, in the case of a crop reaped or raised, before it is begun to be removed from the land.

(5) The tenant must give written notice to the landlord[3] of the particulars of the claim within one month after the end of the calendar year in which the claim arises. A different period of 12 months, may, by agreement between them, be substituted for the calendar year.[4]

If the right to take the game belongs to someone other than the landlord, he is entitled to be indemnified by that person against the claim. Disputes about this or about the amount of compensation are to be settled by arbitration.[5]

---

[1] *E.g.*, a person to whom the tenant lets the sporting rights when these are not reserved to the landlord.

[2] The Act does not say what the contents of the notice are to be. It is suggested that it may be sufficient to indicate intention to make a claim, the situation of the land on which the crops have been damaged, and the kind of game causing it. The substantive claim will follow later under item (5) in the text above.

[3] The notice must be served by delivering it to the landlord, by leaving it at his proper address, or by sending it by registered letter or recorded delivery service to him. It may also be served by any of these means on the agent or employee of the landlord who is responsible for the management of the holding. (A.H.A. 1948, s. 92(1), (3); R.D.S.A. 1962, s. 1, and Sch.)

[4] A.H.A. 1948, s. 14(1).

[5] A.H.A. 1948, s. 14(2), (3). For arbitration procedure, *see* A.H.A. 1948, s. 77 and Sch. 6.

Physical Protection of Game

One of the cases in which the criminal law allows a person to kill or injure another's dog is where the dog was chasing game and the defendant reasonably believed that his action was necessary to protect his interest in the game.[1] However, it seems that there would be no defence to a civil claim by the dog's owner in these circumstances.[2]

Nevertheless, an occupier of land may take steps to protect his game in his absence. For example, it was decided in two old court cases that he was justified in setting dog spears in his woods.[3] But he must not tempt dogs by baiting traps with strong-smelling meat near places where dogs may lawfully be.[4]

It is an offence for an owner of gaming rights to set any spring gun, man trap "or other engine"[5] calculated to destroy human life or inflict grievous bodily harm so that it may destroy or inflict such harm upon a trespasser.[6] Traps for animals may be used within limitations.[7]

When fencing, barbed wire must not be put where it is likely to injure persons or animals using a road; if it is, the local authority may by notice require the occupier of the land to remove it.[8]

---

[1] C.D.A. 1971, s. 5(1)–(3).
[2] See Halsbury's Laws of England, 4th Ed., Vol. 2, para. 265.
[3] Deane v. Clayton (1817); Jordin v. Crump (1841).
[4] Townsend v. Wathen (1809).
[5] This appears to mean any device similar to a spring gun or man trap, but it does not include electrified wires. (R. v. Munks (1963).)
[6] O.P.A. 1861, s. 31.
[7] See pp. 129–131.
[8] H.A. 1980, s. 164(1).

CHAPTER 8

PROTECTION OF ANIMALS

[117]

118 PROTECTION OF ANIMALS

A. INTRODUCTION

Since the first Act of Parliament giving protection to animals was passed in 1822 measures strengthening that protection have appeared intermittently, and frequently in recent years, in the statute book until to-day there is a substantial body of law, both in Acts and regulations made under them, which both prohibits acts considered to be cruel or causing unnecessary suffering and regulates dealings with animals to mitigate suffering. These matters are dealt with in Part B of this Chapter.

In more recent times particular animals have been selected by Parliament as being endangered and thus as meriting their own codes of protection in individual Acts; these are deer, seals and badgers which are considered in Parts C, D and E of this Chapter. This process in turn gave way in 1975 to legislation in the shape of the Conservation of Wild Creatures and Wild Plants Act designed to protect a very limited number of rare animals from deliberate destruction and capture. And now the 1975 Act has been succeeded by Part I of the Wildlife and Countryside Act 1981 whose provisions are described in Part F below.

The Chapter concludes with Part G on the criminal and civil law governing the killing or injuring of one person's animals by another.

Parliament has also made a number of protective laws dealing with animal boarding, breeding and riding establishments and pet shops, and with performances and public exhibitions of animals. These are considered in Chapters 4, 5 and 10.

B. PREVENTION OF CRUELTY

Abandonment

Any person, being the owner or having charge or control of any animal,[1] who without reasonable cause or excuse abandons it, whether permanently or not, in circumstances likely to cause it unnecessary suffering, is guilty of an offence of cruelty.[2] Equally, it is an offence to cause or procure such abandonment or, being the owner, to permit[3] it.[4]

Carriage of Animals

A person who conveys any animal in such manner or position as to cause it any unnecessary suffering is guilty of an offence of cruelty.[2] Likewise if he causes or procures such a conveying or, being the animal's owner, he permits[3] it[5].

There are detailed regulations about the transport of animals by road, rail, sea and air; these are discussed on pages 53 to 60.

Cruelty to Livestock

Any person who causes unnecessary pain or distress to livestock[6] on agricultural land[7] under his control, or who

---

[1] The word "animal" in this and later contexts in this Section (unless otherwise defined) has a lengthily defined meaning which is fully set out in Appendix E at the end of the book. (P.A.A. 1911, s. 15; A.A.A. 1960, s. 2.)

[2] For exceptions and consequences of conviction, see pp. 132–134.

[3] An owner is deemed for the purpose of this offence to permit cruelty if he fails to exercise reasonable care and supervision in protecting the animal from it. (P.A.A. 1911, s. 1(2); A.A.A. 1960, s. 1.)

[4] A.A.A. 1960, s. 1.

[5] P.A.A. 1911, s. 1(1)(b).

[6] "Livestock" means any creature kept for the production of food, wool, skin or for use in the farming of land. The appropriate Minister may by order extend this definition (AA 1968 ss. 8(1), 50(1)), and deer kept for the production of antlers in velvet have been added to the definition (Welfare of Livestock (Deer) Order 1980 (S.I. 1980/593)).

[7] "Agricultural land" is defined as land used for agriculture within the meaning of that word given by AA 1947 s. 109(3) (A.A. 1968 s. 8(1)), for which see note 3 on p. 157.

permits such livestock to suffer unnecessary pain or distress of which he knows or may reasonably be expected to know, is guilty of an offence[1] unless the act is lawfully done under the Cruelty to Animals Act 1876[2] or under a licence from the appropriate Minister for scientific research.[3] To check whether an offence has been committed, an authorised person[4] may enter on land[5] (but not a building used wholly or mainly as a dwelling); he may also take samples of any substance on the land for analysis. The occupier or his employee must, if he can, comply with any request to indicate to the person where livestock or their food is kept and facilitate the person's access to those places. Failure to do so, or wilful obstruction, is an offence.[6]

Docking and Nicking

The docking[7] or nicking[8] of horses'[9] tails is prohibited except in a case where a member of the Royal College of Veterinary Surgeons after examination of the horse has certified in writing that the operation is in his opinion necessary for its health because of disease or injury to its tail. Otherwise, offences are committed both by the person who performed the operation and anyone who causes or permits it.[10]

The docking of tails of sheep, pigs, cattle and dogs is prohibited or restricted as described below, except when the exemptions at items (A) to (C) on page 127 apply. To

---

[1] A.A. 1968, s. 1(1).

[2] For the provisions of the 1876 Act, *see* p. 125.

[3] A.A. 1968, s. 1(2).

[4] This is a person authorised in writing by the appropriate Minister. A person so authorised by the local authority may also enter to take samples. (A.A. 1968, s. 6(1), (2), (4).)

[5] For the definition of "land" see note [6] on p. 142.

[6] A.A. 1968, s. 6(1), (4), (6), (7).

[7] "Docking" means the deliberate removal of any bone or any part of a bone from the tail of a horse. (D.N.H.A. 1949, s. 3.)

[8] "Nicking" means the deliberate severing of any tendon or muscle in the tail of a horse. (D.N.H.A. 1949, s. 3.)

[9] "Horse" includes stallion, gelding, colt, mare, filly, pony, mule and hinny (offspring of a she-ass by a stallion). (D.N.H.A. 1949, s. 3.)

[10] D.N.H.A. 1949, s. 1. For the import of docked horses, *see* p. 35.

cause or permit the docking is likewise prohibited and an offence.[1]

The short-tail docking of sheep is forbidden unless sufficient tail is retained to cover the vulva in the case of female sheep and the anus in the case of male sheep.[2]

The tail docking of pigs is forbidden unless the operation is performed by the quick and complete severance of the part of the tail to be removed and **either**—

(i) the pig is less than 8 days old, **or**
(ii) the operation is performed by a vet who is of the opinion that the operation is necessary for reasons of health or to prevent injury from the vice of tail biting.[3]

Further, the docking of tails of pigs over 7 days old requires an anaesthetic, unless the docking is done in an emergency to save life or relieve pain.[4]

The tail docking of cattle[5] is prohibited,[6] as is the docking of dogs' tails without an anaesthetic after the dogs' eyes are open.[7]

Dogs as Draught Animals

A person who uses any dog[8] for the purpose of drawing or helping to draw any cart, carriage, truck or barrow on any public highway is guilty of an offence.[9] Likewise if he causes or procures such use or, being the dog's owner, permits[10] it.[11]

---

[1] A.A. 1968, s. 2; Welfare of Livestock (Prohibited Operations) Regulations 1982 (S.I. 1982/1884), Arts. 3 and 5.

[2] 1982 Regulations cited above, Art. 3(c). For the docking of lambs' tails without anaesthetics, see item (f) on pp. 128–129.

[3] 1982 Regulations cited above, Art. 3(k).

[4] Docking of Pigs (Use of Anaesthetics) Order 1974 (S.I. 1974/798).

[5] "Cattle" means all bovine animals (1982 Regulations cited above, Art. 2.).

[6] 1982 Regulations cited above, Art. 3(f).

[7] See item (d) on p. 128.

[8] "Dog" includes any bitch, sapling (greyhound in its first year) and puppy. (P.A.A. 1911, s. 15(d).)

[9] For consequences of conviction, see pp. 133–134.

[10] As to permitting, *see* note [3] on p. 119.

[11] P.A.A. 1911, s. 9.

122   PROTECTION OF ANIMALS

Drugs and Poisons

If any person wilfully[1] without any reasonable cause or excuse—

(a) administers any poisonous or injurious drug or substance to any animal[2]; or

(b) causes or procures the administration of such drug or substance; or

(c) being the owner of the animal, permits[3] such administration; or

(d) causes any such substance to be taken by any animal, he is guilty of an offence of cruelty.[4]

A person commits an offence[5] (except where he has the defence mentioned below) if he—

(a) sells; or

(b) offers or exposes for sale; or

(c) gives away; or

(d) causes or procures any person to sell or offer or expose for sale or give away; or

(e) is knowingly a party to the sale or offering or exposing for sale or giving away of

any grain or seed which has been rendered poisonous except for *bona fide* use in agriculture.[6]

A person also commits an offence[5] (except where he has the defences mentioned below) if he—

(a) knowingly puts or places; or

---

[1] "Wilfully" has been interpreted to mean deliberately and intentionally, and not by accident or inadvertence. (*R. v. Senior* [1899] 1 Q.B. at 290–291.)
[2] The definition of "animal" in Appendix E to this book applies.
[3] As to permitting, *see* note [3] on p. 119.
[4] P.A.A. 1911, s. 1(1)(d). For exceptions and consequences of conviction, *see* pp. 132–134.
[5] For consequences of conviction, *see* pp. 133–134.
[6] P.A.A. 1911, s. 8(a).

(*b*) causes or procures any other person to put or place; or

(*c*) knowingly is a party to the putting or placing of,

in or upon any land[1] or building, any poison, or any fluid or edible matter (not being sown seed or grain) which has been rendered poisonous.[2]

It is a defence in the case of the third offence above that the poison, etc., was placed for the purpose of destroying insects and other invertebrates, rats, mice or other small ground vermin where destruction is found to be necessary in the interest of public health, agriculture or the preservation of other animals, domestic or wild, or for the purpose of manuring the land, **and** that the accused took all reasonable precautions to prevent injury thereby to dogs, cats, fowls or other domestic animals[3] and wild birds,[4] provided that the poison is not banned by Government order; at present the use of elementary yellow phosphorus and red squill is banned in all cases and the use of strychnine except for destroying moles.[5]

A person is not guilty of the second or third offences above by reason only that he uses poisonous gas in any hole, burrow or earth for the purpose of killing rabbits, hares or other rodents, deer, foxes or moles, or in places where a substance which, by evaporation or in contact with moisture, generates poisonous gas.[6]

Additionally, Government Ministers have powers to make an order permitting the use of a specified poison against grey squirrels and coypus and describing the way in which it is to be used. The use of that poison in the way described in the order will avoid prosecution under the third offence mentioned above.[7] An order has been made[8]

[1] For the meaning of "land" see note [6] on p. 142.
[2] P.A.A. 1911, s. 8(*b*).
[3] A definition of these kinds of animals is given in Appendix E to this book.
[4] P.A.A. 1911, s. 8, proviso.
[5] A.A. 1962, ss. 1, 2; Animals (Cruel Poisons) Regulations 1963 (S.I. 1963/1278).
[6] PDRA 1939 s.4; AA 1947. s. 98(3).
[7] A.A. 1972, s. 19(1), (2).
[8] Grey Squirrels (Warfarin) Order 1973 (S.I. 1973/744).

approving the use of warfarin and its soluble salts for destroying grey squirrels under the conditions stipulated by the order.

It is an offence to put, or cause to be put, at any time any poison or poisonous ingredient on ground, whether open or enclosed, where game usually resort, or in any highway,[1] with intent to destroy or injure game.[2]

Where the Government Minister concerned is satisfied that a poison cannot be used for destroying animals[3] or animals of any particular description without causing undue suffering, and that other suitable methods of destroying them exist, and are or would in certain circumstances be adequate, he may make regulations[4] prohibiting or restricting the use of that poison for destroying animals generally or particular animals.[5]

It is no criminal offence to use non-poisonous substances as bait for traps[6] for animals. But should the bait be of such a nature or so near a boundary as to attract animals which would not otherwise be likely to have entered the land, the occupier, or whoever set the bait or caused it to be set, may be liable to legal action for the value of the animals destroyed.[7] It is probable, even if he acted merely in defence of his property, that he could be prosecuted for possessing articles with intent to damage or destroy.[8]

The use of poisons against protected wild animals is considered on pages 156 and 157.

---

[1] For the meaning of "highway", see the brief non-statutory description in note [8] on p. 15.

[2] G.A. 1831, s. 3; G.A. 1970, s. 1(1)(a). "Game" in this context is defined to include hares, pheasants, partridges, grouse, heath or moor game and black game. (G.A. 1831, s. 2.)

[3] In this context "animal" means any mammal. (A.A. 1962, s. 3.)

[4] Regulations so made are the Animals (Cruel Poisons) Regulations 1963 (S.I. 1963/1278), for which see p. 123.

[5] A.A. 1962, s. 2(1).

[6] For the use of traps, see pp. 129–131.

[7] Townsend v. Wathen (1808).

[8] Halsbury's Laws of England, 4th Ed., Vol. 2, para. 401. The prosecution could be made under C.D.A. 1971, s. 3.

Experiments

No unlicensed person may perform any experiment calculated to give pain upon any living vertebrate animal.[1] Licences for this purpose are granted by the Home Secretary; they are revocable and may be made subject to conditions.[2] A High Court judge may also grant a licence in a case where he is satisfied that it is essential for the purpose of justice in a criminal case to make an experiment on living animals.[3]

Experiments calculated to give pain may be performed by licensed persons under the restrictions set out in Appendix F at the end of the book.[4]

Special protection is given to dogs, cats, horses, mules and asses. No experiment calculated to give pain may be performed on a dog or cat without anaesthetics except on certificates being given as required in the case of any animal[5] and additionally a certificate[6] that for reasons stated in it the object of the experiment will be necessarily frustrated unless it is performed on an animal similar in constitution and habits to a cat or dog and that no other animal is available. The protection for horses, asses and mules is similar, the special certificate referring to those animals in place of cats and dogs.[7]

Exhibitions to the general public, whether admitted on payment or free, of experiments on living animals calculated to give pain are illegal. Offences are committed by anyone who performs or who aids in performing such experiments, or who publishes any notice of such an intended exhibition by advertisement in a newspaper, placard or otherwise.[8]

---

[1] C.A.A. 1876, ss. 2, 3(2), 22. Vertebrate animals include mammals, birds, fishes, reptiles and amphibians.
[2] C.A.A. 1876, ss. 7, 8.
[3] C.A.A. 1876, s. 12.
[4] C.A.A. 1876, s. 3.
[5] These are the certificates mentioned in paras, 1, 3, 4 and 6 of Appendix F to this book.
[6] The additional certificate must be signed as described in note [3] on p. 226. (C.A.A. 1876, s. 11.).
[7] C.A.A. 1876, s. 5.
[8] C.A.A. 1876, s. 6.

Fighting and Baiting

It is an offence of cruelty[1] for any person—

(a) to cause, procure or assist at the fighting or baiting of any animal[2]; or

(b) to keep, use, manage, or act or assist in the management of, any premises or place for the purpose, or partly for the purpose, of fighting or baiting any animal; or

(c) to permit any premises or place to be kept, managed or used for those purposes; or

(d) to receive, or cause or procure any person to receive, money for the admission of any person to such premises or place.[3]

It is also an offence to keep or use, or act in the management of, any house, room, pit or other place for the purpose of fighting or baiting any animal. Persons found without lawful excuse on premises so kept or used may be arrested and fined.[4]

Myxomatosis

It is an offence knowingly to use or permit the use of a rabbit infected with myxomatosis to spread the disease among uninfected rabbits; but this provision does not prevent a properly authorised experiment in the disease.[5]

Operations and Anaesthetics

Any person who subjects any animal[2] to an operation which is performed without due care and humanity is guilty of an offence of cruelty,[1] as is anyone who causes or procures

---

[1] For exceptions and consequences of conviction, see pp. 132–134.
[2] The full definition of "animal" is given in Appendix E to this book.
[3] P.A.A. 1911, s. 1(1)(c).
[4] M.P.A. 1839 s. 47; TPCA 1847 s. 36.
[5] P.A. 1954, s. 12. For authorised experiments, see p. 125.

such an operation or, being the owner of the animal, permits[1] it.[2]

More specifically, new regulations make it an offence, subject to the exemptions mentioned below, for any person to perform, or cause or permit to be performed, any of the following operations on livestock[3] for the time being on agricultural land[3]—

(a) penis amputation and other penial operations;
(b) freeze dagging[4] of sheep;
(c) tongue amputation in calves;
(d) hot branding of cattle;[5]
(e) removal of any part of the antlers of a deer before the velvet of the antlers is frayed and the greater part of it has been shed.[6]

But no offence will be committed in performing these operations in the following cases:

(A) an act lawfully done under the Cruelty to Animals Act 1876;[7] **or**
(B) the rendering, in emergency, of first aid for the purpose of saving life or relieving pain; **or**
(C) the performance by a vet of an operation where in his opinion—
   (i) disease or injury is present **and**
   (ii) the proper treatment for the disease or injury is, or includes, the operation.[8]

Further legislation regulates the use of anaesthetics in operations on animals. With the exceptions mentioned

---

[1] As to permitting, *see* note [3] on p. 119.
[2] P.A.A. 1911, s. 1(1)(e).
[3] For the definitions of "livestock" and "agricultural land" which apply, see notes [6] and [7] on p. 119 (A.A. 1968 s. 8(1)).
[4] Freeze dagging means treating the skin in the area of the crutch to prevent wool growth.
[5] "Cattle" means all bovine animals (Welfare of Livestock (Prohibited Operations) Regulations 1982 (S.I. 1982/1884) Art. 2.).
[6] A.A. 1968 s. 2; 1982 Regulations cited above, Arts, 3 and 5.
[7] For the provisions of the 1876 Act, see p. 125.
[8] 1982 Regulations cited above. Art. 4.

below, all operations on animals,[1] with or without instruments, involving interference with their sensitive tissues or bone structure without the use of anaesthetics so administered as to prevent any pain during the operation are deemed to be operations performed without due care and humanity and are offences of cruelty.[2] The exceptions are:

(*a*) the making of injections or extractions by means of a hollow needle;

(*b*) any experiment duly authorised under the Cruelty to Animals Act 1876[3];

(*c*) the rendering in emergency of first aid for the purpose of saving life or relieving pain;

(*d*) the docking of a dog's tail, or the amputation of its dew claws, before its eyes are open;

(*e*) the castration of a sheep under the age of 3 months, or of a goat, bull[4] or pig under the age of 2 months, except by the use of a ring or other device to constrict the flow of blood to the scrotum unless applied within the first week of life;

(*f*) any minor operation performed by a vet which by reason of its quickness or painlessness is customarily performed without an anaesthetic, or any minor operation, whether performed by a vet or not, which is not customarily performed only by a vet; none of these exceptions, however, permits castration, de-horning of cattle[5] or disbudding of calves except by chemical cauterisation in the first week of life, nor the docking of lambs' tails by

---

[1] Animals in this context do not include fowls or other birds, fishes or reptiles, but otherwise the word has the meaning given in Appendix E at the end of the book. (P.A. (An.) A. 1954, s. 1(4).)

[2] P.A. (An.) A. 1954, s. 1(1), (2); P.A.A. 1911 s. 1(1)(*e*).

[3] For such experiments, *see* p. 125.

[4] The relevant age for a bull was altered from 3 months to 2 months by the Protection of Animals (Anaesthetics) Act 1954 (Amendment) Order 1982 (S.I. 1982/1626).

[5] "Cattle" means bulls, cows, bullocks, heifers, calves, steers or oxen. (P.A.A. 1964 s. 1(5)).

the use of a rubber ring unless applied in the first week of life.[1]

Government Ministers may alter the ages of the animals mentioned in paragraph (e) above[2] and may extend the classes of operations in which anaesthetics must be used so as to include other operations.[3] An operation now so included is one for removing any part of a deer's antlers while in velvet, unless this is done as an experiment authorised under the Cruelty to Animals Act 1876[4], or unless it is done in an emergency to save life or relieve pain.[5]

The law on experiments on animals and the connected use of anaesthetics is set out in page 125.

Traps

With the two exceptions mentioned below, a person commits an offence if—

(a) for the purpose of killing or taking animals[6] he uses, or knowingly permits the use of, any spring trap other than an approved trap; or

(b) he uses, or knowingly permits the use of, an approved trap for animals in circumstances for which it is not approved; or

(c) he sells, or exposes or offers for sale, any spring trap other than an approved trap with a view to its being used for a purpose which is unlawful under the last two paragraphs; or

(d) he has any spring trap in his possession for a purpose which is unlawful under any of the foregoing paragraphs.[7]

[1] P.A. (An.) A. 1954, s. 1(2) and First Schedule.
[2] P.A. (An.) A. 1954, s. 1(3).
[3] A.A. 1968, ss. 5, 51(1).
[4] For such experiments, see p. 125.
[5] Removal of Antlers in Velvet (Anaesthetics) Order 1980 (S.I. 1980/685).
[6] The word "animals" is not defined in this context, but for its meaning generally in law, see p. 3.
[7] P.A. 1954, s. 8(1).

References to an approved trap in these paragraphs mean a trap of a type and make approved by Government Ministers, either generally or subject to conditions as to the animals for which or the circumstances in which it may be used.[1] A list of traps presently so approved and the conditions under which each may be used are set out in Appendix G at the end of the book.[2]

The two cases in which the acts described do not amount to an offence are:—

(i) The experimental use of a spring trap under and in accordance with a licence or authority given by Ministers to enable a trap to be developed or tested with a view to its becoming an approved trap.[3]

(ii) Traps of any description detailed in an order of Ministers as being adapted solely for the destruction of rats, mice or other small ground vermin.[4] Traps of the following descriptions have been so authorised: spring traps known as break-back traps and commonly used for the destruction of rats, mice and other small ground vermin; and spring traps of the kind commonly used for catching moles in their runs.[5]

Any person who sets, or causes or procures to be set, any spring trap for the purpose of catching any hare or rabbit, or which is so placed as to be likely to catch any hare or rabbit, must inspect, or cause some competent person to inspect, the trap at reasonable intervals of time and at least once every day between sunrise and sunset; failure to do so is an offence.[6] It is also an offence if a person—

(a) sets in position any snare which is of such a nature and so placed as to be calculated to cause bodily injury to any wild animal[7] coming into contact with it; **and**

---

[1] P.A. 1954, s. 8(3), (8).
[2] Spring Traps Approval Order 1975 (S.I. 1975/1647).
[3] P.A. 1954, s. 8(4).
[4] P.A. 1954, s. 8(5).
[5] Small Ground Vermin Traps Order 1958 (S.I. 1958/24).
[6] P.A.A. 1911, s. 10. For consequences of conviction, *see* pp. 133–134.
[7] For the definition of "wild animal", see p. 153–154.

(b) while the snare remains in position, fails, without reasonable excuse, to inspect it, or cause it to be inspected, at least once every day.[1]

It is an offence to use, or knowingly permit the use of, a spring trap for the purpose of killing or taking hares or rabbits elsewhere than in a rabbit hole;[2] though guilt is avoided if the trap is used in accordance with Ministers' regulations[3] or under licence from them.[4] The licence may be embodied in a rabbit clearance order[5] or in a notice by Ministers[6] requiring action to prevent pest damage, and is revocable by notice.[7] It should be noted that a spring trap, though placed in a rabbit hole, is unlawful under offence (a) on page 129 unless of an approved type.

Other restrictions on the use of traps and snares against protected and other wild animals are considered on pages 156 and 157.

Other Cases of Cruelty

If a person cruelly—

(a) beats, kicks, ill-treats, over-rides, over-drives, over-loads, tortures, infuriates or terrifies any animal;[8] or

(b) causes or procures or, being the owner, permits[9] any animal to be so used; or

(c) by wantonly or unreasonably doing or omitting to do any act, or causing or procuring the commission or omission of any act, causes any unnecessary suffering to any animal; or

---

[1] W.C.A. 1981 s. 11(3).

[2] This means the part of the burrow which is inside the ground and covered by a roof, and not the ground which is scraped away outside. (*Brown v. Thompson* (1882). It does not mean a hole scooped out under a wire fence with no roof of soil. (*Fraser v. Lawson* (1882)).

[3] No such regulations have to date been made.

[4] P.A. 1954, s. 9(1), (3).

[5] For rabbit clearance orders, *see* pp. 190–192.

[6] For such a notice, *see* pp. 186–188.

[7] P.A. 1954, s. 9(4).

[8] The full definition of "animal" is given in Appendix E to this book.

[9] As to permitting, *see* note [3] on p. 119.

(*d*) being the owner, permits[1] any unnecessary suffering
to be caused as last described,

he is guilty of an offence of cruelty.[2]

This collection of wide-ranging offences may benefit from
some commentary. In those cases where it is an explicit
ingredient of the offence that the act or omission be done
cruelly, the accused can be guilty without proof of his intention to commit cruelty. The questions are whether pain or
suffering was inflicted and, if so, whether it was inflicted
without good reason; affirmative answers to both questions
should lead to conviction. A simple definition of the cruelty
aimed at is "the unnecessary abuse of the animal". On
the other hand, if the charge is causing or procuring the
commission or omission of an act, guilty knowledge must
be shown; it is not enough to show that a defendant would
have known of the animal's suffering had he properly
performed his duties.[3]

Exceptions to Cruelty Offences

A number of offences which has been examined in the
previous pages are expressed to be offences of cruelty.
Where this is the case, it is provided that the following acts
are permissible so as to legalise what would otherwise be
offences:—

(*a*) Any act lawfully done under the Cruelty to Animals
Act 1876.[4]

(*b*) The commission or omission of any act in the course
of the destruction, or the preparation for destruction,
of any animal as food for mankind, unless such
destruction or preparation was accompanied by the
infliction of unnecessary suffering.

(*c*) The coursing or hunting of any captive animal,[5] unless

---

[1] As to permitting, *see* note [3] on p. 119.
[2] P.A.A. 1911, s. 1(1)(*a*). For exceptions and consequences of conviction, *see*
pp. 132–134.
[3] *Halsbury's Laws of England*, 4th Ed., Vol. 2, paras 385–386.
[4] For such acts, *see* p. 125.
[5] For the meaning of "captive animal", *see* Appendix E at the end of the book.

such animal is liberated in an injured, mutilated or exhausted condition; but a captive animal shall not be deemed to be coursed or hunted before it is liberated for that purpose, or after it has been re-captured, or if it is under control; nor if it is in an enclosed space from which it has no reasonable chance of escape.[1]

Consequences of Conviction for Offences of Cruelty

In addition to fining and/or imprisoning offenders for offences of cruelty, the court has a number of other powers. First, the court may, if satisfied that it could be cruel to keep the animal alive, direct that it be destroyed and assign it to any person for that purpose; but no such direction shall be given except upon the evidence of a registered vet unless the animal's owner assents. The court may order the owner to pay the reasonable expenses of destroying the animal.[2]

The court may also, in addition to any other punishment, deprive the offender of the ownership of the animal and may order its disposal, but only if it is shown by evidence as to a previous conviction or to the character of the owner or otherwise that the animal, if left to him, is likely to be exposed to further cruelty.[3] If convicted again of a cruelty offence, the court may disqualify him for a stated period from having custody of any animal or of any animal of a particular kind.[4] Disqualification may be suspended by the court for so long as it thinks necessary for arrangements to be made for the alternative custody of the animal or animals involved, or to allow an appeal to be made.[5] After 12 months from the date of disqualification the offender may apply to the court to remove it[6]; the court may, instead of refusing or granting the application, vary the order to make it apply to animals of a particular kind. When considering

---

[1] P.A.A. 1911, s. 1(3).

[2] P.A.A. 1911, s. 2.

[3] P.A.A. 1911, s. 3.

[4] P.A. (Am.) A. 1954, s. 1(1). Breach of a disqualification order is an offence leading to a fine and/or imprisonment. (P.A. (Am.) A. 1954, s. 2).

[5] P.A. (Am). A. 1954, s. 1(2).

[6] If unsuccessful, he must wait at least 12 months before applying again, and so on for subsequent applications. (P.A. (Am.) A. 1954, s. 1(3), proviso.)

an application the court will have regard to the applicant's character and his conduct since disqualification, the nature of the offence and any other circumstances of the case.[1]

For any offence, whether of cruelty or not, the convicting court may order the offender to pay compensation up to £1000[2] for any loss or damage resulting from that offence.[3] This does not affect punishment for the offence[4] but may affect damages awarded in civil proceedings.[5]

A person disqualified from having the custody of animals cannot, while the disqualification lasts, obtain a licence to keep boarding kennels,[6] riding stables,[7] a pet shop[8] or dog breeding kennels.[9] Furthermore, when a person holds one of these licences and is convicted of any offence under the Protection of Animals Act 1911[10] (or the corresponding Scottish Act), the convicting court may cancel the licence and disqualify him from keeping the kind of animal establishment to which it relates.[11] The same will apply in the case of a guard dog kennel licence except that the holder may not be disqualified.[12]

The particular consequences of a conviction for cruelty to a dog are described on pages 63 and 64.

---

[1] P.A. (Am.) A. 1954, s. 1(3).

[2] A different sum may from time to time be substituted by Government order (M.C.A. 1980, s. 143(1)(2)).

[3] P.C.C.A. 1973 s. 35(1)(3)(4); M.C.A. 1980 s. 40(1).

[4] *E.g.*, fine and/or imprisonment.

[5] P.C.C.A. 1973, s. 38.

[6] A.B.E.A. 1963, s. 1(2).

[7] R.E.A. 1964, s. 1(2)(*e*).

[8] P.A.A. 1951, s. 1(2).

[9] B.D.A. 1973, s. 1(2).

[10] *I.e.* all offences in this Chapter described as offences of cruelty and also: failure to feed and water animals in pounds (*see* pp. 15–16); putting down and dealing in poisonous substances (*see* pp. 122–123); using dogs as draught animals (*see* p. 121); and failure to inspect spring traps (*see* p. 130).

[11] P.A.A. 1951, s. 5(3); A.B.E.A. 1963, s. 3(3); R.E.A. 1964, s. 4(3); B.D.A. 1973, s. 3(3). For the licensing of these establishments *see* pp. 73–77, 81–85.

[12] G.D.A. 1975, s. 3(4); the Act's provisions about these licences are not yet operative: *see* p. 78.

Dealing with Diseased or Injured Animals

A police constable must take the following action if he finds any animal[1] so diseased or so severely injured or in such a physical condition that in his opinion, having regard to the means available for removing the animal, there is no possibility of doing that without cruelty. If the owner is absent or refuses to consent to the destruction of the animal, the constable must at once summon a registered vet if one lives without a reasonable distance. If the vet gives a certificate that the animal is mortally injured, or so severely injured, or so diseased, or in such physical condition, that it is cruel to keep it alive, the constable may without the owner's consent arrange for the slaughter of the animal in such a way as to inflict as little suffering as practicable.[2] If the animal is so slaughtered on a public road, the constable may arrange for the removal of the carcase from the road.[3]

If the vet on being summoned certifies that the animal can be removed without cruelty, the person in charge of it must remove it at once with as little suffering as possible. If he does not, the constable may cause the animal to be removed at once without that person's consent.[4]

Any reasonable expenses of the constable in carrying out his duties, including the vet's expenses and regardless of whether or not the animal is slaughtered under these provisions, may be recovered[5] from the animal's owner as a civil debt.[6]

---

[1] In this context "animal" means any horse, mule, ass, bull, sheep, goat or pig. (P.A.A. 1911, s. 11(4).)

[2] In practice, the constable would ask the vet humanely to put down the animal. It appears that if no vet is accessible the constable is powerless to put down the animal without the owner's consent.

[3] P.A.A. 1911, s. 11(1);

[4] P.A.A. 1911, s. 11(2).

[5] Recovery is presumably by the police authority for which action can be taken in the magistrates' court.

[6] P.A.A. 1911, s. 11(3).

C. DEER

Close Seasons

There are close seasons for four species of deer and these are:—

Red deer (*cervus elaphus*) stags, fallow deer (*dama dama*) buck, and sika deer (*cervus nippon nippon*) stags.	1st May to 31st July inclusive,[1]
Roe deer (*capreolus capreolus*) buck.	1st November to 31st March inclusive.[2]
Red deer hinds, fallow deer doe, sika deer hinds and roe deer doe.	1st March to 31st October inclusive.[1]

It is an offence to take[3] or wilfully[4] kill deer[5] of these species, or to attempt to do so, during their respective close seasons,[6] except where one of the following defences is available. One of these defences is available only to "an authorised person", and this means—

(*a*) the occupier of the land on which the action is taken; or

(*b*) any member of the occupier's household[7] normally resident on the occupier's land, acting with the written authority of the occupier; or

---

[1] D.A. 1963, s. 1(1) and Sch. 1. Further species of deer with close seasons for them may be added by order of the Home Office. (D.A. 1963, s. 1(2).)

[2] R.D.A. 1977, ss. 1, 2(2).

[3] For the meaning of "take", see p. 100.

[4] For the meaning of "wilfully", see note [1] on p. 122.

[5] The word "deer" includes the carcase of any deer or any part of the carcase (D.A. 1963, s. 9). It will also include deer of either sex and of all ages (*R. v. Strange* (1843)) and tame deer as well as wild deer.

[6] D.A. 1963 ss. 1(1)(4), 4(1).

[7] For comment on the meaning of these words, see note [7] on p. 108. Though this is derived from the law relating to ground game, it may serve as a guide pending any courts' decisions on the words' meaning in the text above which is new law.

(c) any person in the ordinary service[1] of the occupier on the occupier's land, acting as above; or

(d) any person having the right to take or kill deer on the land[2] on which the action is taken; or

(e) any person acting with the written authority of a person at (d) above.[3]

The defences are:—

(A) That the deer was killed or taken, or was injured in an attempt to kill or take it, by an authorised person by means of shooting, and the act was done on any cultivated land, pasture or enclosed woodland.[4] But this defence cannot be relied upon unless the authorised person shows that—

(i) he had reasonable grounds for believing that deer of the same species were causing, or had caused, damage to crops, vegetables, fruit, growing timber or any other form of property on the land;[5] and

(ii) it was likely that further damage would be so caused **and** such damage was likely to be serious; **and**

(iii) his action was necessary for the purpose of preventing any such damage.[6]

(B) That any of the prohibited acts was done for the purpose of preventing suffering by an injured or diseased deer.[7]

(C) That any of the prohibited acts was done in pursuance of a Government Minister's requirement under Section 98 of the Agriculture Act 1947.[8]

[1] For comment on the meaning of these words, see note [1] on p. 109. Though this is derived from the law relating to ground game, it may serve as a guide pending any courts' decisions on the words' meaning in the text above which is new law.
[2] As to landlords' and tenants' rights to take game on land, see pp. 110–114.
[3] DA 1963 s. 10A(6).
[4] DA 1963 s. 10A(1).
[5] I.e., the land on which the act was done, being land of one of the three descriptions given earlier in the text.
[6] DA 1963 s. 10A(3).
[7] DA 1963 s. 10(1).
[8] DA 1963 s. 10(2). For details of this requirement, see pp. 186–188.

(D) That the prohibited act was done for the purpose of moving deer from one area to another or of taking deer alive for scientific or educational purposes under the authority (in both cases) of a licence[1], using one or more of the following methods:

  (i) a net, trap, stupefying drug or muscle-relaxing agent of a type authorised by the licence;

  (ii) a missile carrying or containing such a drug or agent, the missile being discharged by a means authorised by the licence.[2]

Killing Deer at Night

It is an offence to take[3] or wilfully[4] kill a deer[5] at night[6], or to attempt to do so,[7] except where one of the defences described at (B), (C) and (D) above is available.[8].

Use of Unlawful Methods and Illegal Possession of Objects

Subject to the defences later described, which are available in the instances below which are asterisked, the following acts done in relation to deer,[5] and attempts to commit those acts,[9] are offences:—

(1) Setting in position any trap, snare, or poisoned or stupefying bait which is of such a nature and so placed as to be calculated to cause bodily injury to any deer coming into contact with it.[10]

(2) Using, for the purpose of killing or taking[3] any deer,

---

[1] See p. 141 for further particulars about licences.
[2] DA 1963 s. 11(1).
[3] For the meaning of "take" and "taking", see p. 100.
[4] For the meaning of "wilfully" , see note [1] on p. 122.
[5] For the meaning of "deer", see note [5] on p. 136. In this context the word will include deer of any species (D.A. 1963 s. 9).
[6] "Night" extends from one hour after sunset to one hour before sunrise. (D.A. 1963 s. 2).
[7] DA 1963 ss. 2, 4(1).
[8] DA 1963 ss. 10(1)(2), 11(1).
[9] DA 1963, s. 4(1).
[10] DA 1963 s. 3(1)(a).

any of the articles described in (1) above, whether or not of such a nature or so placed as there described, or any net.[1]

(3) Using, for the purpose of killing or taking[2] any deer,—
   *(a) any smooth bore gun or any cartridge for use in it,

   (b) any rifle of a calibre less than .240 inches or a muzzle energy of less than 1,700 foot pounds,

   (c) any bullet for use in a rifle, other than a soft-nosed or hollow-nosed bullet,

   (d) any air gun, air rifle, or air pistol,[3]

   (e) any arrow, spear or similar missile,

   (f) any missile, whether discharged from a firearm[4] or otherwise, carrying or containing any poison, stupefying drug or muscle-relaxing agent.[5]

*(4) Discharging any firearm[4] or projecting any missile from any mechanically propelled vehicle or aircraft at any deer.[6]

*(5) Using any mechanically propelled vehicle or aircraft for the purpose of driving deer.[7]

(6) Possessing,[8] for the purpose of committing any of the offences described on pages 136 to 139 inclusive,

---

[1] DA 1963 s. 3(1)(b).

[2] For the meaning of "take" and "taking", see p. 100.

[3] The descriptions of guns and ammunition in sub-paras (a)–(d) may be varied by order of the Home Office (D.A. 1963, s. 3(4)).

[4] A firearm, basically, is "a lethal barrelled weapon of any description from which any shot, bullet or other missile can be discharged" (D.A. 1963 s. 9; FA 1968 s. 57(1)).

[5] DA 1963 s. 3(1)(c).

[6] DA 1963 ss. 3(2)(a), 9.

[7] DA 1963 ss. 3(2)(b), 9.

[8] For some notes on the meaning of "possessing", see p. 65.

any firearm[1] or ammunition[2] or any weapon or article which is described at items (2) or (3) above.[3]

The defences which are available in some instances are:

(A) In the case of the offence at (3)(*a*) above, that the gun was used[4] for the purpose of killing any deer if the user can show that it had been so seriously injured, otherwise than by his unlawful act,[5] or was in such a condition, that to kill it was an act of mercy.[6]

(B) In the case of the offence at (3)(*a*) above, that the gun was used as a slaughtering instrument to kill deer, provided the gun—

(i) was of not less gauge than 12 bore, **and**

(ii) had a barrel less than 24 inches (609.6 mm.) in length, **and**

(iii) was loaded with a cartridge purporting to contain shot none of which was less than .203 inches (5.16 mm.) in diameter (size AAA or larger).[7]

(C) In the case of the offence at (3)(*a*) above, that a gun of not less gauge than 12 bore was used by an authorised person[8] to take or kill deer on any land, and the gun was loaded with—

---

[1] For the meaning of "firearm', see note [4] on p. 139.

[2] "Ammunition" means ammunition for any firearm and includes grenades, bombs and other like missiles, whether capable of use with a firearm or not, and any ammunition containing, or designed or adapted to contain, any noxious liquid, gas or other thing (DA 1963, s.9; FA 1968 s. 57(2)(4)).

[3] DA 1963 ss. 3(1)(*b*)(*c*), 4(2), 9. To secure a conviction for this offence, it would be necessary for the prosecution to prove to the court's satisfaction a link between possession and the commission, or intended commission, of one of the offences.

[4] This defence is in fact restricted to the use of a smooth bore gun and does not extend to cartridges for it. For cartridges which may be used with it, see items (B) and (C) following.

[5] The words "unlawful act" are not restricted to acts made unlawful by the Deer Act of 1963, and will thus, it seems, embrace acts which are otherwise unlawful, e.g., the improper use of a gun without a shotgun certificate.

[6] DA 1963 s. 10(3).

[7] DA 1963 s. 10(4).

[8] For the meaning of "authorised person", see pp. 136–137.

(i) a cartridge containing a single non-spherical projectile weighing not less than 350 grains (22.68 grammes); or

(ii) a cartridge as described at (B)(iii) above.[1]

But this defence cannot be relied upon unless the authorised person can show the existence of the three points described in items (i), (ii) and (iii) on page 137.[2]

(D) In the cases of the offences at (4) and (5) above, that the prohibited act was done by, or with the written authority of, the occupier of any enclosed land[3] where deer are usually kept and was done in relation to deer on that land.[4]

Licences

As we have seen at (D) on page 138, a licence can be obtained for taking deer by certain means for the purposes there described. The licence will exempt the person to whom it is issued, and any other person acting with his written authority, from liability for acts within the terms of the licence which would otherwise be offences.

Such a licence is issued by the Nature Conservancy Council.[5] It may be revoked by them at any time, and may be granted subject to conditions. Contravention of, or failure to comply with, any condition is itself an offence.[6]

Powers of Court on Conviction of Offences

Offences are punishable with substantial fines, imprisonment, or both. If an offence is committed with respect to more than one deer, the maximum fine shall be determined

---

[1] DA 1963 s. 10A(2). Government Ministers may by order alter in any way the types of guns or ammunition in item (C) or apply the provisions in it to particular areas or species of deer (DA 1963 s. 10A (4)(6)).

[2] DA 1963 s. 10A(3).

[3] No definition is given of "enclosed land", but see p. 103.

[4] DA 1963 s. 3(3).

[5] The address of the Council is 19–20 Belgrave Square, London S.W.1.

[6] DA 1963 s. 11.

as if there had been a separate offence against each of them.[1]

A convicting court may order the forfeiture of—

(*a*) any deer in respect of which the offence was committed or which was found in the accused's possession;[2] and

(*b*) any vehicle[3], animal, weapon or other thing which—

    (i) was used to commit the offence, or

    (ii) was capable of being used to take,[4] kill or injure deer and was found in the accused's possession.[5]

Deer Poaching

With the purpose of preventing the poaching of deer, the following acts are, subject to the exemptions mentioned below, made offences by the Deer Act of 1980:—

(1) To enter land[6] in search or pursuit of any deer[7] with the intention of taking,[4] killing or injuring it.[8]

(2) While on any land—

    (*a*) intentionally to take, kill or injure, or attempt to take, kill or injure, any deer;

    (*b*) to search for or pursue any deer with the intention of taking, killing or injuring it;

    (*c*) to remove the carcase of any deer.[9]

---

[1] DA 1963 s. 6(1)(2).

[2] For some notes on the meaning of "possession", see p. 65.

[3] "Vehicle" includes an aircraft, hovercraft or boat (DA 1980 ss. 7, 8).

[4] For the meaning of "take" and "taking", see. p. 100.

[5] DA 1963 s. 6(3). For the powers of the police in connection with offences under the Deer Act of 1963, see pp. 143–144.

[6] "Land" includes buildings and other structures and land covered with water (IA 1978 s. 5, Sch. 1).

[7] "Deer" in the context of this and the ensuing offences means deer of any species and includes the carcase of any deer or any part of the carcase (DA 1980 s. 8).

[8] DA 1980 s. 1(1).

[9] DA 1980 s.1(2)

But these offences are not perpetrated if the person committing the act—

(*a*) has the consent[1] of the owner or occupier of the land; or

(*b*) has lawful authority[2] to do it;[3] or

(*c*) believes that he would have the consent of the owner or occupier of the land if the owner or occupier knew of his doing the act and the circumstances of it; or

(*d*) believes that he has other lawful authority[4] to do the act.[5]

If an authorised person[6] suspects with reasonable cause that another person is committing or has committed any of these offences on any land, he may require that person to give his full name and address and to leave the land at once; failure to do so is an offence.[7]

Constables[8] are given wide powers by the 1980 Act to stop, search and arrest suspected persons, to examine vehicles,[9] weapons, animals and other things for evidence, to seize and detain things which are such evidence and deer,

---

[1] Although written consent is not required, the possession of it is surer protection.

[2] No definition or explanation of "lawful authority" is given, but these words would cover acts by a tenant with sporting rights over the land (for which, generally, see pp. 110–114), or by Ministry of Agriculture officers acting under powers given to them to deal with animal diseases; see pp. 169–170, 177–180.

[3] D.A. 1980 s. 1(1)(2).

[4] The difference between this defence and that at (*b*) above is that the former relies only on the defendant's belief that he had lawful authority of some kind other than that described at (*c*) above; for examples, see note [2] above. For the belief to be effective as a defence, it is thought that, though the belief may be mistaken, it must be honestly and reasonably held.

[5] D.A. 1980 s.1(3).

[6] "Authorised person" is defined as the owner or occupier of the land or a person authorised by either of them, and includes any person having the right to take or kill deer on the land (D.A. 1980, s. 1(7)).

[7] D.A. 1980 s.1(4). This provision does not enable an authorised person to eject the suspected person, but an owner or occupier of the land, or an employee acting under their orders, may eject a trespasser at common law, using only such force as is necessary.

[8] For the meaning of "constables", see note [5] on p. 162.

[9] For the meaning of "vehicles", see note [3] on p. 142.

venison,[1] vehicles, animals, weapons and other things which a court may order to be forfeited on conviction, and to enter land[2] (except a dwelling) to exercise the foregoing powers. Deer or venison so seized may be sold and the proceeds forfeited.[3] All these powers are also now available where offences under the 1963 Act are suspected.[4]

The maximum punishments for offences and the powers of a convicting court under the 1980 Act are the same as those under the 1963 Act,[5] but additionally in the former case the court may cancel any firearm or shotgun certificate held by the accused.[6]

The 1980 Act also regulates sales of venison and requires licensed game dealers to keep records of their sales of it.[7]

The need for a game licence to take deer is considered on pages 102 to 104, and tenants' compensation for damage to crops by deer is looked at on pages 114 to 115. The removal of deers' antlers while in velvet is mentioned on page 129.

D. SEALS

The protection afforded to seals by the Conservation of Seals Act 1970 is similar to that available for deer in that the use of certain kinds of guns and ammunition for killing them are prohibited, they are protected during close seasons, and licences to take them are available for limited purposes; exceptions are made in the first two cases.

Taking these aspects in order, it is an offence to use or attempt to use—

---

[1] "Venison" includes the carcase, or any edible part of the carcase, of a deer (DA 1980 s.8).
[2] For the definition of "land", see note [6] on p. 142.
[3] DA 1980 ss. 4, 5(1)(a)(b).
[4] DA 1980 s. 7, Sch. 2, para. 5.
[5] DA 1980 ss. 1(5)(6), 5(1)(a)(b). For the 1963 Act's provisions, see pp. 141–142.
[6] DA 1980 s. 5(1)(c)(d).
[7] DA 1980 ss. 2, 3.

(*a*) for the purpose of killing or taking[1] any seal[2], any poisonous substance; or

(*b*) for the purpose of killing, injuring or taking[1] any seal, any firearm[3] other than a rifle using ammunition[3] having a muzzle energy of not less than 600 foot pounds and a bullet weighing not less than 45 grains.[4]

The following defences will be available in a prosecution for offence (b):—

(1) In the case of killing a seal, that it had been so seriously disabled otherwise than by an act of the killer that there was no reasonable chance of its recovering[5]:

(2) That the act done was authorised by a licence granted by the Home Office[6];

(3) That the act was done outside the seaward limits of the territorial waters adjacent to Great Britain.[7]

The annual close seasons for seals are as follows:—

Grey seals (*Halichoerus grypus*): 1st September to 31st December inclusive.

Common seals (*Phoca vitulina*): 1st June to 31st August inclusive.[8]

It is an offence wilfully[9] to kill, injure or take[1], or attempt to kill, injure or take, these seals during their close seasons or at any time in an area which is designated by an order

---

[1] For an interpretation of "taking", *see* p. 100.

[2] Although this means all seals, the grey and common seals are the only species known to inhabit the coast of Britain.

[3] For the meanings of these terms, *see* note [4] on p. 139 and note [2] on p. 140.

[4] C.S.A. 1970, ss. 1(1), 8(1). The description given of firearms and ammunition may be altered by order of the Home Office. (C.S.A. 1970, s. 1(2).).

[5] C.S.A. 1970, ss. 1(1), 9(2).

[6] C.S.A. 1970, ss. 1(1), 10. For details of such licence, *see* pp. 146–147.

[7] C.S.A. 1970, s. 17(2). The question of the extent of territorial waters is much disputed in international law and practice, but the United Kingdom adheres to the rule of the 3-mile limit measured, in general, from low-water mark.

[8] C.S.A. 1970, s. 2(1).

[9] This means deliberately and intentionally, and not by accident or inadvertence. (*R. v. Senior* [1899] 1 Q.B. 283, at pp. 290–291).

made by the Home Office[1] and which prohibits these acts in it.[2] The following defences are available to an accused in the case of a prosecution:—

(i) That the killing or injuring of the seal was unavoidable and the incidental result of a lawful action[3];

(ii) That the killing or attempted killing of any seal was to prevent it from causing damage to a fishing net or fishing tackle in the accused's possession[4] or in the possession of a person at whose request he killed or attempted to kill the seal, or to any fish for the time being in such fishing net, provided that at the time[5] the seal was in the vicinity of such net or tackle.[6]

(iii) In the case of taking or attempted taking, that the seal had been disabled otherwise than by the accused's act and it was taken or to be taken solely for the purpose of tending it or releasing it when no longer disabled;

(iv) The defences described in items (1), (2) and (3) on page 145.[7]

The Home Office may grant licences[8] for specific purposes to kill or take seals and, provided this is done within the terms and conditions of the licence, no offence will be committed.

The purposes are:—

(a) Purposes of any zoological gardens or collection;

---

[1] Such an order may be made if the Home Office, after consulting the Nature Conservancy Council, consider it necessary for the conservation of seals, (C.S.A. 1970, s. 3(1)). No other details are given in the 1970 Act, and no such order has yet been made.
[2] C.S.A. 1970, ss. 2(2), 3, 8(1).
[3] C.S.A. 1970, ss. 2(2), 3(2), 9(1)(b).
[4] For some notes on the meaning of "possession", see p. 65.
[5] I.e., at the time of killing or attempted killing.
[6] C.S.A. 1970, ss. 2(2), 3(2), 9(1)(c).
[7] C.S.A. 1970, ss. 2(2), 3(2), 9(1)(a), (2), 10, 17(2).
[8] Enquiries about a licence should be addressed to the Home Office at Queen Anne's Gate, London, SW1H 9AT.

(*b*) Scientific or educational purposes;

(*c*) Preventing damage to fisheries, reducing a population surplus of seals for management purposes, or using a population surplus of seals as a resource;

(*d*) Protecting flora or fauna in special areas.[1]

In all cases the licence will authorise a killing or taking in the area described in the licence which will also specify the means to be used and the number of seals to be killed or taken.[2] The licence may be revoked at any time by the Home Office, and a person who contravenes, or attempts to contravene, or fails to comply with, any condition of the licence commits an offence.[3]

Any person who, for the purpose of committing any of the offences described,[4] has in his possession,[5] or attempts to have in his possession, any poisonous substance or any prohibited firearm or ammunition[6] commits an offence.[7]

A court convicting a person of any of the offences described[8] may order the forfeiture of any seal or seal skin in respect of which the offence was committed, or any seal, seal skin, firearm, ammunition or poisonous substance in his possession[5] at the time of the offence.[9]

The powers which police and other constables[10] can use when with reasonable cause they suspect an offence are similar to those available to them in cases of offences against

---

[1] These special areas are: nature reserves; areas of special scientific interest; marine nature reserves (NPA 1949 s. 15; C.S.A. 1970 s. 10(4); WCA 1981 ss. 28(1), 29(1)(3), 36).

[2] C.S.A. 1970, s. 10(1). The use of strychnine cannot be authorised by a licence.

[3] C.S.A. 1970, s. 10(2).

[4] And also the offences of obstructing or attempting to obstruct the entry on land or water of a person authorised in writing to enter by the Minister of Agriculture. (C.S.A. 1970, s. 11).

[5] For some notes on the meaning of "possession", *see* p. 65.

[6] *I.e.*, any firearm or ammunition other than the types described in item (b) on p. 145.

[7] C.S.A. 1970, s. 8(2).

[8] Including those mentioned in note [4] above.

[9] C.S.A. 1970, s. 6.

[10] For the meaning of "other constables", see note [5] on p. 162.

the Deer Acts of 1963 and 1980.[1] Additionally, they may without warrant search any vehicle or boat which the suspected person may be using, but their power to arrest a suspect without warrant can only be exercised if he fails to give his name and address to a constable to his satisfaction.[2]

E. BADGERS

Special protection for badgers was given by the Badgers Act of 1973. The Act starts by making it an offence for anyone wilfully[3] to kill, injure or take,[4] or to attempt to kill, injure or take, any badger.[5] The Act later enumerates a number of defences available to those prosecuted for this offence, and these are:—

(1) In the case of a killing or taking, or attempts at either, or in the case of injuring a badger in the course of taking it or attempting to kill or take it, that the defendant can show[6] that his action was necessary for the purpose of preventing serious damage to land,[7] crops, poultry or any other form of property; **but** this defence is **not** available in relation to any action taken at any time if it had become apparent, before that time, that that action would prove necessary for the purpose mentioned, **and**

    either (a) a licence authorising that action had not been applied for as soon as reasonably practicable after the fact of the action proving necessary had become apparent;

    or (b) an application for such a licence had been determined[8]

---

[1] See pp. 143–144.

[2] C.S.A. 1970, s. 4(1), (2).

[3] This means deliberately and intentionally, and not by accident or inadvertence. (R. v. Senior [1899] 1 Q.B. 283 at pp. 290–291.)

[4] For an interpretation of "take", see p. 100.

[5] B.A. 1973, s. 1(1). "Badger" is defined to mean any animal of the species Meles meles. (B.A. 1973, s. 11.)

[6] I.e., can satisfy the court before whom he is prosecuted.

[7] "Land" is defined to include, amongst other things, buildings and other structures and land covered with water (IA. 1978, s. 5, Sch. 1.).

[8] BA 1973, s. 8 (1A), (1B). For comment on this defence, see note [3] on p. 156.

(2) That it was a taking or attempted taking of a badger which had been disabled otherwise than by the act of the accused, **and** it was taken or to be taken solely for the purpose of tending it.[1]

(3) That it was a killing or attempted killing of a badger which appeared to be so seriously injured or in such a condition that to kill it would be an act of mercy.[2]

(4) That it was an unavoidable killing or injuring as an incidental result of a lawful action.[3]

(5) That the act was done in connection with an experiment on a living badger which was not a contravention of the Cruelty to Animals Act 1876.[4]

(6) That the act was done under the authority of, and within the conditions of, a licence the provisions for which are next considered.[5]

Licences may be granted for the following purposes:—

(i) For scientific or educational purposes or for the conservation of badgers, to kill or take within the area and by the means described in the licence, or to sell or have in the licensed person's possession, the number of badgers stipulated by the licence;

(ii) for the purpose of any zoological gardens or collection named in the licence, to take within the area and by the means described in the licence, or to sell or have in the licensed person's possession, the number of badgers stipulated by the licence;

(iii) for the purpose of ringing and marking, to take badgers within the area described in the licence, to mark them and to attach to them any ring, tag or other marking device as specified in the licence;

---

[1] B.A. 1973, s. 8(1)(*a*).

[2] B.A. 1973, s. 8(1)(*b*).

[3] B.A. 1973, s. 8(1)(*c*). An example of this defence would be an accident between a vehicle and a badger on a road.

[4] B.A. 1973, s. 8(3). For the provisions of the 1876 Act, *see* p. 125.

[5] B.A. 1973, s. 9(1).

(iv) for the purpose of preventing the spread of disease, to kill or take badgers within the area and by the means described in the licence;

(v) for the purpose of preventing serious damage to land,[1] crops, poultry or any other form of property, to kill or take badgers within the area and by the means described in the licence.[2]

In the first three cases licences are granted by the Nature Conservancy Council[3] and in the last two cases by the Minister of Agriculture or, in Scotland, the Secretary of State for Scotland.[4] A licence may be revoked at any time, and breach of any of its conditions is an offence.[5]

The 1973 Act creates a number of other offences related to badgers, some with special defences, and these will now be considered.

Unless permitted by or under the 1973 Act,[6] it is an offence for any person to have in his possession[7] or under his control any dead badger or any part of, or anything derived from, a dead badger.[8] It is a defence if the person shows that—

(a) the badger had not been killed; **or**

(b) it had been killed otherwise than in contravention of the Act; **or**

(c) the object in the person's possession or control had been sold (whether to him or any other person) **and**, at the time of purchase, the purchaser had had no

---

[1] For the definition of "land", see note 6 on p. 142.

[2] B.A. 1973, s. 9(1).

[3] Applications should be made to the Council at 19–20 Belgrave Square, London, S.W.1.

[4] B.A. 1973, s. 9(2). Applications to the Minister should be made to the Divisional Executive Officer at the Ministry's local Divisional Office. In Scotland applications should be sent to the Divisional Veterinary Officer at the local Animal Health Office.

[5] B.A. 1973, s. 9(3).

[6] E.g., under the terms of a licence.

[7] For some notes on the meaning of "possession", see p. 65.

[8] B.A. 1973, s. 1(2).

reason to believe that the badger had been killed in contravention of the Act[1]

Described as offences of cruelty, the following acts are forbidden—

(a) cruelly to ill-treat any badger;

(b) to use any badger tongs in the course of killing or taking, or attempting to kill or take, any badger;

(c) to dig for any badger, except as permitted by or under the 1973 Act[2]

(d) to use, for the purpose of killing or taking any badger, any firearm[3] other than a smooth bore weapon of not less than 20 bore or a rifle using ammunition[3] having a muzzle energy of not less than 160 foot pounds and a bullet weighing not less than 38 grains.[4]

It is an offence for any person to sell,[5] offer for sale,[5] or have in his possession[6] or under his control any live badger[7] unless—

(i) it has been kept in captivity by that person for a continuous period beginning before 25th July 1973[8]; **or**

(ii) it is in the person's possession or under his control in the course of his business as a carrier; **or**

(iii) the badger was taken when disabled otherwise than by the act of the accused solely for the purpose of

---

[1] B.A. 1973, s. 1(3).
[2] E.g., under the terms of a licence.
[3] For the definitions of "firearm" and "ammunition" which are applicable, see note [4] on p. 139 and note [2] on p. 140. (B.A. 1973, s. 11).
[4] B.A. 1973, s. 2.
[5] The word "sale" includes hire, barter and exchange, and "sell" is to be interpreted accordingly (B.A. 1973, s. 11).
[6] For some notes on the meaning of "possession", see p. 65.
[7] B.A. 1973, s. 3.
[8] This date is selected as the date on which the Badgers Act 1973 was passed.

tending it, **and** it is necessary for that purpose for it to remain in the accused's possession or under his control,[1] or

(iv) the possession or control of the badger was covered by a licence granted under the Act.[2]

It is also an offence if any person marks, or attaches any ring, tag or other marking device to, any badger unless:he is authorised to do so by, or has possession of the animal by virtue of, a licence under the Act; or he has kept it in captivity for a continuous period beginning before the 25th July 1973.[3]

Police and other constables[4] are given wide powers by the Act to search suspects, vehicles and articles, to arrest suspects and to seize and detain anything which may be evidence of an offence under the Act or which may be forfeited by a court.[5] On conviction of any offence under the Act the court **must** order forfeiture of any badger or skin in respect of which the offence was committed, and **may** order forfeiture of weapons and articles connected with the offence.[6]

If any person is found on land committing any of the offences mentioned below, the owner or occupier of the land, or an employee of either of them, or a constable[4], may require that person to leave the land at once and to give his name and address. If that person then deliberately refuses to comply with either requirement, he commits an offence.[7] The offences in question are: killing, injuring or taking a badger, or attempting to do so; and having posses-

---

[1] B.A. 1973, s. 8(1)(*a*), (2).
[2] B.A. 1973, s. 9(1).
[3] B.A. 1973, ss. 4, 8(2)(*a*), 9(1).
[4] For the meaning of "constables", see note [5] on p. 162.
[5] B.A. 1973, s. 10(1).
[6] B.A. 1973, s. 10(3).
[7] B.A. 1973, s. 5. Note that the Act gives no right to the persons named forcibly to eject the offender from the land, but at common law the owner and occupier have the right if the offender is a trespasser, as also will their employees and a constable if (in either case) they are exercising it under the direction of the owner or occupier.

sion or control of a dead badger, or part of it, or anything
derived from it.[1]

The powers of Government Ministers to destroy wild
badgers for the purpose of combating disease are discussed
on pages 169 to 171.

F. PROTECTION OF OTHER WILD ANIMALS

Introduction

This Section describes the provisions for protecting other
wild animals which are now to be found in Part I of the
Wildlife and Countryside Act of 1981. That Part is the
successor to the Conservation of Wild Creatures and Wild
Plants Act 1975, which it repeals, but it is also wider in its
scope, in relation to both the variety of wildlife which it
protects and the protective measures enacted.[2] Its provisions
extend to the territorial waters[3] adjacent to Great Britain.[4]

Since the expression "wild animals" frequently recurs in
the pages following, it will be convenient at this point to
examine the scope of its meaning. The words "wild animal"
are defined to mean any animal (other than a bird) which
is or (before it was killed or taken) was living wild.[5] The
word "animal", as a part of this expression, will itself have
a wide meaning: first, any reference in the Act to an animal
of any kind is to include, unless the context otherwise
requires, a reference to an egg, larva, pupa, or other immature stage of an animal of that kind.[6] Secondly, as a matter

---

[1] B.A. 1973, s. 1. These offences are fully set out on pp. 148 and 150 and the
defences available for them in the respective following passages. Difficulties may
arise in practice because of the problem of establishing on the spot whether a
defence is available which would prevent an apparent offence from being a real
one and thus nullify the rights to make the two requirements which, on the wording
of the Act, depend on an offence being committed.

[2] The Act also protects many wild birds and wild plants, and its wildlife provisions extend to Scotland.

[3] For the extent of territorial waters, see note [7] on p. 145.

[4] WCA 1981 s. 27(5). For the meaning of "Great Britain", see note [3] on p. 30.

[5] WCA 1981 s. 27(1).

[6] WCA 1981 s. 27(3).

of general law, the term "animals" includes all creatures not belonging to the human race.

Specially Protected Wild Animals

The 1981 Act names 39 different kinds of wild animal as meriting special protection.[1] Their names are given in Appendix H at the end of the book. They are regarded[2] as animals in danger of extinction in Great Britain or likely to become so endangered unless conservation measures are taken. The Government may by means of orders[3] add further names to, or remove names from, this list.[4]

Apart from the defences next mentioned, it is an offence for any person intentionally to kill, injure or take[5] any wild animal[6] included in Appendix H, or to attempt to do so.[7]

The defences available[8] are:—

(A) That the act was done in pursuance of a requirement by a Government Minister under Section 98 of the Agriculture Act 1947.[9]

(B) That the act was done under, or in pursuance of an order made under, the Animal Health Act 1981.[10]

(C) That the defendant can show[11] that the animal taken

---

[1] WCA 1981 Sch. 5.

[2] Judged by the principal criteria used in WCA 1981 s. 22(3) used for altering the listing.

[3] These orders and others related to wild life protection are to be made by the Secretary of State for the Environment. Advice is to be given to him in this and other instances by the Nature Conservancy Council (WCA 1981 ss. 22(3) 24(1)–(3)).

[4] WCA 1981 s. 22(3), (4)(a). Enquiries to check whether the listing has been altered should be addressed to the Department of the Environment, Tollgate House, Houlton Street, Bristol BS2 9DJ.

[5] For an interpretation of the word "take", see p. 100.

[6] In proceedings for the offence, the animal is to be presumed to have been wild unless the contrary is shown (WCA 1981, s. 9(6)).

[7] WCA 1981 ss. 9(1), 18(1).

[8] It should be noted that in some instances a defence will apply to all acts which may be the subject of this offence, i.e., killing, injuring, taking and attempts, whereas in other instances a defence applies only to one or two of these acts.

[9] WCA 1981 s. 10(1)(a). For details of this requirement, see pp. 186–188.

[10] WCA 1981 s. 10(1)(b). For the provisions of AHA 1981 and its orders, see Chaps. 3 and 9, especially pp. 169–171.

[11] I.e., can satisfy the court before whom he is prosecuted.

had been disabled otherwise than by his unlawful act[1] **and** that it was taken solely for the purpose of tending it and releasing it when no longer disabled.[2]

(D) That the defendant can show[3] that the animal killed had been so seriously disabled otherwise than by his unlawful act[1] that there was no reasonable chance of its recovering.[4]

(E) That the defendant can show[3] that the act was the incidental result of a lawful operation and could not reasonably have been avoided.[5] But, in the case of anything done to a bat (except in the living area of a dwelling house), this defence will not be available unless the defendant had notified the Nature Conservancy Council[6] of what act he intended to do and allowed them a reasonable time to advise him as to whether that should be done and, if so, the method to be used.[7]

(F) That the animal was killed or injured by an authorised person[8] who can show[3] that his action was necessary for the purpose of preventing serious damage to livestock,[9] foodstuffs for livestock,[9] crops, vege-

---

[1] The words "unlawful act" are not restricted to acts made unlawful by WCA 1981 and will thus, it seems, embrace acts which are otherwise unlawful, e.g., the improper use of a gun without a shotgun certificate.

[2] WCA 1981 s. 10(3)(*a*).

[3] *See* note [11] on last page.

[4] WCA 1981, s.10(3)(*b*).

[5] WCA 1981, s. 10(3)(*c*).

[6] The address of the Council is 19–20 Belgrave Square, London SW1X 8PY.

[7] WCA 1981 s. 10(5).

[8] "Authorised person" means: the owner or occupier of the land on which the action authorised is taken; any person authorised by either of them (writing is not required but will be advisable for that person's protection); a person authorised in writing by the local authority for the area (WCA 1981 s. 27(1)). "Occupier", except for the foreshore, includes any person having any right of hunting, shooting, fishing or taking game or fish; and "local authority" means a county, district, or London borough council and the Greater London Council (WCA 1981 s. 27(1)).

[9] "Livestock" includes any animal which is kept for: the provision of food, wool, skins or fur; the purpose of its use in carrying on any agricultural activity; or the provision or improvement of shooting or fishing (WCA 1981, s. 27(1)).

156 PROTECTION OF ANIMALS

tables, fruit, growing timber or any other form of property or to fisheries.[1] **But** this defence will **not** be available for any action taken at any time if it had become apparent, before that time, that the action would prove necessary for one of the purposes mentioned **and—**

(i) **either** a licence[2] authorising the action had not been applied for as soon as reasonably practicable after the fact of the action proving necessary had become apparent; **or**

(ii) an application for such a licence had been determined.[3]

(G) That the act was done under and in accordance with the terms of a licence[2] issued to the defendant.[4]

(H) That the act was not done intentionally.[5]

Prohibited Methods of Killing or Taking Wild Animals

The Wildlife and Countryside Act 1981 contains a long list of methods of killing or taking wild animals which are prohibited. Some of these are applicable to all wild animals, and others only to those named. The list, divided in this way, is reproduced in Appendix I at the end of the book, which also contains a list of the named animals.[6] The list of prohibited methods may be altered by government order by adding further methods or omitting methods presently in it, and methods may be made to apply to particular kinds of animals.[7]

It is an offence to use, or to attempt to use, any of these

---

[1] WCA 1981 s. 10(4).
[2] For licences, see pp. 160–161.
[3] WCA 1981 s. 10(6). This is a rather involved qualification of the defence which must in some circumstances render it nugatory. An application for a licence should be submitted as soon as possible, and the defence will then not be vitiated for any action taken thereafter, irrespective of the outcome of the application.
[4] WCA 1981s. 16(3).
[5] It is a necessary ingredient of the offence that it be done intentionally—see p. 154.
[6] WCA 1981, s. 11(1)(2), Sch. 6.
[7] WCA 1981 s. 11(4).

methods.[1] Only two defences are available, one of which is restricted to a particular method. The defences are:—

(A) In the case of item 4 in Appendix I, that the defendant can show[2] that the article was set in position by him for the purpose of killing or taking, in the interests of public health, agriculture,[3] forestry, fisheries or nature conservation, any wild animals which could be lawfully killed or taken by the means described in item 4, **and** that he took all reasonable precautions to prevent injury by those means to the wild animals listed in Part III of Appendix I.[4]

(B) In the case of all methods, that the method was used under and in accordance with the terms of a licence[5] issued to the defendant.[6]

Introduction of New Species into the Wild

A person commits an offence if he releases or allows to escape into the wild any animal[7] which—

(*a*) is of a kind which is not ordinarily resident in, and is not a regular visitor to, Great Britain[8] in a wild state;
or

(*b*) is included in the list of animals at Appendix J[9] at the end of the book.[10]

---

[1] WCA 1981 ss.11(1)(2), 18(1).

[2] *I.e.*, can satisfy the court before whom he is prosecuted.

[3] Though not defined in this context, the word "agriculture" is defined in AA 1947 s. 109(3) so as to include horticulture, fruit growing, seed growing, dairy farming, livestock breeding and keeping, the use of land as grazing land, meadow land and osier land, market gardens and nursery grounds, and the use of land for woodlands where that is ancillary to the farming of land for other agricultural purpose. This serves as a guide, but no more, to its meaning in the present context.

[4] WCA 1981 s. 11(6). Put another way, this means that the defendant may use the methods in item 4 against any wild animals except those in Part III, if used in the interests described and if the precautions described are taken.

[5] For licences, see pp. 160–161.

[6] WCA 1981, s. 16(3).

[7] *I.e.*, domestic or wild. See pp. 153–154 for the wide meaning of the word "animal".

[8] For the meaning of "Great Britain", see note [3] on p. 30.

[9] The Appendix is reproduced from WCA 1981, Sch. 9., Part I. The list may be varied by Government order (WCA 1981, s. 22(5)(*a*)).

[10] WCA 1981 s. 14(1). It is also an offence to attempt to commit either of the offences mentioned (WCA 1981 s. 18(1)).

The defences available in this instance are:—

(A) That the defendant can prove that he took all reasonable steps and exercised all due diligence to avoid committing the offence.[1]

(B) That the act was done under and in accordance with the terms of a licence issued to the defendant.[2]

A person with the written authority (to be produced if required) of the Minister[3] may enter any land,[4] except a dwelling, to find out whether this offence is being, or has been, committed on that land.[5] The intentional obstruction of such a person is an offence.[6]

Other Offences relating to the Protection of Wild Animals

In the case of the specially protected animals whose names appear in Appendix H, the following further offences are created. Attempts to commit them are also offences.[7] The defences available are listed after the description of each offence or group of offences. The offences are:—

(1) Intentionally to damage or destroy, or obstruct access to, any structure or place which a specially protected animal uses for shelter or protection.

(2) Intentionally to disturb such an animal while it is occupying a structure or place so used.[8]

Defences for items (1) and (2):

(i) that the act was done in a dwelling-house, but this is qualified in the case of a bat as stated in item (E) on page 155;[9]

---

[1] WCA 1981 s. 14(3). If this defence relies on an allegation that another person was responsible for the offence, certain procedural requirements must be followed (WCA 1981 s. 14(4)).

[2] WCA 1981 s. 16(4)(c). For licences, see pp. 160–161.

[3] *I.e.*, the Secretary of State for the Environment, for Wales or for Scotland, as appropriate.

[4] For the definition of "land", see note [6] on p. 142.

[5] WCA 1981 s. 14(5).

[6] WCA 1981 s. 14(6).

[7] WCA 1981 s. 18(1).

[8] WCA 1981 s. 9(4).

[9] WCA 1981 s. 10(2)(5).

(ii) the defences stated at items (A), (B), (E), (G) and (H) on pages 154 to 156.[1]

(3) To sell,[2] offer or expose for sale, or to have in one's possession,[3] or to transport for the purpose of sale,—

(a) any live or dead animal in Appendix H, or

(b) any part of such an animal, or

(c) anything derived from such an animal.[4]

(4) To publish, or cause to be published, any advertisement[5] likely to be understood as conveying that the advertiser buys or sells, or intends to buy or sell, any of the things mentioned in item (3) above.[6]

The only defence for items (3) and (4) is that the act was done under and in accordance with the terms of a licence issued to the defendant.[7]

(5) To have in one's possession[3] or control any live or dead wild animal named in Appendix H, or any part of, or anything derived from, such an animal.[8]
Defences available in this case are:

(i) That the defendant is able to show[9] that—

(a) the animal had not been killed or taken;[10] or

(b) the animal had been killed or taken other-

---

[1] WCA 1981 ss. 10(1)(3)(c), 16(3).

[2] The words "sell" and "sale" in this and the next offence include hire, barter and exchange (WCA 1981 s. 27(1)).

[3] For some notes on the meaning of "possession", see p. 65.

[4] WCA 1981 s. 9(5)(a). Note 6 on p. 154 applies to this offence.

[5] "Advertisement" includes a catalogue, a circular and a price list (WCA s. 27(1)).

[6] WCA 1981 s. 9(5)(b).

[7] WCA 1981 s. 16(4)(b). For licences, see pp. 160–161.

[8] WCA 1981 s. 9(2). Note 6 on p. 154 applies to this offence.

[9] I.e. can satisfy the court before whom he is prosecuted.

[10] This defence refers to any killing or taking by any person, from which the apparent conclusion is that the defence is restricted to the case of possession or control of a dead animal which died from natural causes. For an interpretation of the word "take", see p. 100.

wise than in contravention of any of the provisions in the Wildlife and Countryside Act 1981 for the protection of wildlife[1] or the provisions of the Conservation of Wild Creatures and Wild Plants Act 1975;[2] or

(c) the animal or other thing in the defendant's possession or control had been sold[3] (either to the defendant or any other person) otherwise than in contravention of the provisions of the Acts mentioned at (b) above;[4]

(ii) the defences stated at items (A) to (G) on pages 154 to 156.[5]

And lastly, it is made an offence if any person, for the purpose of committing any of the offences described in this Section, has in his possession[6] anything capable of being used to commit one of those offences.[7]

Licences

In the case of all the offences, except the last, described in the preceding pages of this Section the possession of a licence authorising an act which would otherwise be an offence will exculpate the licence-holder, if the act is done under and in accordance with the terms of the licence.

Licences are issued, either for specified purposes or to

[1] These provisions will strictly include, not only those described in this Section F of this Chapter, but also the provisions in Part I of WCA 1981 which protect wild birds.

[2] The 1975 Act was the predecessor of WCA 1981—see p. 153. A reference to it is necessary to cover instances of possession or control following a killing or taking which occurred when the 1975 Act was in force.

[3] The word "sold" is to be interpreted in the same way as the cognate expressions in note [2] on p. 159.

[4] WCA 1981 s. 9(3).

[5] WCA 1981 ss. 10, 16(3). Items (A)–(G), as set out on the pages mentioned, provide defences to what are otherwise offences of killing, taking or injuring the Appendix H animals. It appears that the intention of WCA 1981 s. 10 is to make the same defences available for possession or control of an animal subsequent to its killing, taking or injuring in circumstances which are exonerated by items (A)–(G).

[6] For some notes on the meaning of "possession", see p. 65.

[7] WCA 1981 s. 18(2). The comment at note [3] on p. 140 will apply to this offence.

cover acts which would otherwise be offences,[1] by one of the Secretaries of State for the Environment, for Wales or for Scotland, or the Nature Conservancy Council, or the Minister of Agriculture, according to the subject matter of the licence and the location of the activity to be licensed.[2] These details can be conveniently set out in tabular form, and this is provided in Appendix K at the end of the book.

A licence may be: general or specific; granted to persons of a class[3] or to a particular person; subject to compliance with specified conditions; and modified or revoked at any time by the issuing authority. It will be valid for the period stated in it unless previously modified or revoked, and a reasonable charge may be made for it.[4]

A licence authorising the killing of wild animals for specified purposes will lay down the area within which, and the methods by which, the animals may be killed, and it cannot be granted for more than two years.[5]

A person commits an offence if, for the purpose of obtaining (for himself or another person) the grant of a licence, he—

(*a*) makes a statement or representation, or furnishes a document or information, which he knows to be false in a material particular; or

(*b*) recklessly makes a statement or representation, or furnishes a document or information, which is false in a material particular.[6]

Powers of the Court and of the Police

A substantial fine may be imposed on conviction of the offences which have been described, varying with the type

---

[1] WCA 1981 s. 16(3), (4)(*b*)(*c*).

[2] WCA 1981 s. 16(9)(*b*)—(*e*).

[3] The definition of a class of persons may be framed by reference to any circumstances whatever, including persons being authorised by any other person (WCA 1981 s. 16(8)).

[4] WCA 1981 s. 16(5).

[5] WCA 1981 s. 16(6). It can be modified or revoked during its currency.

[6] WCA 1981 s. 17. Attempts to commit any of the acts described are also offences (WCA 1981 s. 18(1)).

of offence.[1] If the offence relates to more than one animal or other thing, the maximum fine is determined as if there had been a separate offence for each animal or thing.[2]

On conviction of any of the offences described, the court—

(a) **shall** order the forfeiture of any animal or other thing in respect of which the offence was committed;

(b) **may** order the forfeiture of any vehicle, aircraft, hovercraft, boat, animal, weapon or other thing which was used to commit the offence;

(c) in the case of the offences of releasing certain animals into the wild or allowing them to escape there,[3] **may** order the forfeiture of any animal which is of the same kind as that in respect of which the offence was committed **and** which was found in the possession of the accused.[4]

Constables[5] are given wide powers, exercisable without a warrant, to stop and search persons suspected of committing offences, to search or examine anything which a suspect may then be using or have, to arrest a suspect if he fails satisfactorily to give his particulars, and to seize and detain things which may be evidence of an offence or which may be forfeited by the court as described above.[6] For these purposes constables may enter any land[7] except a dwelling house,[8] for the entry of which a warrant may be granted on certain grounds.[9]

---

[1] WCA 1981 s. 21(2)–(4).

[2] WCA 1981 s. 21(5);

[3] For these offences, see pp. 157–158.

[4] WCA 1981 ss. 21(6), 27(1).

[5] As well as police constables, including special police constables, the word "constables" includes others holding that office, e.g., harbour constables. The hallmark of a constable is his attestation as such before, usually, a J.P.

[6] WCA 1981 s. 19(1).

[7] For the definition of "land", see note [6] on p. 142.

[8] WCA 1981 s. 19(2).

[9] WCA 1981, s. 19(3).

G. KILLING OR INJURING OTHER PERSONS' ANIMALS

The destruction or damage by one person of another's property is a criminal offence governed by rules in the Criminal Damage Act of 1971. Domestic animals, since they are capable of ownership,[1] are always treated as property for this purpose; wild animals are so treated only if—

(1) they have been tamed; **or**

(2) they are ordinarily kept in captivity; **or**

(3) they or their carcases have been reduced into possession[2] which has not been lost or abandoned; **or**

(4) they are in course of being reduced into possession.[3]

The offence is committed if a person without lawful excuse destroys or damages any property belonging to[4] another intending to destroy or damage any such property[5], or being reckless as to whether any such property[5] would be destroyed or damaged.[6] A person is treated as having a lawful excuse—

(*a*) if at the time of the offence he believed[7] that the person or persons whom he believed[7] to be entitled to consent to the destruction or damage—

(i) had so consented, **or**

---

[1] *See* pp. 3–4

[2] No definition is given of the phrase "reduced into possession", but *see* note [6] on p. 5.

[3] C.D.A. 1971, s. 10(1)(*a*).

[4] Property is treated as belonging to any person (*a*) having the custody or control of it; or (*b*) having in it any proprietary right or interest (not being an equitable interest arising only from an agreement to transfer or grant an interest); or (*c*) having a charge (*e.g.*, a mortgage) on it. (C.D.A. 1971, s. 10(2).)

[5] *I.e.*, any property belonging to any other person, not necessarily the property destroyed or damaged.

[6] C.D.A. 1971, s. 1(1).

[7] It is immaterial whether the belief is justified or not if it is honestly held. (C.D.A. 1971, s. 5(3).)

    (ii) would have so consented if he or they had known of the destruction or damage and its circumstances; **or**

  (b) if he destroyed or damaged the property in question in order to protect property belonging to[1] himself or another or a right or interest in property which was or which he believed[2] to be vested in himself or another, **and** at the time of the offence he believed[2]—

    (i) that the property, right or interest was in immediate need of protection; **and**

    (ii) that the means of protection adopted or proposed to be adopted were or would be reasonable having regard to all the circumstances.[3]

A number of allied offences is also created. It is made a more serious offence if, when destroying or damaging any property (including the offender's), there is an intention to endanger another's life or recklessness in that regard.[4] It is an offence without lawful excuse[5] to make a threat to another, intending that the other would fear it would be carried out,—

  (a) to destroy or damage any property belonging to[1] that other or a third person; or

  (b) to destroy or damage his own property in a way which he knows is likely to endanger the life of the other or a third person.[6]

---

[1] Property is treated as belonging to any person (a) having the custody or control of it; or (b) having in it any proprietary right or interest (not being an equitable interest arising only from an agreement to transfer or grant an interest); or (c) having a charge (e.g., a mortgage) on it. (C.D.A. 1971, s. 10(2).)

[2] It is immaterial whether the belief is justified or not if it is honestly held. (C.D.A. 1971, s. 5(3).)

[3] C.D.A. 1971, s. 5(1), (2).

[4] C.D.A. 1971, s. 1(2).

[5] "Lawful excuse" has the meaning discussed in the text above.

[6] C.D.A. 1971, s. 2.

A person commits an offence if he has anything in his custody or control intending without lawful excuse[1] to use it, or cause or permit another to use it, to destroy or damage: another's property or his own or the user's property in a way which he knows is likely to endanger another's life.[2]

The killing or injuring of one's own animal is not **by itself** an offence.[3]

A person convicted of killing or injuring an animal belonging to[4] another person may be ordered by the court to pay compensation to that person.[5] A person who kills[6] a tame or domestic animal belonging to another makes himself liable to be sued for its value unless he can show that he had no other means of protecting his property.[7] To kill or take[8] wild animals on another's land which are not reduced into the possession[9] of that other person is a trespass for which the trespasser can be sued.[10] If the animals are game,[11] he may be prosecuted.

The particular rules about killing or injuring dogs are discussed on pages 71 and 73.

---

[1] "Lawful excuse" has the meaning discussed in the text on pp. 163–164
[2] C.D.A. 1971, s. 3.
[3] But it could be an offence if, for example, accompanied by cruelty (for which *see* earlier passages in this Chapter).
[4] For the meaning of "belonging to", *see* note [4] on p. 163.
[5] *See*, further, p. 134.
[6] Injury of the animal would presumably also justify a claim if thereby loss to its owner could be proved.
[7] *Cresswell v. Sirl* (1947); *Hamps v. Darby* (1948).
[8] For an interpretation of "take", *see* p. 100.
[9] For an explanation of the phrase "reduce into possession", *see* note [6] on p. 5.
[10] *See* p. 5 for theft of wild animals.
[11] Hares, rabbits and deer are the only four-legged game animals.

CHAPTER 9

ANIMAL DISEASES

Introduction

Modern times have seen the introduction of a large volume of legislation aimed at the eradication and prevention of diseases in animals, and for these purposes statutory controls have been established over the whole field of animal movement, treatment and slaughter. The main provisions are found in the Animal Health Act 1981 and in a host of regulations made under that Act and its predecessors. This legislation confers wide powers on the Minister of Agriculture, Fisheries and Food and the Scottish and Welsh Secretaries of State (who in this Chapter are referred to as "the Minister") and on local authorities.[1]

The expression "animals" in the 1981 Act means cattle,[2]

---

[1] These authorities are generally: the Common Council of the City of London for its area and, as regards imported animals, for the whole of Greater London; the London borough councils for their areas, except for imported animals; county councils in the remainder of England and Wales; and regional or island councils in Scotland (A.H.A. 1981, s. 50(1)–(4)). They and the police are obliged to enforce the Act and regulations. (A.H.A. 1981, ss. 50(5), 60(1).)

[2] "Cattle" means bulls, cows, steers, heifers, and calves. (A.H.A. 1981, s. 89(1)).

sheep and goats and all other ruminating[1] animals and swine.[2] The word may be further extended in meaning by orders of the Minister.[3] The expression "disease" in the Act, so far as applying to animals, means cattle plague,[4] pleuro-pneumonia,[5] foot-and-mouth disease, sheep-pox, sheep scab or swine fever.[6] Other diseases may be included by the Minister's order,[7] and those so added for all or certain purposes are:—

African horse sickness	Equine virus abortion
African swine fever	Equine encephalomyelitis
Anjeszky's disease of swine	Glanders, including farcy
Anthrax	Infectious equine anaemia
Blue tongue disease	Leptospirosis
Bovine leutosis	Parasitic mange in horses
Brucella suis	Rabies
Brucellosis	Swine vesicular disease
Brucellosis in cattle (epizootic abortion)	Teschen disease
	Tuberculosis
Brucellosis melitensis	Tularaemia
Dourine	Vesicular exanthema
Encephalomyelitis	Warble fly
Epizootic lymphangitis	

The control of animal diseases necessarily implies restrictions on the import, export and movement of animals, and these are dealt with in Chapter 3. Further provisions relating to diseased animals may be found on other pages as follows: owner's liability for diseased animals (9–10); selling diseased animals (10, 26); police powers to deal with them (135); and diseased deer (137).

---

[1] *I.e.*, chewing cud.
[2] A.H.A. 1981, s. 87(1).
[3] A.H.A. 1981, s. 87 (2)(3).
[4] "Cattle plague" means rinderpest or the disease commonly called cattle plague (A.H.A. 1981 s. 89(1)).
[5] "Pleuro-pneumonia" means contagious pleuro-pneumonia of cattle (A.H.A. 1981 s. 89(1)).
[6] A.H.A. 1981, s. 88(1). "Swine fever" means the disease known as typhoid fever of swine, soldier purples, red disease, hog cholera or swine plague. (A.H.A. 1981, s. 89(1)).
[7] A.H.A. 1981, s. 88(2).

The total volume of animal diseases legislation is such that a large volume on its own would be needed to cover the topic fully. This Chapter can hope to do no more than broadly indicate the range of the subject.

Powers of Ministry's Vets

To obtain information necessary to eradicate animal diseases, the Minister may authorise in writing any vet or other Ministry officer to inspect cattle, sheep, goats, all other ruminating animals, swine and horses[1]. A person so authorised may at all reasonable times enter on any land or premises to make his inspection, and may apply such tests and take such samples as he considers necessary; he must produce his written authority on demand.[2] Anyone who obstructs or impedes an authorised person is liable to prosecution.[3]

When a vet suspects certain diseases he is empowered to make enquiries and to examine animals, animal products and carcases on the premises concerned. He has powers of entry for this purpose, and those concerned must afford him the necessary facilities.[4]

To prevent disease spreading, the Minister may cause to be treated with serum or vaccine or both any animals[5] which have been in contact with a diseased animal or bird, or which appear to him to be or to have been exposed to the infection of disease, or which are in an infected area.[6] These powers include the taking of any action necessary for the treatment to be administered or otherwise required in

---

[1] A.H.A. 1981, ss. 3(2), 87(1). "Horses" includes asses and mules (A.H.A. 1981 s. 89(1)).

[2] A.H.A. 1981, s. 3(3).

[3] A.H.A. 1981, s. 4(2).

[4] These powers, contained in the respective regulations, apply in the case of the following diseases: anthrax, cattle plague, epizootic lymphangitis, foot-and-mouth disease, glanders or farcy, parasitic mange, pleuro-pneumonia, rabies, sheep-pox, sheep scab, swine fever, swine vesicular disease, Teschen disease and infectious diseases of horses. The particular powers in relation to rabies are discussed on pp. 177–180.

[5] "Animals" means cattle, sheep, goats, all other ruminating animals and swine (A.H.A. 1981 s. 87(1)).

[6] For infected areas, *see* pp. 173–175.

connection with the treatment. An authorised officer of the Ministry may for the purpose enter any land[1] or premises and take with him any other persons he requires. He must produce his written authority on demand.[2]

Powers to Destroy Wild Life

The Minister may make orders providing for the destruction of wild members of any species[3] of mammal (except man) in an area when he is satisfied that: there is a disease[4] which has been or is being transmitted from that species to any kind of animals[5] or poultry in that area; and that destruction of the species is necessary to eliminate, or substantially reduce the incidence of, that disease in such animals or poultry.[6] Methods of destruction otherwise unlawful may be used if the Minister is satisfied on certain matters.[7]

Orders so made may provide for: ensuring that the destruction is properly and effectively carried out; preventing persons from taking into captivity, harbouring, concealing or otherwise protecting wild life with intent to prevent their destruction, or obstructing or interfering with the processss of destruction; and regulating the ownership and disposal of carcases.[8]

Before beginning destruction on any land[1] the Minister must take all reasonable steps to inform the occupier and anyone else who may be there of his intention and the proposed methods of destruction which must be carried out as safely as possible.[9] When an order is in force the Minister

---

[1] For the definition of "land", see note 6 on p. 142.
[2] A.H.A. 1981, s. 16.
[3] References to wild members of any species in an area means members of the species in the area that are neither domesticated nor held in captivity. (A.H.A. 1981 s. 21 (9).)
[4] For the kinds of disease for which these powers may be operated, see p. 167. But rabies, for which there are special powers (see pp. 177–180), is excluded. (A.H.A. 1981 ss. 1(a), 21(1)(a)).
[5] "Animals" includes horses (A.H.A. 1981, s. 21(9)).
[6] A.H.A. 1981 s. 21(2))
[7] A.H.A. 1981, s. 21(4).
[8] A.H.A. 1981, s. 21(5).
[9] A.H.A. 1981, s. 21(6).

may "take such measures" (including the erection of fences or other obstacles) as he considers appropriate for preventing: the movement of living creatures[1] into or out of the destruction area, or any part of it, while destruction is being carried out; or the recolonisation of an area of destruction by the species being destroyed.[2] When, in the Minister's opinion, these measures are no longer necessary, he must remove anything erected or placed on the land and carry out any reasonably practicable reinstatement of the land.[3]

To implement these destruction orders "authorised officers"[4] are given powers of entry to any land[5]—

(i) to take samples of wild life, their excreta and materials they may have been in contact with;

(ii) to carry out other investigations;

(iii) to destroy wild life which is the subject of an order;

(iv) to take any of the measures described in the last paragraph;

(v) to ascertain whether destruction has been effectively carried out.[6]

If required by the owner, occupier or person in charge of the land, an authorised officer must produce a duly authenticated document showing his authority and state in writing his reasons for entering.[7] His powers of entry to certain nature reserves are subject to conditions.[8]

---

[1] *I.e.*, living creatures of any kind, domestic or wild, and whether of the species to be destroyed or not.
[2] A.H.A. 1981 s. 21(7),
[3] A.H.A. 1981, s. 21(8).
[4] An authorised officer is an officer of the Minister, a veterinary inspector, or another person authorised by the Minister to exercise the powers described in the text. (A.H.A. 1981 s. 22(1).)
[5] "Land" includes land covered with water, buildings and other structures (I.A. 1978, s. 5, Sch. 1), but there is no power of entry to a dwelling (A.H.A. 1981, ss. 22(5).)
[6] A.H.A. 1981, s. 22(2)(3)(4). The purposes for which these powers of entry may be exercised are much abbreviated in the text. Some powers are exercisable before an order is made and others up to 2 years after its revocation.
[7] A.H.A. 1981, s. 22(6).
[8] A.H.A. 1981, s. 22(7).

An order[1] made under the powers described is now in force in the County of Avon and parts of Cornwall, Devon, Gloucestershire and Wiltshire, because tuberculosis is being transmitted from badgers to cattle in these areas. It permits the poisoning of wild badgers by hydrocyanic acid gas and the shooting of them with a .22 pistol. The order prohibits the harbouring, etc., of badgers and any obstruction or interference with the destruction process. Badgers' carcases are not to be removed from where they are destroyed without Ministerial approval.

Giving Notice of Disease and Separating Diseased Animals

Every person having in his possession or under his charge an animal[2] affected with disease[3] shall—

(a) as far as practicable keep that animal separate from animals not so affected; and

(b) with all practicable speed give notice[4] to a local police constable that he has an affected animal.[5]

Failure so to act in either case is an offence.[6] A person prosecuted is presumed to have known of the existence of the disease unless and until he shows to the satisfaction of the court that he had no knowledge of it **and** could not with reasonable diligence have obtained that knowledge.[7]

The following persons, if required in writing by the Ministry, the local authority or an inspector, must give all information in their possession about diseased animals, their movements and the persons into or through whose hands

---

[1] The Badgers (Control Areas) Order 1977 (S.I. 1977/1721).

[2] For the definition of "animal", see pp. 166–167.

[3] For the definition of "disease", see p. 167.

[4] The notice must be in writing and delivered to the police constable personally or left at his house. (A.H.A. 1981, s. 83(3).). Although the Act allows the notice to be sent through the post, it is suggested that this would be quite unsatisfactory in the circumstances. It will be advisable to have a copy of the notice receipted by the constable and endorsed by him with the time and date of receipt; the onus of proving that the notice was given rests upon the person giving it (*Huggins v. Ward* (1873)).

[5] A.H.A. 1981, s. 15(1).

[6] A.H.A. 1981, s. 15(7).

[7] A.H.A. 1981, s. 79(2).

the animals have passed. Those required to give this information[1] are—

(1) Every person who has or has had in his possession[2] or under his charge any animal[3] affected with or suspected of disease or any animal which has been in any way in contact with such an animal; and

(2) Any auctioneer who has sold or offered for sale any animal as described in (1).[4]

Infected Places

When a local authority or Ministry inspector has been told or suspects that an animal disease exists or has existed within a limited time on premises, he may serve notice on the occupier of the premises, and they become an infected place until the notice is withdrawn.[5] Movement and activity in infected places are governed by rules which vary according to the disease. For example, the rules may prohibit: the movement of animals except under licence; the removal of carcases,[6] fodder,[7] litter,[8] dung and other things except under licence or with permission; the removal of milk; the removal of fleeces without permission; and the tending without permission of unaffected animals by a person who has attended diseased or affected animals. The rules may require persons leaving infected premises to disinfect their clothing in disinfectant provided and to wash their hands; and may require liquid manure to be disinfected before

[1] Failure to give it or to give false information is an offence. (Animals (Miscellaneous Provisions) Order 1927 (S.R. & O. 1927/290), Art 12(1).)

[2] For some notes on the meaning of "possession", see p. 65.

[3] "Animal" in this context means cattle, sheep, goats, all other ruminating animals, swine, horses, asses, mules, dogs and other canine animals. (1927 Order cited above, Art. 1.).

[4] 1927 Order cited above, Art. 12(1).

[5] Ministerial orders giving authority for individual diseases to be dealt with in this way are made under A.H.A. 1981, s. 17(1). For a list of relevant diseases, see p. 167.

[6] "Carcase" means the carcase of an animal and includes parts of a carcase, and the meat, bones, hide, skin, hooves, offal or other part of an animal, separately or otherwise, or any portion thereof. (A.H.A. 1981 s. 89(1)).

[7] "Fodder" means hay or other substance commonly used for food of animals. (A.H.A. 1981, s. 89(1)).

[8] "Litter" means straw or other substance commonly used for bedding or otherwise for or about animals. (A.H.A. 1981, s. 89(1)).

being drained away. Places where animals affected with disease have been kept must or may be required by the rules to be disinfected and cleansed in the ways described in the rules.

A person owning or having charge of any animals in an infected place may put up a notice, at or near the entrance to a building or enclosure in which the animals are, forbidding entry without permission. It then becomes an offence for anyone to enter those places without permission unless he has by law a right of entry.[1]

Infected and Controlled Areas

An infected area is an area surrounding an infected place with defined boundaries a certain number of miles from the infected place. A controlled area, which operates only in cases of foot-and-mouth disease and, exceptionally, swine vesicular disease, is normally much larger than an infected area. It is imposed (usually, but not always, around an infected area) when there is a risk of widespread dissemination of disease, for instance when disease is believed to have been present in animals in a market which have been moved over a wide area from it. Both types of area are declared as such by special order of the Minister. The following are the main provisions which operate in these areas.

In cases of foot-and-mouth disease and swine vesicular disease[2] no animal[3] may be moved out of an infected area at all, or out of a controlled area except under licence into a contiguous infected area. No animal may be moved into an infected or controlled area, except under licence direct to a farm (where it must be detained for 14 days) or to a slaughterhouse (where it must be slaughtered) not less than two miles from an infected place. No animal may be moved by road, rail or water within an infected or controlled area

---

[1] A.H.A. 1981 ss. 27, 72(6). A person having such a right would be an inspector of the Ministry or local authority.

[2] Swine Vesicular Disease Order 1972 (S.I. 1972/1980), Art. 3.

[3] "Animal" in this context means cattle, sheep, goats, pigs and deer. (Foot-and-Mouth Disease (Infected Areas Restrictions) Order 1938 (S.R. & O. 1938/1434), Art. 21).

except under licence, which will not be granted for
movement to an unlicensed market or sale, or to farm
premises for sale there, or from a licensed market or sale
except to a slaughterhouse in the same area, or by road or
water within two miles of an infected place.[1] Animals may
however be moved directly through an infected or controlled
area provided they are not untrucked within the area.

Orders made by the Minister for foot-and-mouth disease
and African swine fever also regulate the movement of
imported animals in infected and controlled areas, the
holding of markets for such animals there, the disposal of
slaughterhouse manure there, and the prohibition of
hunting. In an infected area cattle, sheep, goats and pigs
must not be allowed to stray on roads; persons clipping or
dipping sheep or using vehicles to transport animals must
take special disinfection precautions; inspectors may
prohibit entry to footpaths, fields, sheds and other places
except under licence or with permission; all dogs within five
miles of any infected place must at all times be confined,
chained up or under effectual personal control except when
in a house; and an inspector may require the occupier of
premises in an infected area in which dogs or poultry are
kept to control them in particular ways.[2] Milk originating
in a controlled area, and whey or other liquid derived from
it, may not be fed to animals on other premises unless the
milk has been pasteurised or boiled.[3]

In the case of swine fever, no person may move swine
into or out of an infected area, or within an infected area
by road or water, except under licence or by rail through
the area provided they are not untrucked within it; and no
one may cause or permit swine to stray on a road within
the area. A licence may permit the movement of swine
through an infected area provided they are transported in
a mechanically-propelled vehicle, are not unloaded during
the journey, and are being taken to a slaughterhouse or
bacon factory, to premises used for keeping swine other

[1] Licences are granted by local authority inspectors.
[2] Foot-and-Mouth Disease (Infected Areas Restrictions) Order 1938.
[3] Diseases of Animals (Milk Treatment) Order 1967 (S.I. 1967/1714), Art. 3.

than in connection with their sale, or to a vessel on which they are to be shipped abroad.[1]

In the case of sheep scab, there are restrictions on movement of sheep out of an infected area (sometimes known as "a movement area" or "a dipping area") and on the marketing of sheep in the area. All sheep in the area may be required to be dipped in a stated period unless slaughtered during the period. Infected areas may be of any size up to the whole of Great Britain.

Movement of Animals

The Minister is given very wide powers[2] to make orders prohibiting and regulating the movement of animals in almost all circumstances in which they are not in an enclosed field, e.g., when being driven, transported, sold or awaiting sale, awaiting slaughter, or grazing on unenclosed land. The main purposes of the orders are to prevent the spread of disease and unnecessary suffering.

By way of example, a local authority inspector finding a diseased animal or one suspected of being affected, may seize it with other animals in the same place, and may detain and isolate them where they are or move them to an isolated place for detention. They can then only be moved under the Minister's direction or licence. It is an offence for a person to expose an animal affected or suspected of being affected with certain diseases[3] in a market or other place where animals are commonly exposed for sale or exhibited, to move it by road rail or water, to place it or allow it to stray on common, unenclosed or insufficiently fenced land, or to graze it on roadside verges.[4]

The movement of animals generally is discussed on pages 53 to 60.

---

[1] Swine Fever (Infected Areas Restrictions) Order 1956 (S.I. 1956/1750), Arts. 5, 6, 7.

[2] By A.H.A. 1981, ss. 7(1)(a)(b), 8(1), 25, 26, 37.

[3] The diseases are: cattle plague, epizootic lymphangitis, foot-and-mouth disease, glanders or farcy, parasitic mange, pleuro-pneumonia, sheep-pox, sheep scab, swine fever and swine vesicular disease.

[4] See the respective orders dealing with the diseases listed in note [3] above and A.H.A. 1981, s. 25.

Slaughter of Animals

The Minister has power to slaughter diseased animals and those suspected of disease or exposed to infection. In some cases slaughter is compulsory, and in others there is a discretion.[1]

Except in some cases,[2] compensation will be paid for animals slaughtered. The rate varies according to the disease for which the animal was slaughtered and according to whether the animal was actually affected with the disease or not. In the case of some diseases the amount of compensation is regulated by the Act of 1981[3] or orders made under it. Where it is not, the procedure is for the Minister to give a notice of value to the owner and that becomes the compensation payable unless the owner within 14 days serves a counter-notice disputing it. In that event the sum is settled by arbitration.[4]

The carcase of an animal belongs to the Minister when he orders its slaughter, and will be buried, sold or otherwise disposed of at his direction.[5] If the sum received on sale of the carcase exceeds the compensation paid, the excess is due to the animal's owner after deducting reasonable expenses.[6] The Minister is entitled to bury the carcase in any suitable ground in the possession or occupation of the animal's owner or in any common or unenclosed land.[7] It is an offence to dig up the carcase except with a licence from the Minister.[8]

---

[1] A.H.A. 1981 ss. 31, 32, Sch. 3.

[2] These are, briefly; a diseased or suspect animal slaughtered in an export quarantine station (A.H.A. 1981 s. 12(2)); cases provided for by orders which the Minister may make under A.H.A. 1981, s. 10(2)(d) and Schedule 2, para. 12; and where the animal, being imported, was diseased on landing, or, coming from the E.E.C., had been exposed to infection, when the Minister may withhold compensation wholly or partly. (A.H.A. 1981 s. 34(6)).

[3] A.H.A. 1981, ss. 31, 32(3), Sch. 3, paras 1(4), 2(3), 3(2), 4(2).

[4] Diseases of Animals (Ascertainment of Compensation) Order 1959 (S.I. 1959/1335), Art. 3.

[5] A.H.A. 1981 s. 34(2).

[6] A.H.A. 1981, s. 34(3).

[7] A.H.A. 1981, s. 34(4).

[8] Animals (Miscellaneous Provisions) Order 1927 (S.R. & O. 1927/290), Art. 16.

Insurers of animals slaughtered on the Minister's orders may deduct compensation paid by the Minister from payments to the owner for which they are liable.[1]

Rabies

Concern with the increasing risk of rabies spreading to Great Britain led to the passing of the Rabies Act[2] in 1974 to strengthen the powers relating to animal diseases then contained in the Disease of Animals Act 1950. The extra powers so given merit particular attention.

Where the Minister has declared an area to be infected[3] for rabies purposes, he may take steps to secure the destruction of foxes in the area, except those held in captivity. Officers of the Ministry and persons authorised in writing by the Minister may enter any land[4] (other than a dwelling-house) to destroy foxes or to decide whether to destroy them. Methods of destruction otherwise unlawful may be used. The occupier and anyone else on the land must be warned beforehand by the Minister that he proposes to destroy foxes and the methods to be used. The warning will be by service of a written notice or "such other method as may be appropriate in the circumstances". The Minister may erect fences or other obstacles on the land, as part of the destruction operation, to restrict the movement of animals into and out of the infected area. The Minister also has power to forbid the movement of animals[5] into or out of an infected area, to control their movements within the area, to seize, detain and destroy uncontrolled animals, and to introduce compulsory vaccination. The carcase of every fox destroyed belongs to the Minister and is to be disposed of as he determines.[6]

---

[1] A.H.A. 1981, s. 34(5).

[2] Now repealed and re-enacted by A.H.A. 1981.

[3] For infected areas, generally, see pp. 173–175.

[4] "Land" will include buildings. (Rabies (Control) Order 1974 (S.I. 1974/2212), Art. 2(2).)

[5] "Animal" means an animal (other than man) belonging to any of the orders of mammals listed in Appendix C at the end of the book. (Rabies (Control) Order 1974. Art. 2(1) and Sch. 1.)

[6] Rabies (Control) Order 1974, Arts, 9, 10 and Sch. 3.

By further order the powers described in the last paragraph may be extended to apply to any wild animal in an infected area not held in captivity.[1]

The holding of sporting and recreational activities on land in an infected area may be prohibited by serving a written notice on the person responsible for holding the activity. A veterinary inspector of the Minister may serve such notices when in his opinion the activity might cause the spread of rabies.[2]

A person who knows or suspects that an animal[3] (whether in captivity or not) is affected with rabies, or was so affected at its death, must with all practicable speed give notice[4] of the fact to an inspector[5] or a police constable, unless he reasonably believes that someone else has done so. Further, a person who knows or suspects that an animal in his possession or under his charge is, or was at the time of death, affected with rabies must as far as practicable keep that animal or the carcase separate from any other animal.[6]

When a veterinary inspector suspects that rabies exists, or has within the previous 56 days existed, at any premises[7] or that there is an animal there who has been or may have been exposed to the infection of that disease, he has to make enquiries about the correctness of his information and examine any animal or carcase found at the premises. For these two purposes the inspector may—

(a) enter on any part of the premises; and

(b) remove from the premises any animal affected, or suspected of being affected, with rabies, or another

---

[1] A.H.A. 1981 s. 19(1).

[2] 1974 Order, Art. 11.

[3] "Animal" means an animal (other than man) belonging to any of the orders of mammals listed in Appendix C at the end of the book. (1974 Order, Art. 2(1) and Sch. 1.)

[4] Written notice is required. (A.H.A. 1981 s. 83(1).

[5] This is a diseases of animals inspector of the Ministry or local authority. (1974 Order, Art. 2(1).)

[6] 1974 Order, Art. 4(1), (2). These provisions do not apply in cases prescribed by order for the purpose of regulating the keeping, import or use of rabies virus. (1974 Order, Art. 4(4).)

[7] "Premises" includes land, with or without buildings. (1974 Order, Art. 2(1).)

animal which has been in contact with such an animal, or the carcase of any of these kinds of animals, to a place for veterinary observation or diagnostic tests; and

(c) take samples for diagnosis from any animal on the premises, whether or not it is one of the kinds of animals described in (b) above.

The occupier of the premises and his employees must give the inspector such reasonable assistance as may be required in performing these tasks. If there is or has been on premises an animal or carcase as described in (b) above, the following people must give all reasonable facilities for the inspector's inquiries, for the removal of any animal or carcase and for the taking of samples:—

(i) the occupier of those premises;

(ii) the vet (if any) who has been attending or has been consulted about the animal or carcase;

(iii) any person who has been in charge of the animal or carcase or in any manner in contact with it.

Further, the persons described above must, if required to do so by an officer of the Ministry, give such information as they possess about the animal or carcase, about the location or movements of any other animal in their possession or under their charge, or about any other animal with which any animal described in (b) above may have been in contact.[1]

The extent of the powers described shows the serious view taken of the dangers of rabies. A little thought will show how wide these powers are. By way of illustration, a veterinary inspector need only suspect (though he must have grounds for his suspicion) that there is on premises an animal which **may** have been exposed to rabies to give him the right—without notice or warning—to enter those premises (which includes houses and other buildings as well as bare land). Having entered, he has the right to remove

---

[1] 1974 Order, Art. 6.

an animal (which includes pet dogs and cats) which has been in contact with another animal suspected of rabies. There is no right of redress or appeal. Indeed, those involved must give the inspector every assistance in doing these and the other things described, and will be liable to prosecution if they do not comply in any way.[1] Further, an animal affected, suspected of being affected or exposed to the infection of rabies may be slaughtered by Ministry officials. Prior written notice may be served requiring the animal to be surrendered for slaughter or detained pending slaughter. Compensation is payable.[2]

The restrictions aimed at preventing the introduction of rabies into the country through imported animals are discussed on pages 42 to 44.

---

[1] 1974 Order, Art. 13.
[2] A.H.A. 1981, s. 32(1)–(3); 1974 Order, Arts, 3, 8. If the animal was affected with rabies when slaughtered, compensation is payable at the rate of 50% of its market value immediately before it contracted the disease. In all other cases, the full market value immediately before slaughter is payable. (Rabies (Compensation) Order 1976 (S.I. 1976/2195) Art. 3.)

PERFORMANCES AND PUBLIC EXHIBITIONS

Exhibition and Training of Performing Animals

With the exceptions later mentioned, it is an offence for anyone to exhibit[1] or train[2] any performing animal[3] unless he is registered with the county council[4] in whose area he lives.[5] Applications for registration must contain particulars of the animals and of the general nature of the performances for which they are to be exhibited or trained. Unless the applicant is prohibited from being registered,[6] he will receive a certificate of registration on payment of a fee of such amount as the council may charge.[7] There appears to

---

[1] "Exhibit" means exhibit at any entertainment to which the public are admitted whether on payment of money or otherwise. (P.A.A. 1925, s. 5(1).)

[2] "Train" means train for the purpose of such an exhibition as is defined by reference to the meaning of "exhibit" above (P.A.A 1925, s. 5(1).)

[3] The only restriction on the meaning of "animal" is that it is not to include invertebrates (P.A.A. 1925, s. 5(1).) Thus, all mammals, birds, fishes, reptiles and amphibians are included in the meaning.

[4] In the City of London the registration authority is the Common Council of the City; in the Inner Temple, the Sub-Treasurer; in the Middle Temple, the Under Treasurer; elsewhere in London, the London Borough Councils (P.A.A. 1925, s. 5(1); L.G.A. 1963, s. 4(2)(b); Temples Order 1971 (S.I. 1971/1732) Art. 3).

[5] A person having no fixed place of residence in Great Britain may apply for registration to the council of such one of the following districts as he may choose: the City of London, Birmingham, Bristol, Cardiff, Kingston-upon-Hull, Leeds, Liverpool, Manchester, Newcastle upon Tyne, Plymouth and Southampton in England and Wales; and Aberdeen, Dundee, Edinburgh and Glasgow in Scotland. (P.A.A. 1925, s. 1(2); Performing Animals Rules 1925 (S.R. & O. 1925/1219).

[6] As to such prohibition, or disqualification as it is there called, see p. 183.

[7] P.A.A. 1925, s. 1(2).

be no discretion for the council to refuse registration if the applicant is not prohibited from being registered and the application correctly made out and the fee paid.

The particulars on the application form are entered in the council's register (which is open to inspection) and recorded in the certificate issued. An applicant may apply to have the particulars varied, when the council will cancel the existing certificate and issue a new one.[1]

There is no need to register for the training of animals for *bona fide* military, police, agricultural or sporting purposes, or for the exhibition of animals so trained.[2]

If a magistrates' court is satisfied on complaint made by the police or a council officer that the training or exhibition of any performing animal has been accompanied by cruelty and should be prohibited or allowed only subject to conditions, the court may make an order accordingly. There is a right of appeal to the Crown Court. The order comes into force seven days after it is made or, if an appeal is lodged within that time, when the appeal is determined. Particulars of the order will be endorsed on the issued certificate and entered in the council's register.[3]

A police officer or an authorised officer of the council[4] has power to enter premises, to inspect them and performing animals there, and to request the production of a registration certificate, but may not get on or behind the stage during a public performance.[5]

Offences punishable with a fine have been created if a person does any of the following things:—

(1) Exhibits or trains a performing animal without being registered.

(2) Exhibits or trains such an animal outside the terms of registration.

---

[1] P.A.A. 1925, s. 1. No fee is payable for a certificate in this case.
[2] P.A.A. 1925, s. 7.
[3] P.A.A. 1925, s. 2.
[4] *I.e.*, the council who has registration powers (*see* p. 181) in the area.
[5] P.A.A. 1925, s. 3.

(3) Fails to comply with an order of the magistrates' court.

(4) Obstructs or wilfully[1] delays an officer when exercising his powers of entry and inspection.

(5) Conceals any animal to avoid its inspection.

(6) Fails to produce his certificate to the court for endorsement.

(7) Applies to be registered when prohibited from being registered by a court.[2]

When a person is convicted of any of these offences, or of offences against the Protection of Animals Act 1911,[3] the convicting court may, as well as or instead of fining the offender,—

(a) if he is registered under the Act, order that his name be removed from the register; and

(b) order him to be disqualified from being registered, either permanently or for such time as the order may stipulate.

The same provisions about appeal, the effective date of the order and the recording of the order as apply to an order made after complaint to the court[4] will apply to the orders described above.[5]

Public exhibitions of experiments on living animals are dealt with on page 125.

---

[1] This means deliberately and intentionally, and not by accident or inadvertence. (*R. v. Senior* [1899] 1 Q.B. 282 at pp. 290–291.)

[2] P.A.A. 1925, s. 4(1).

[3] For these offences, *see* pp. 119–132.

[4] *See* p. 182.

[5] P.A.A. 1925, s. 4(2).

Performances Involving Bulls or Horses

No person shall promote, or cause or knowingly permit to take place, any public performance[1] which includes any episode consisting of or involving—

(a) throwing or casting, with ropes or other appliances, any unbroken horse[2] or untrained bull[3]; or

(b) wrestling, fighting or struggling with any untrained bull; or

(c) riding, or attempting to ride, any horse or bull which by the use of any appliance or treatment involving cruelty is, or has been, stimulated with the intention of making it buck during the performance.

No person shall take part in any of the episodes described in a public performance.[4]

The foregoing are offences punishable by fine or imprisonment or both.[5] In cases (a) and (b) if an animal appears to be, or is represented to spectators to be, unbroken or untrained, it is for the person prosecuted to prove to the court that it is in fact broken or trained. In case (c) the defendant will be entitled to be acquitted if he is able to prove to the court that he did not know, or could not reasonably be expected to know, that an appliance or treatment was to be or was used on the horse before or during the performance. No such defence is available if the animal is a bull.[6]

---

[1] Unlike the provisions described in the last section and in the next, there is no definition in this case of what constitutes a public performance. It is suggested that it is enough if the performance is available to the public with or without payment. It does not include a public cinema performance (P.A.A. 1934, s. 1(3)), for which see the next Section.

[2] "Horse", includes any mare, gelding, pony, foal, colt, filly or stallion. (P.A.A. 1911, s. 15(d); P.A.A. 1934, s. 1(3).)

[3] "Bull" includes any cow, bullock, heifer, calf, steer, or ox. (P.A.A. 1911, s. 15(d); P.A.A. 1934, s. 1(3).)

[4] P.A.A. 1934, s. 1(1).

[5] P.A.A. 1934, s. 2.

[6] P.A.A. 1934, s. 1(2).

Films

No person is to exhibit to the public,[1] or supply to another person for public exhibition (whether by the person supplied or someone else), any film, wherever produced, if in connection with its production any scene represented in the film was organised or directed in such a way as to involve the cruel infliction of pain or terror on any animal[2] or the cruel goading of any animal to fury.[3] Contravention is an offence punishable with fine or imprisonment or both.[4]

In a prosecution the court may (without prejudice to any other mode of proof) infer from the film as exhibited or supplied that a scene represented in it was organised or directed in such a way as to involve the cruel infliction of pain or terror on an animal or the cruel goading of it to fury. Whether or not the court draws such an inference, the defendant will be entitled to be acquitted if he proves to the court that he believed, and had reasonable cause to believe, that no scene represented in the film was organised or directed as described above.[5]

---

[1] A film is deemed to be exhibited to the public when, and only when, it is exhibited in a place to which for the time being members of the general public as such have access, whether on payment of money or otherwise. (C.F.A. 1937, s. 1(4)(*a*).)

[2] The long definition of "animal" is to be found in Appendix E at the end of the book. (P.A.A. 1911, s. 15; C.F.A. 1937, s. 1(4)(*b*).)

[3] C.F.A. 1937, s. 1(1).

[4] C.F.A. 1937, s. 1(3).

[5] C.F.A. 1937, s. 1(2).

CHAPTER 11

PESTS

Destructive Animals Generally

By operating the procedure described below Government Ministers[1] can take steps to clear land of destructive animals.

The Minister may serve a written notice[2] if it appears to him that it is expedient to do so for the purpose of preventing damage to crops, pasture,[3] animal or human foodstuffs, livestock.[4] trees, hedges, banks or any works on land.[5] The notice will require the person served to take such steps (including any steps specified in the notice) as may be necessary for the killing, taking[6] or destruction on the land described in the notice of such of the following animals as the notice

---

[1] The functions of Ministers under the provisions discussed in the first, second and fourth sections of this Chapter are variously divided between the Minister of Agriculture and the Secretaries of State for Scotland and Wales. In these Sections, for convenience, the expression "the Minister" is used to cover all situations.

[2] Notice must be served by delivering it personally to the person to be served, by leaving it at his last known address, or by posting it to him by registered letter or recorded delivery service. If an incorporated company or other body is to be served, notice must be given by one of the means described to its secretary or clerk at its registered or principal office. (A.A. 1947, s. 107(1)–(3); R.D.S.A. 1962, s. 1(1).)

[3] "Pasture" includes meadow. (A.A. 1947, s. 109(3).)

[4] "Livestock" includes any creature kept for the production of food, wool, skins or fur, or for the purpose of its use in the farming of land. (A.A. 1947, s. 109(3).)

[5] A.A. 1947, s. 98(1).

[6] For an interpretation of the meaning of taking an animal, see p. 100.

may detail: rabbits,[1] hares and other rodents,[2] deer, foxes and moles.[3] The land in question may be land of any kind.

The person to be served with the notice is the person who has the right to kill, take or destroy the kind of animal described in the notice on the land identified by it.[4] This will generally be the occupier of it, but the rights will sometimes belong to someone else, *e.g.*, a shooting tenant or a landlord who has reserved gaming rights.[5] So far as rabbits are concerned, the notice may be served on the occupier whether or not he has the right to kill them.[6]

The notice may require that the steps to be taken shall be taken within the time stipulated in it.[7]

The Minister may assist in complying with the notice by providing such services and equipment, appliances and other materials as he thinks may be required. A charge may be made for this assistance and recovered from the person requesting it.[8] He may also make financial contributions towards the cost of complying with a notice. Both forms of aid may extend to destroying or reducing breeding places or cover for rabbits or excluding rabbits from them, and preventing rabbits living in any place from spreading to or doing damage in another place.[9]

With the three exceptions mentioned below, the notice cannot require any killing, taking or destruction which would otherwise be prohibited by law.[10] The exceptions are:—

---

[1] For the particular provisions dealing with the destruction of rabbits, *see* pp. 190–193.

[2] Rodents, being animals of the order *Rodentia*, will include rats, mice and squirrels; further examples may be found in Part II of Appendix C at the end of the book. Other measures against rats and mice are dealt with on pp. 193–197.

[3] A.A. 1947, s. 98(1), (4). Other animals may be added to the list by Ministerial regulations (A.A. 1947, s. 98(4)), but none has yet been so added.

[4] A.A. 1947, s. 98(1).

[5] *See* pp. 110–114 for a discussion of these rights.

[6] P.A. 1954, s. 1(6). He will anyhow have the right under the Ground Game Act 1880, for which *see* pp. 107–110.

[7] A.A. 1947, s. 98(1).

[8] A.A. 1947, s. 101.

[9] P.A. 1954, ss. 2(2), 3(1).

[10] A.A. 1947, s. 98(2).

H1

(a) Game may be killed out of season, and the person served with a notice may not use the excuse for non-compliance with it that the game he is required to kill is out of season.[1]

(b) A game licence need not be held when complying with a notice, and a person who has had a notice may sell game destroyed in the course of complying with it as if he had held a game licence.[2]

(c) The use of poisonous gas and substances generating it in the holes, burrows or earths of the animals to be destroyed is permitted.[3]

If the Minister considers it expedient, for the purpose of preventing damage to crops, pasture,[4] animal or human foodstuffs, livestock,[4] trees, hedges, banks or any works on land, to prevent the escape of any animals[5] from any land, he may serve[6] written notice on the occupier requiring him, within the time given in the notice, to take such steps as may be necessary to prevent the animals' escape, including any steps which may be detailed in the notice.[7]

There is no right of appeal against either of the two kinds of notice which have been considered. Failure to comply with their requirements is an offence punishable by fine.[8] Additionally, on failure to comply, a person authorised by

---

[1] A.A. 1947, s. 98(2), proviso. As to close seasons for game, see pp. 101, 136.

[2] A.A. 1947, s. 100(4). As to game licences and the selling of game, see pp. 102–107.

[3] A.A. 1947, s. 98(3). Apart from this provision, the use of these methods is permitted only for the extermination of rabbits. The methods may not be used on any animals added to those listed, for which see note [3] and the text thereto on p. 187. (A.A. 1947, s. 98(4), proviso.)

[4] For the meaning of "pasture" and "livestock", see notes [3] and [4] on p. 186.

[5] The Act puts no restriction on the meaning of "animals", but for the meaning in law generally, see p. 3.

[6] As to the means of serving notice, see note [2] on p. 186. In this case, if the land is used for agriculture, the notice may be served on the agent or employee of the occupier who is responsible for the control of the farming of the land, instead of on the occupier himself. (A.A. 1947, s. 100(6).)

[7] A.A. 1947, s. 99.

[8] A.A. 1947, s. 100(1). This includes a daily fine while the default continues.

the Minister may enter[1] the land and take such steps as the Minister may direct to secure compliance with the notice. The reasonable cost of taking these steps is recoverable by the Minister from the person served with the notice.[2]

If a person incurs expense in complying with either kind of notice or if the Minister recovers money from him as just described, and he considers that the expense should be borne wholly or partly by someone else having an interest in the land, he may apply to the County Court for a full or partial indemnity from the other person.[3] No other grounds are given upon which the application to the court may be made. It would seem to be justified if for any reason a person, other than the recipient of the Minister's notice, was partly or wholly responsible for the state of affairs giving rise to the notice. Thus, an occupier, receiving notice about the escape of animals and not having the right under the terms of his tenancy to destroy them, might justifiably claim that the cost of measures to prevent their escape should be borne by the person having that right.

The Minister may give such directions "as appear to him to be expedient" authorising the keeping of animals killed or taken under these provisions (except those dealing with escape) and their disposal for use for food or otherwise.[4] This appears to give the Minister unfettered control over the animals' carcases some of which will have appreciable value as food; there is no provision for compensation.

The Forestry Commissioners have separate powers to prevent damage to trees by pests. These powers may be operated if they are satisfied that trees or tree plants are being, or are likely to be, damaged by rabbits, hares or

---

[1] The person must, if required, produce authentication of his authority and, if the land is used for residential purposes, give 24 hours notice of intended entry. (A.A. 1947, s. 106(2), (3).) He need hold no game licence and may sell game as if he had a licence. (A.A. 1947, s. 100(4).)

[2] A.A. 1947, s. 100(2). Any dispute over the amount of the cost is settled by arbitration.

[3] A.A. 1947, s. 100(5).

[4] A.A. 1947, s. 100(3).

vermin[1] owing to the failure of an occupier[2] of land to destroy sufficiently those animals on his land, or otherwise to take steps for the prevention of damage by them.[3] In such a case the Commissioners may authorise in writing any competent person to enter on the land and kill or take the animals described. But, before doing so, they must give the occupier **and** owner of the land such opportunity[4] as the Commissioners think reasonable of destroying the animals or taking steps to prevent the damage.[5]

The net cost of the action so taken by the Commissioners is recoverable from the occupier[6] of the land as a civil debt.[7] The person authorised to enter the land must produce his written authority if required; obstruction of him is an offence punishable with a fine.[8]

The Commissioners' officers and others authorised by them may at any time enter land for any purpose connected with the exercise of these powers, *e.g.*, to assess the quantity of vermin on it. Written authority must again be produced if asked for, and obstruction is similarly punishable.[9]

Rabbits

The Minister may make orders known as "rabbit clearance orders". They designate areas as rabbit clearance areas to be freed, so far as practicable, of wild rabbits, and may provide for and regulate the steps to be taken to that end.[10]

---

[1] The expression "vermin" *includes* squirrels. (F.A. 1967, s. 7(5)(b)). It is suggested that the general meaning of the word is so wide as to embrace in this context any creature capable of damaging trees.

[2] The person entitled to kill rabbits, hares or vermin on common land is deemed to be the occupier of that land. (F.A. 1967, s. 7(5)(*a*).) For a definition of "common land", *see* note [2] on p. 15, though this is not expressly applied to the 1967 Act.

[3] F.A. 1967, s. 7(1).

[4] Neither the kind of opportunity nor the means of giving it are detailed, thus leaving both to the Commissioners' discretion.

[5] F.A. 1967, s. 7(2).

[6] There is no right of recovery from the owner, if he is not the occupier, or other sanction available against him.

[7] F.A. 1967, s. 7(3).

[8] F.A. 1967, s. 7(4).

[9] F.A. 1967, s. 48(1), (3).

[10] P.A. 1954, s. 1(1). The orders may be varied or revoked by later orders of the Minister.

By Rabbit Clearance Order No. 148 the Minister has designated the whole of England and Wales (excluding the City
of London, the Scilly Isles and Skokholm Island) as a rabbit
clearance area.

An occupier of land[1] in a rabbit clearance area must take
the necessary steps to kill or take[2] wild rabbits on his land.
Where it is not reasonably practicable to destroy them,
he must take steps to prevent them causing damage. In
particular, he must comply with any directions in the order
about the steps to be taken towards these ends and about
the time in which they are to be taken.[3]

No additional right is given to the occupier to authorise
others to kill rabbits on his land with firearms, but the
Minister may on the occupier's request permit the occupier
to authorise more persons to kill rabbits in this way than is
otherwise permitted[4] if the Minister is satisfied—

(a) that the circumstances make necessary a greater use
of firearms than the occupier has the right to authorise; **and**

(b) that the occupier has tried to obtain the sanction of
the persons who, apart from the Ground Game Act
1880, have the right to take rabbits on his land[5]; **and**

(c) that their sanction has been unreasonably withheld.[6]

This sanction will not be treated as unreasonably withheld
if, so far as the use of firearms is required, the persons
asked for it are themselves taking or proposing to take
adequate steps to destroy the rabbits.[7]

---

[1] The expression "occupier" in relation to unoccupied land means the person
entitled to occupy it. (P.A. 1954, s. 1(13).)

[2] For an interpretation of the word "take", see p. 100.

[3] P.A. 1954, s. 1(2).

[4] Under the Ground Game Act 1880 the occupier may authorise only one other
person to kill rabbits by shooting on his land—see p. 108.

[5] I.e., the persons to whom the shooting is let, or the landlord if the shooting
is held by him.

[6] P.A. 1954, s. 1(4). Additional persons so authorised are subject to the same
provisions (for which see p. 109) about production of their authorisations given
by the occupier as the person authorised under the 1880 Act.

[7] P.A. 1954, s. 1(5).

Persons authorised by the occupier to take rabbits in order to comply with a rabbit clearance order cannot be prosecuted for the unlawful destruction or pursuit of game[1] whilst acting in accordance with their authorisations[2].

There is no right of appeal or other action which can be taken against a rabbit clearance order or its requirements except, as mentioned below, to object to the proposal to make the order. The following provisions dealt with earlier in this Chapter when considering notices by the Minister to deal with pests apply to rabbit clearance orders:—

(1) Game licences and selling of game (page 188).

(2) The results of failure to comply with requirements (pages 188–189).

(3) Obtaining indemnity from another person (page 189)

(4) Disposal of animals by the Minister (page 189).[3]

Authorised officers of the Minister may enter land at all reasonable times to see whether a rabbit clearance order should be made or to check whether the order's requirements are being met.[4]

The Minister must give notice of a proposal to make a rabbit clearance order so as to inform persons interested in land in the area and, when it is made, publish it,[5] take steps to bring it to the notice of persons likely to be affected, and enable them to buy copies of it.[6] The notice of a proposal must allow at least 14 days for representations to be made to the Minister; when making the order the Minister may, but need not, give effect to the representations.[7]

The Minister has further powers by which he can require

---

[1] This is a reference to poaching offences such as are created by N.P.A. 1828, ss. 1 and 9 and G.A. 1831, ss. 30 and 32.
[2] P.A. 1954, s. 1(7).
[3] P.A. 1954, s. 1(9).
[4] P.A. 1954, s. 1(8).
[5] E.g., by notices on public notice boards and in the local press.
[6] P.A. 1954, s. 1(10), (11)(b).
[7] P.A. 1954, s. 1(12).

an occupier to deal with rabbits. If the Minister thinks it expedient for the purpose of preventing damage by rabbits to crops, pasture,[1] trees, hedges, banks or any works on land, he may by written notice served[2] on the occupier of any land[3] require him to take the steps detailed in the notice within the time given to destroy or reduce the breeding places or cover for rabbits, or to exclude rabbits from them, or to prevent rabbits living in any place on the land from spreading to or doing damage in any other place. But this notice is provisional; the occupier and others interested in the land may make written objections to it which must be considered by the Minister before serving a final and effective notice on the occupier. If the occupier holds the land under a contract of tenancy, copies of both notices must be served also on the person to whom he pays rent.[4]

The provisions considered on pages 187 to 189 dealing with game licences, the selling of game, the results of failure to comply with requirements, the disposal of animals by the Minister, the steps for obtaining indemnity from another person, and with assistance from the Minister all apply to the situation created by the type of notice just considered.[5]

Rats and Mice

District councils[6] have a duty to keep their areas, so far as practicable, free from rats and mice[7] and to that end have been given certain powers.

The occupier of any land[8] must at once give written notice[9] to the district council when he knows that rats or mice are

---

[1] "Pasture" includes meadow. (A.A. 1947, s. 109(3).)
[2] As to the service of notices, see note [2] on p. 186 and note [6] on p. 188.
[3] If the land is unoccupied, notice can be served on the person entitled to occupy it. (A.A. 1947, s. 98(7).)
[4] A.A. 1947, s. 98(7).
[5] A.A. 1947, ss. 100, 101, 106(1)–(3); P.A. 1954, ss. 2, 3.
[6] The Common Council of the City of London has this duty in its area and the London borough councils elsewhere in London. (P.D.P.A. 1949, s. 1(1).)
[7] P.D.P.A. 1949, s. 2(1).
[8] "Land" includes land covered with water and any building or part of a building. (P.D.P.A. 1949, s. 28(1).)
[9] No particular form of notice is required.

living on or resorting to his land in substantial numbers,[1] but need not do so if—

(a) his land is agricultural land[2]; **or**

(b) a notice of infestation (*see* pages 195 to 196) is given.[3]

Whether or not notice by an occupier is served on them, if the district council consider that steps should be taken for the purpose of destroying rats or mice on land or keeping it free from them, they may serve written notice on the owner or occupier requiring him to take, within such reasonable time as may be given by the notice, such reasonable steps for those purposes as may be detailed in the notice.[4] In particular, the notice may require a form of treatment to be applied to the land at particular times and the carrying out of structural repairs or other works.[5]

If the owner of the land is not the occupier, the council may serve a notice on both[6]; the owner is entitled to complain to a magistrates' court (if he considers that such is the case) that the occupier is preventing him from doing the work which the owner's notice requires, when the magistrates may order the occupier to permit the work to be done.[7]

An owner or occupier receiving a notice requiring structural works to be done may appeal to a magistrates' court, but only on particular grounds.[8] Those grounds and the appeal procedures relating to them are set out in full in Appendix L at the end of the book. An appeal must be

---

[1] P.D.P.A. 1949, s. 3(1). Failure to give notice is punishable by fine. There appear to be no indications of the meaning of "substantial numbers".

[2] "Agricultural land" means land used for agriculture as that word is defined in AA 1947 s. 109(3). (A.A. 1947, s. 109(1); PDPA 1949. s. 28(1).) The definition is given in note [3] on p. 157. The Minister may by regulations exempt other kinds of land from the requirement (P.D.P.A. 1949, s. 3(2)) but has not yet done so.

[3] P.D.P.A. 1949, s. 3(2), (3).

[4] P.D.P.A. 1949, s. 4(1).

[5] P.D.P.A. 1949, s. 4(2).

[6] P.D.P.A. 1949, s. 4(1).

[7] P.D.P.A. 1949, s. 4(4).

[8] P.H.A. 1936, s. 290(3); P.D.P.A. 1949, s. 4(5).

made within 21 days from receiving the notice,[1] and there is a further right of appeal to the Crown Court.[2] It appears that there is no right of appeal against requirements in a notice which do not relate to structural works.

If an owner or occupier served with a notice fails to take the steps which it requires at the time or within the period given in the notice, the council may take those steps themselves and recover their reasonable expenses from the person in default. Also, the person defaulting commits an offence punishable by fine.[3]

Where land affected by rats or mice[4] is in multiple occupation and the council consider that it should be dealt with as one unit, the council may enter the land and take the necessary steps (except structural works) to deal with the vermin without serving the notices just considered. At least 7 days' notice of entry must be given, and this must show the steps proposed to be taken. The council's expenses in this are recoverable from the occupiers in proportion to the expenditure on their individual properties.[5]

Powers similar to those just described are given to the Minister of Agriculture to deal with cases of infestation of food and things associated with it. With the exceptions mentioned below, every person whose business consists of or includes the manufacture,[6] storage, transport or sale of food[7] must at once give written notice to the Minister when he knows that infestation[8] is present—

(a) in any premises or vehicle, or any equipment belong-

---

[1] The notice itself must state the right of appeal and the time limit. (P.H.A. 1936, s. 300(3); P.D.P.A. 1949, s. 4(5).)

[2] P.H.A. 1936, ss. 300(2), 301.

[3] P.D.P.A. 1949, ss. 5, 7(1).

[4] *I.e.*, land on which rats or mice are living or resorting to in substantial numbers.

[5] P.D.P.A. 1949, ss. 6, 7(1). Unoccupied land is treated as being occupied by the owner.

[6] "Manufacture" includes processing. (P.D.P.A. 1949, s. 28(1).)

[7] "Food" includes any substance ordinarily used in the composition or preparation of food, the seeds of any cereal or vegetable, and any feeding stuffs for animals, but does not include growing crops. (P.D.P.A. 1949, s. 28(1).)

[8] "Infestation" means the presence of rats, mice, insects or mites in numbers or under conditions which involve an immediate or potential risk of substantial loss of or damage to food. (P.D.P.A. 1949, s. 28(1).)

ing to either, used or likely to be used in the course of that business for the manufacture, storage, transport or sale of food; **or**

(*b*) in any food manufactured, stored, transported or sold in the course of that business, or in any other goods for the time being in his possession[1] which are in contact or likely to come into contact with any such food.[2]

Similarly, but again with exceptions, as mentioned below, every person whose business consists of or includes the manufacture, sale, repair or cleaning of containers must at once give written notice to the Minister when he knows that there is any infestation in any container[3] in his possession[1] which is to be used for the reception of food in the course of any business of the kind mentioned in the last paragraph.[4]

The exceptions referred to earlier are exceptions which may be made by the Minister in regulations.[5] Regulations so made relax the requirements to give notice when, briefly[6]; named types of food or premises are infested with insects or mites only; a carrier in certain circumstances is involved; or the Minister decides on an application to him to relax or exclude the requirements.[7] The Minister is empowered[8] to prohibit or restrict the delivery of food or other goods for which notice is to be given as described above and has done so in the same regulations.[9]

Whether or not such notices are given, the Minister may give directions, for preventing or mitigating damage to food, to persons whose business is involved with it or with food containers. If he thinks the infestation cannot be remedied

---

[1] As to the meaning of "possession", see p. 65.
[2] P.D.P.A. 1949, s. 13(1).
[3] "Container" includes sacks, boxes, tins and other similar articles. (P.D.P.A. 1949, s. 28(1).)
[4] P.D.P.A. 1949, s. 13(2).
[5] P.D.P.A. 1949, s. 13(3)(*a*).
[6] For full details, the text of the regulations must be referred to.
[7] Prevention of Damage by Pests (Infestation of Food) Regulations 1950 (S.I. 1950/416).
[8] P.D.P.A. 1949, s. 13(3)(*b*).
[9] 1950, Regulations cited above, Arts. 5 and 8.

by any treatment, his directions may require the destruction of the food or containers involved.[1]

When the directions require any structural work to be done or any food or container to be destroyed, any person aggrieved may appeal to the magistrates[2] and thence, in a case of structural works only, to the Crown Court.[3]

In default of compliance with directions, the Minister may by order authorise the person named in it to take the steps necessary for compliance. The expenses of this are recoverable from the person in default who also commits an offence by non-compliance.[4]

The Minister may make regulations for controlling the methods for keeping down or destroying rats, mice, insects or mites which may be used by persons carrying on business in pest destruction and control.[5]

The application of the earlier provisions in this Section for dealing with rats and mice has been extended so as to apply the provisions, wholly or partly, to ships, vessels and hovercraft and places connected with them.[6]

Destructive Foreign Animals

The Destructive Imported Animals Act of 1932 is designed to prohibit or control the import into, and the keeping in, Great Britain[7] of destructive non-indigenous mammals. The controls which the Act gives are exercised by the Minister through the making of regulations and the granting of licences.

The only animals which the Act names are musk rats

---

[1] P.D.P.A. 1949, s. 14.

[2] Within 21 days from receipt of the directions in the case of structural work, or 7 days in the other case. (P.D.P.A. 1949, s. 15(1).)

[3] P.D.P.A. 1949, s. 15. The directions must state the right of appeal and the time limits.

[4] P.D.P.A. 1949, ss. 16(1), (2), 17.

[5] P.D.P.A. 1949, s. 19(1). No such regulations have yet been made.

[6] Prevention of Damage by Pests (Application to Shipping) Order 1951 (S.I. 1951/967); H.A. 1968, Schedule, para. 3.

[7] *I.e.*, England, Wales and Scotland.

(*Fiber zibethicus*) and musquash (*Ondatra zibethica*),[1] but it allows the Minister to make orders bringing other animals into its orbit; these further animals can only be drawn from species of mammals which on 17th March 1932[2] were not established in a wild state in Great Britain, or had only become so established within the preceding 50 years, but excluding species which on that date were commonly kept in Great Britain in a domesticated state.[3] To date, the animals added in this way are mink, grey squirrels, rabbits other than the European rabbit and coypus. The Minister's orders may prohibit absolutely the importing[4] and keeping[5] of the animals or allow their import and keeping under licence.

The present position is that the keeping of musk rats, musquash, grey squirrels (*Sciurus carolinensis*) and rabbits other than the European rabbit (*Oryctolagus Cuniculus*) is absolutely prohibited,[6] *i.e.*, no licence can be granted. To keep them is an offence punishable by fine, and on conviction the court may order the animals to be forfeited and destroyed.[7] Mink (*Mustela vison*) and coypus (*Myocastor coypus*) may only be kept if a licence to do so is issued by the Minister.[8] Keeping without a licence, or contravening or failing to comply with the terms of a licence or with any

---

[1] D.I.A.A. 1932, s. 1(1).

[2] This is the date on which the Act was passed.

[3] D.I.A.A. 1932, s. 10. Also, the Minister is required to be satisfied that because of their destructive habits it is desirable to prohibit or control these mammals' import or keeping and to destroy any which may be at large.

[4] For the importing of these kinds of animals, *see* pp. 36–38.

[5] There is no definition of "keeping" in the Act but its wording and that of the regulations indicate that the word signifies a deliberate maintaining of the animals as distinct from merely letting them exist at large. The measures which can be taken against them when they do so exist are described on p. 200.

[6] Musk Rats (Prohibition of Importation and Keeping) Order 1933 (S.R. & O. 1933/106); Grey Squirrels (Prohibition of Importation and Keeping) Order 1937 (S.R. & O. 1937/478); Non-indigenous Rabbits (Prohibition of Importation and Keeping) Order 1954 (S.R. & O 1954/927).

[7] D.I.A.A. 1932, ss. 1(1), 6(1), 10(1); the three Orders cited in the last footnote.

[8] Mink (Keeping) Order 1982 (S.I. 1982/1745), Art. 3; Coypus (Keeping) Order 1982 (S.I. 1982/1744), Art. 3. Both orders cease to have effect on 1st January 1988 but may, as has been done previously, be re-enacted.

regulation made under the Act,[1] are offences with a liability to a fine and a court order as before.[2]

A licence to keep coypus or mink will be issued on payment of the fee laid down,[3] will be in force for 12 months and may be renewed, but may be revoked if the licence holder fails to comply with any of its terms or the regulations dealing with keeping, or if he commits an offence under the Act.[4] The terms of the licence will require the licensee—

(1) In the case of coypus, to inform the Minister of the name and address of any person to whom he disposes of the coypus.

(2) In the case of mink, to inform persons to whom he disposes of them of their obligation to obtain a licence to keep them.

(3) In the case of mink, to inform the Minister of any alteration, at the place where they are kept, to a guard fence or to a baffle attached to it at least 14 days before he proposes to make the alteration.

(4) In both cases, to inform the Minister of any change of occupancy of the premises where the animals are kept or if they cease to be kept there.

(5) In both cases, to make returns to the Minister when required stating the number of each sex of animal kept.

(6) In both cases, to give immediate notice to the Minister if any animal escapes.

(7) In both cases, to permit persons authorised by the Minister at reasonable times to enter and inspect the premises where the animals are kept.[5]

---

[1] *I.e.*, the regulations about keeping the animals cited in note 3 below.
[2] D.I.A.A. 1932, ss. 1(1), 6(1), 10(1); the two Orders cited in note 8 on p. 198.
[3] These fees are presently: £43 for coypus (Coypus (Keeping) Regulations 1967 (S.I. 1967/1873), Art. 4); £58 for mink (Mink (Keeping) Regulations 1975 (S.I. 1975/2223), Art. 5(3).)
[4] D.I.A.A. 1932, ss. 2, 3.
[5] Coypus and Mink Keeping Regulations cited in note 3 above.

The licensee will also be required to comply with the regulations about the manner in which the animals are to be kept. Coypus, when not being transported, must be confined in enclosures[1] constructed so as to prevent their escape. They must only be transported in closed cages or other containers similarly constructed.[2] The requirements for mink are much lengthier and more detailed; briefly, they must be kept in escape-proof cages or other containers which in turn must be kept in enclosures or buildings constructed in accordance with the regulations' specifications.[3] The requirements for their transport are the same as those for coypus.[4]

The occupier[5] of any land[6] who knows that musk rats (or musquash), grey squirrels, rabbits other than the European rabbit, mink or coypus (other than those which may be and are kept under licence) are to be found[7] on his land must give notice[8] at once to the Minister. As soon as the Minister becomes aware of this situation[9] he may take the steps he considers necessary for the animals' destruction, and it is the occupier's duty to afford all such facilities as he can to persons employed by the Minister for destroying the animals.[10]

---

[1] "Enclosures" includes cages, hutches, pens, sties, stockades, buildings and parts of buildings. (1967 Coypu Regulations, Art. 2(1).)

[2] 1967 Coypus Regulations, Art. 3.

[3] 1975 Mink Regulations, Art. 4(1), Schedule 2.

[4] 1975 Mink Regulations, Art. 4(2).

[5] "Occupier" means, in the case of unoccupied land, the owner of the land. (D.I.A.A. 1932, s. 11).

[6] "Land" includes land covered with water and any buildings and any other erection on land and any cellar, sewer, drain or culvert in or under land. (D.I.A.A. 1932, s. 11).

[7] Note that there is no indication of the numbers necessary to require a notice to be given, unlike the case for rats and mice where "substantial numbers" are mentioned: see pp. 193–194.

[8] Written notice is not required, but is advisable since failure to give it is an offence.

[9] This may happen either through the notice given to the Minister by the occupier or through other sources of information.

[10] D.I.A.A 1932, ss. 1(1), 5(1)–(3), 10(1), 11; the Orders cited in notes 6 and 8 on p. 198.

The occupier is not required to pay for or towards the cost of destruction. There can be no action for damages for the killing or wounding of any of these animals found at large. (D.I.A.A. 1932, s. 5(5).)

A special licence may be given by the Minister to anyone
who wants to keep the animals described in the last paragraph for exhibition or scientific research or other exceptional purposes. The licence, which is revocable at any time,
will require the animals to be kept in such manner and upon
such conditions as it may specify.[1]

As mentioned earlier,[2] other animals may be brought into
the orbit of the Act by Ministerial orders. If this happens,
any person who on the date of the relevant order is keeping
animals described in it for profit in Great Britain[3] is entitled
to receive compensation from the Minister for his losses
which will ensue as a result of the order being made.[4]

In addition to the offences described on pages 198–199,
the following offences, all punishable by fines, are created
by the Act:—

(1) Turning loose any musk rat (or musquash), grey
    squirrels, non-European rabbits, mink or coypus, or
    wilfully[5] allowing them to escape.[6]

(2) Obstructing any officer of, or person authorised or
    employed by, the Minister in the execution of his
    duty under the Act.

(3) An occupier failing to give the required notice that
    the animals described in (1) above are to be found
    on his land.[7]

---

[1] D.I.A.A. 1932, ss. 1(1), 8(1), 10(1), 11.
[2] On p. 198.
[3] *I.e.* England, Wales and Scotland.
[4] D.I.A.A. 1932, ss. 1(1), 7, 10(1), 11.
[5] This means deliberately and intentionally, and not by accident or inadvertence.
(*R. v. Senior* (1899) 1 Q.B. 283 at pp. 290–91.)
[6] From what the animals are to escape in order for an offence to occur is not
clear. It is perhaps intended to refer to the enclosures, containers, cages, etc., in
which licensed mink and coypus must be kept (see p. 200) and to the doubtless
similar requirements under a special licence (*see* text above).
[7] D.I.A.A. 1932, ss. 1(1), 6(1), 10(1), 11; the Orders cited in notes [6] and [8] on
p. 198.

CHAPTER 12

BYELAWS

Introduction

Byelaws are a form of subordinate legislation having the force of law[1]; they supplement the general law. They can be made by many different kinds of organisations and sometimes by groups of people; but in each case the power to make byelaws must be granted by an Act of Parliament which will define the purposes for which the byelaws can be made and often require them to be approved by a Government Department. No byelaw otherwise made can be effective.

The purpose of byelaws may be said to be, in general terms, the regulation of the conduct of people in particular places or circumstances; in some cases this affects animals[2] also. Because the total range of operation of byelaws is so wide, a comprehensive coverage of byelaws affecting animals is not attempted here. The purpose of this Chapter is to indicate the more common situations in which byelaws concern animals and to give details of those byelaws which are of more general application.

---

[1] Though the validity of a byelaw can be attacked on specific legal grounds.
[2] The word "animal" is frequently used in byelaws without definition. In law generally the term includes all creatures not belonging to the human race.

In some situations notices with the text of the byelaws are posted on the land or in the buildings to which the byelaws apply. In other cases enquiries will have to be made.

Penalties for the non-observance of byelaws are generally exacted by prosecution in the magistrates' courts. The maximum penalty is usually a moderate fine, but occasionally a further small fine can be imposed for each day of non-compliance after conviction.

Byelaws for Good Rule and Government

A district council[1] may make byelaws for the good rule and government of, and for the suppression of nuisances[2] in, the whole or any part of their area.[3] The byelaws must be confirmed by the appropriate Government Department, but otherwise each council will decide what byelaws to make. The following three byelaws about animals are commonly found:

(1) A person in charge of a dog must not allow it to foul the footway of any street or public place by deposit of its excrement. It is usually provided that it is a defence if the person in charge satisfies the court that the fouling of the footway was not due to culpable neglect or default on his part, and the byelaw may go on to provide that the owner of the dog shall be deemed to be in charge of it unless the court is satisfied that at the time the dog fouled the footway it was in the charge of some other person.

Notices warning of the byelaw are usually displayed adjacent to the footways affected but this cannot be relied upon.

(2) A person must not keep in any house, building or premises any noisy animal which causes a serious nuisance to residents in the neighbourhood. To this

---

[1] In London byelaws may be made by the borough councils (L.G.A. 1972, s. 235(1)) or, in the city of London, by the City Corporation. (C.L.A. 1961).

[2] For common law and statutory nuisances, see pp. 19–20.

[3] L.G.A. 1972, s. 235(1).

byelaw is usually added a provision that there is to
be no prosecution unless the nuisance continues after
the expiration of a fortnight from the date on which
a notice alleging a nuisance is served[1] on the person
keeping the animal, the notice to be signed by at
least three householders living within hearing of the
animal.

(3) A person must not drive or lead, or cause to be driven
or led, in any street or public place any bull more
than a year old unless it is properly secured and kept
under proper control.

These byelaws are required to be available at the district
council offices for free inspection at all reasonable hours;
copies are to be made available on payment.[2]

Public Open Spaces

Local authorities and other bodies who manage public
open spaces have powers to make byelaws regulating users'
conduct. As with the byelaws considered in the last section,
no standard set of byelaws applies universally except in the
case of Forestry Commission land. Some of these byelaws
will affect animals. Copies are often displayed on the land.
They may provide for the removal of offenders.

As well as urban public parks and the like, these byelaws
can be made for: national parks; areas of outstanding
natural beauty; land and waterways to which the public
are given access by agreements or orders; National Trust
property; nature reserves; common land; and large forest
areas such as Epping Forest and the New Forest.

Land under the management or control of the Forestry
Commissioners to which the public have, or may be permitted to have, access is governed by a standard set of byelaws.[3]

---

[1] It is unlikely that the byelaw will stipulate the method of service. It is suggested
that the posting or personal delivery of the notice to the person keeping the animal
will suffice; this will have to be proved by the prosecution.
[2] L.G.A. 1972, s. 236(8).
[3] The Forestry Commission Byelaws 1982 (S.I. 1982/648).

These provide that a person shall not, except with the Commissioners' written authority,—

(a) turn out to graze or feed or allow to remain on the land any animal.[1]

(b) permit any animal in the person's charge to be out of control;

(c) ride or lead any horse except:
(i) in the New Forest,

(ii) on public bridleways,[2] or

(iii) on bridleways specified by the Commissioners;

(d) permit a dog for which the person is responsible to disturb, worry or chase any bird or animal or, on being requested by an officer of the Commissioners, fail to keep the dog on a leash;

(e) wilfully[3] disturb, injure, catch, net, destroy or take[4] any bird, fish, reptile or animal, or attempt to do so;

(f) wilfully[3] disturb, damage or destroy the burrow, den, set or lair of any wild animal;

(g) play or practise any game or sport in such a manner as to endanger animals.[5]

In the New Forest and the Forest of Dean there is a general prohibition, except with the Commissioners' written authority or, in some cases, other lawful authority, against turning out animals or fowls to graze or feed or allowing

---

[1] This byelaw does not apply to the New Forest or the Forest of Dean (1982 Byelaws, Art. 3(1)), for which separate byelaws are made— see below.

[2] Public bridleways are not defined in the 1982 Byelaws, but, as a guide, see items (ii) and (iii), on p. 93; see note [6] on that page for the means of checking recorded public bridleways.

[3] This means deliberately and intentionally, and not by accident or inadvertence (*R. v. Senior* (1899) 1 Q.B. 283 at pp. 290–91).

[4] For an interpretation of "take", *see* p. 100.

[5] 1982 Byelaws, Arts. 3(3), 5(xi)–(xiv), (xviii), (xx), (xxiv).

them to remain. But in the Forest of Dean sheep are allowed in some circumstances.[1]

Railways

The byelaws of the British Railways Board contain the following provisions affecting animals:

(1) No person shall take or cause to be taken on to, or cause or allow to remain upon, the Railway,[2] if requested not to do so by an authorised person,[3] any animal which by reason of its nature is in the opinion of the authorised person likely to cause, or in fact does cause, annoyance or damage to any passenger or damage to any property.

(2) No person in charge of an animal shall permit it to stand, lie down or walk on any escalator or moving platform while in motion in breach of a warning exhibited on it.[4]

(3) No person in charge of any animal in or upon the Railway shall—

(a) leave or place it in or upon the Railway—

(i) in any manner or place so as to cause an obstruction or hindrance to the Railways Board or to persons using the Railway, **or**

(ii) otherwise than in accordance with any reasonable direction of an authorised person, **or**

(iii) where parking or waiting[5] is prohibited; **or**

---

[1] 1982 Byelaws, Arts. 11, 12. The Verderers of the two Forests may themselves make byelaws which affect animals (F.A. 1967, s. 47), and these are unaffected by the Forestry Commissioners' byelaws (1982 Byelaws, Art. 3(4)).

[2] "The Railway" means the railways and railway premises of the Board, including stations and the approaches to stations. (1971 Byelaws.)

[3] "An authorised person" means any officer, employee or agent of the Board, and any constable, acting in the execution of his or her duty upon or in connection with the Railway. (1971 Byelaws).

[4] Byelaw 18.

[5] The seemingly inappropriate references to parking and waiting are due to the byelaw applying also to vehicles.

(*b*) leave or place any animal in or upon the Railway (otherwise than in a car park[1] or other place expressly authorised by the Board) for a period longer than necessary for the person in charge to transact any lawful business upon the Railway at or adjacent to the place at which the animal has been left or placed; **or**

(*c*) leave or place any animal in or upon the Railway (otherwise than in a place expressly appointed by the Board) unattended; **or**

(*d*) conduct himself or herself in a disorderly manner.[2]

An authorised person may remove an animal contravening Byelaws (1), (2) or (3), but in the case of Byelaws (1) and (2) only after the person in charge of it has failed to do so after a request by the authorised person to remove it immediately. Under Byelaw (3) the person in charge of the animal is liable to pay the cost of removal to the Board. These provisions do not affect liability to a monetary penalty for contravention of the byelaws.[3]

Inland Waters

The British Waterways Board's byelaws apply to every canal and inland navigation in England and Wales belonging to or under the control of the Board except the Gloucester

---

[1] The seemingly inappropriate reference to a car park is due to the byelaw applying also to vehicles.

[2] Byelaw 25.

[3] Byelaws 18 and 25.

Other regulations of the British Railways Board which affect animals may be found in the following publications of the Board: *"Conditions of Carriage of Livestock by Rail Express Parcels Services"*, *"Regulations governing the Transport of Unaccompanied Animals by British Rail"* and *"Conditions of Carriage of Passengers and their Luggage"*.

For Government orders regulating the movement of animals by rail, *see* pp. 57–58.

The information in this Section of the Chapter is supplied by courtesy of the Press and Public Relations Officer of the Board.

and Sharpness Canal and the River Severn Navigation. The following byelaws affect animals:

(1) Any person in charge of any animal on any moveable bridge shall remove it immediately on being warned that the bridge is about to be opened; and no person shall permit any animal under his control to go upon a moveable bridge, or attempt to drive any animal on to it, after receiving warning that the bridge is about to be opened until the bridge has been closed[1] after such opening.[2]

(2) No person shall permit any horse used for towing vessels to be used upon the towing path[3] unless such horse is accompanied by and under the control of a competent driver.[4]

(3) No person shall wash any animal in any canal.[5]

Water authorities and internal drainage boards may make byelaws applying to reservoirs, waterways, other inland waters and land under their control.[6] These may deal with such matters as—

(1) Prohibiting the washing of animals in the water.

(2) Prohibiting the destruction, injury or disturbance of wild animals.

(3) Ordering dog owners and others in charge of them to keep them under proper control and to restrain them from causing annoyance to other people, from

---

[1] This byelaw provides that the bridge shall be deemed to be closed only when it is secured in position to allow persons and traffic to pass in safety over the canal by means of the bridge.

[2] British Waterways Board's General Canal Byelaws, No. 27(2).

[3] "Towing path" includes any way alongside a canal provided for hauling or towing boats along the canal together with any gantries, bridges or other works on it (The same Byelaws, No. 2.)

[4] The same Byelaws, No. 33.

[5] The same Byelaws, No. 42, "Canal" includes any inland navigation belonging to the Board or under its control. (The same Byelaws, No. 2.)

The information in this Section of the Chapter is supplied by courtesy of the Amenity Services Division of the British Waterways Board.

[6] By virtue of powers in the Water Act 1973 and the Land Drainage Act 1976. Further powers may be given by water authorities' private Acts of Parliament.

worrying other animals or waterfowl and from entering the water.

(4) Requiring persons grazing animals on the banks of watercourses to take necessary and practicable steps to prevent them damaging the banks or the channels of watercourses. This byelaw may however provide that drinking places for stock may be made with the approval of the authority making the byelaw.

Pleasure Fairs, Markets, Fairs and Public Health Byelaws

District councils' byelaws controlling pleasure fairs[1] may require that any person having control of an animal which would be dangerous to the public if at large shall take all reasonable steps to secure or cage it so as to prevent that danger. Other byelaws regulating markets or fairs may deal with the accommodation to be provided for animals.[2]

Under public health legislation local authorities may make byelaws to prevent any keeping of animals which is a nuisance or which is injurious, or likely to cause injury, to health.[3]

---

[1] Made under P.H.A. 1961, s. 75.
[2] M.F.A.. 1847, s. 42.
[3] P.H.A. 1936, ss. 81(b), 343(1); L.G.A. 1963, s. 40. For common law and other statutory nuisances, see pp. 19–20.

APPENDICES

APPENDIX A

**Endangered kinds of mammals which cannot be imported or
exported without a licence[1]**

**ALL kinds of mammals EXCEPT the kinds specified in the first column
below:—**

Excepted kind[2]	Common name or names[2]
	Marsupials
Macropus giganteus	Eastern grey kangeroo
Macropus fuliginosus	Western grey kangaroo
	Insectivores
Talpa europaea	Common European mole
	Rabbits
Oryctolagus cuniculus	European rabbit (otherwise known as domestic rabbit)
	Rodents
Castor canadensis	Canadian beaver
Rattus norvegicus	Common rat (otherwise known as laboratory rat)
Mus musculus	House mouse (otherwise known as laboratory mouse)
Any domestic form of Mesocricetus auratus	Domestic golden hamster

---

[1] E.S.A. 1976, Sch. 1, Part I. *See* pp. 38–42, 53 for further details.

[2] The second column of this schedule gives a common name or names, where available, and is included by way of guidance only; in the event of any dispute or proceedings, only the first column is to be taken into account. (Note to E.S.A. 1976, Sch. 1.).

Any domestic form of Ondatra zibethicus — Domestic muskrat (otherwise known as musquash)

Any domestic form of Cavia — Domestic guinea pig

Any domestic form of Chinchilla laniger — Domestic chinchilla

Carnivores

Canis familiaris — Domestic dog

Vulpes vulpes — Common fox and silver fox

Procyon lotor — North American racoon

Procyon cancrivorus — Crab-eating racoon

Mustela vison — North American mink

Mustela furo — Domestic ferret

Martes zibellina — Sable

Felis catus — Domestic cat

Odd-toed ungulates

Equus caballus — Domestic horse

Equus asinus — Domestic donkey

Equus caballus x asinus — Mule and hinny[1]

Even-toed ungulates[2]

Any domestic form of Sus scrofa — Domestic pig

Lama glama — Domestic llama

Lama pacos — Domestic alpaca

Any domestic form of Camelus bactrianus — Domestic bactrian camel

Camelus dromedarius — Arabian camel

Dama dama — European fallow deer

Cervus elaphus (except Cervus elaphus bactrianus, Cervus elaphus hanglu and Cervus elaphus barbarus) — Red deer (except Bactrian deer, the Kashmir stag and Barbary deer).

Any domestic form of Rangifer tarandus — Domestic reindeer

Capreolus capreolus — Roe deer

Any domestic form of Bubalus bubalis — Domestic water buffalo

Bos taurus — Domestic ox

Bos indicus — Domestic zebu

---

[1] *I.e.*, offspring of she-ass by stallion.

[2] The mammals listed under this heading nevertheless require an import licence under the Importation of Animals Order 1977, as to which *see* pp. 30–32.

Bos frontalis	Domestic gayal
Any domestic form of Bos grunniens	Domestic yak
Any domestic form of Capra hircus	Domestic goat
Ovis aries	Domestic sheep

APPENDIX B

Endangered Kinds of Mammals the sale etc. of which is restricted[1]

Marsupials

Kind[2]	*Common Name[2]*
Bettongia	Rat Kangaroo
Caloprymnus campestris	Desert rat-kangaroo
Lagorchestes kirsutus	Western hare-wallaby
Lagostrophus fasciatus	Banded hare-wallaby
Onychogalea fraenata	Bridle nail-tailed wallaby
Onychogalea lunata	Crescent nail-tailed wallaby
Lasiorhinus krefftii	Queensland hairy-nosed wombat
Chaeropus ecaudatus	Pig-footed bandicoot
Macrotis lagotis	Rabbit-bandicoot
Macrotis leucura	Lesser rabbit-bandicoot
Perameles bouganville	Western barred bandicoot
Sminthopsis longicaudata	Long-tailed dunnart
Sminthopsis psammophila	Sandhill dunnart
Thylacinus cynocephalus	Tasmanian wolf.

Primates

Allocebus	Hairy-eared dwarf lemur
Cheirogaleus	Dwarf lemurs
Hapalemur	Gentle lemurs
Lemur	Lemurs
Lepilemur	Sportive and weasel lemurs
Microcebus	Mouse lemurs

[1] ESA 1976 Sch. 4. Birds, fish and molluscs listed in that Schedule are not included in this Appendix. The Schedule may be modified from time to time by the Secretary of State (ESA 1976 s. 3). For further details, see pp. 40–42.

[2] The second column of this Appendix gives a common name or names, where available, and is included by way of guidance only; in the event of any dispute or proceedings, only the first column is to be taken into account (Note to ESA 1976 Sch. 4).

Phaner	Fork-marked mouse lemurs
Avahi	Avahis (otherwise known as Woolly indris)
Indri	Indris
Propithecus	Sifakas
Daubentonia madagascariensis	Aye-aye
Callimico goeldii	Goeldi's marmoset (otherwise known as Goeldi's tamarin)
Callithrix aurita	White eared marmoset
Callithrix flaviceps	Buff-headed marmoset
Leontopithecus	Maned tamarin (otherwise known as Golden tamarin)
Saguinus bicolor	Pied tamarin
Saguinus geoffroyi	Geoffroy's tamarin
Saguinus leucopus	White-footed tamarin
Saguinus oedipus	Cotton-headed tamarin
Alouatta palliata (otherwise known as Alouatta villosa)	Mantled howler
Ateles geoffroyi frontatus	Black-browed spider monkey
Ateles geoffroyi panamensis	Red spider monkey
Brachyteles arachnoides	Woolly spider monkey
Cacajao	Uakaris
Chiropotes albinasus	White-nosed saki
Saimiri oerstedii	Red-backed squirrel monkey
Cercocebus galeritus galeritus	Tana River mangabey
Circopithecus diana	Diana monkey
Colobus badius kirkii	Kirk's red colobus (otherwise known as Zanzibar red colobus)
Colobus badius rufomitratus	Tana River red colobus
Macaca silenus	Lion-tailed macaque
Nasalis larvatus	Proboscis monkey
Papio leucophaeus (otherwise known as Mandrillus leucophaeus)	Drill
Papio sphinx (otherwise known as Mandrillus sphinx)	Mandrill
Presbytis entellus	Langur (otherwise known as Entellus langur or True langur)
Presbytis geei	Golden langur
Presbytis pileatus	Caped langur
Presbytis potenziani	Mentawi leaf monkey
Pygathrix nemaeus	Douc langur
Rhinopithecus roxellanae	Snub-nosed langur
Simias concolor	Mentawi snub-nosed langur
Hylobates	Gibbons
Symphalangus syndactylus	Siamang
Pongidae	Great apes

Edentates

Priodontes giganteus (otherwise known as Priodontes maximus)	Giant armadillo

Pangolins

Manis temmincki	South African pangolin

Rabbits and hares

Caprolagus hispidus	Assam rabbit (otherwise known as Hispid hare)
Romerolagus diazi	Volcano rabbit

Rodents

Cynomys mexicanus	Mexican prairie marmot
Leporillus conditor	Australian sticknest rat
Pseudomys fumeus	Smoky mouse
Pseudomys praeconis	Shark Bay mouse
Xeromys myoides	False water rat
Zyzomys pendunculatus	Central thick-tailed rat
Chinchilla (except any domestic form of Chinchilla laniger)	Chinchilla

Cetaceans

Lipotes vexillifer	Chinese river dolphin
Physeter catodon (otherwise known as Physeter macrocephalus)	Sperm whale
Platanista minor	Indus river dolphin
Platanista gangetica	Ganges dolphin
Sotalia	Humpbacked dolphins
Sousa	Humpbacked dolphins
Neophocaena phocaenoides	Finless porpoise
Phocoena sinus	Cochito
Balaena mysticetus	Greenland right whale (otherwise known as Bowhead whale)
Balaenoptera borealis	Sei whale
Balaenoptera musculus	Blue whale
Balaenoptera physalus	Common rorqual
Eschrichtius	Grey whales
Eubalaena	Right whales
Megaptera novaeangliae	Humpback whale

Carnivores

Speothos venaticus	Bush dog
Vulpes velox hebes	Northern kit fox
Helarctos malayanus	Sun bear
Selenarctos thibetanus	Asiatic black bear
Tremarctos ornatus	Spectacled bear
Ursus arctos isabellinus	Brown bear
Ursus arctos nelsoni	Mexican brown bear
Ursus arctos pruinosus	Tibetan brown bear
Aonyx microdon	Cameroon clawless otter
Enhydra lutris nereis	Southern sea otter
Lutra felina	Marine otter
Lutra longicaudis	South American otter
Lutra lutra	Eurasian otter
Lutra provocax	Southern river otter
Mustela nigripes	Black-footed ferret
Pteronura brasiliensis	Giant otter
Prionodon pardicolor	Spotted linsang
Hyaena brunnea	Brown hyaena
Acinonyx jubatus	Cheetah
Felis bengalensis bengalensis	Leopard cat
Felis concolor coryi	Florida puma
Felis concolor costaricensis	Costa Rica puma
Felis concolor cougar	Eastern puma
Felis jacobita	Andean cat
Felis rufa escuinapae	Mexican bobcat
Felis marmorata	Marbled cat
Felis nigripes	Black-footed cat
Felis pardalis mearnsi	Costa Rica ocelot
Felis pardalis mitis	Brazilian ocelot
Felis planiceps	Flat-headed cat
Felis rubiginosa	Rusty spotted cat
Felis temmincki	Asiatic golden cat
Felis tigrina oncilla	Little spotted cat
Felis wiedii salvinia	Guatemalan margay
Felis wiedii nicaraguae	Nicaraguan margay
Felis yagouaroundi cacomitli	Jaguarundi
Felis yagouaroundi fossata	Jaguarundi
Felis yagouaroundi panamensis	Jaguarundi
Felis yagouaroundi tolteca	Jaguarundi
Neofelis nebulosa	Clouded leopard
Panthera leo persica	Asiatic lion
Panthera onca	Jaguar
Panthera pardus	Leopard
Panthera tigris	Tiger
Panthera uncia	Snow leopard

218 APPENDIX B

Seals

Arctocephalus townsendi — Guadelupe fur seal
Monachus — Monk seals

Elephants

Elephas maximus — Asian elephant

Sea-cows

Dugong dugon — Dugong (otherwise known as Sea-cow)
Trichechus inunguis — Amazonian manatee
Trichechus manatus — West Indian manatee

Odd-toed ungulates

Equus grevyi — Grevy's zebra
Equus hemionus hemionus — Mongolian wild ass
Equus hemionus khur — Indian wild ass
Equus przewalskii — Przewalski's horse
Equus zebra zebra — Cape mountain zebra
Tapirus bairdii — Central American tapir
Tapirus indicus — Malayan tapir (otherwise known as Indian tapir).
Tapirus pinchaque — Mountain tapir (otherwise known as Woolly tapir)
Rhinocerotidae — Rhinoceroses

Even-toed ungulates

Babyrousa babyrussa — Babirusa
Sus salvanius — Pygmy hog
Vicugna vicugna — Vicugna
Axis calamianensis — Calamian deer
Axis kuhli — Bawean deer
Axis porcinus annamiticus — Thai hog deer
Blastocerus dichotomus — Marsh deer
Cervus duvauceli — Swamp deer
Cervus elaphus hanglu — Kashmir stag (otherwise known as Hanglu)
Cervus eldi — Brow-antlered stag
Dama mesopotamica — Persian fallow deer
Hippocamelus antisiensis — Peruvian huemal
Hippocamelus bisulcus — Chilean huemal
Moschus moschiferus moschiferus — Himalayan musk deer

Ozotoceros bezoarticus	Pampas deer
Pudu pudu	Chilean pudu
Antilocapra americana peninsularis	Lower California pronghorn
Antilocapra americana sonoriensis	Sonoran pronghorn
Bison bison athabascae	Wood bison
Bos gaurus	Gaur
Bos mutus	Wild yak
Bubalus depressicornis	Lowland anoa
Bubalus mindorensis	Tamaraw
Bubalus quarlesi	Mountain anoa
Capra falconeri chiltanensis	Markhor
Capra falconeri jerdoni	Markhor
Capra falconeri megaceros	Markhor
Capricornis sumatraensis	Serow
Hippotragus niger variani	Giant sable antelope
Nemorhaedus goral	Goral
Novibos sauveli	Koupray
Oryx leucoryx	Arabian oryx
Ovis ammon hodgsoni	Great Tibetan sheep
Ovis orientalis ophion	Cyprian mouflon
Ovis vignei	Urial
Pantholops hodgsoni	Tibetan antelope
Rupicapra rupicapra ornata	Abrussi chamois

APPENDIX C

Animals affected by the Rabies (Importation of Dogs, Cats and Other Mammals) Order 1974[1]

PART I
Animals subject to quarantine for life

Order		Common name of some species[2]
Chiroptera	Desmodontidae only	Vampire bats

PART II
Animals subject to 6 months' quarantine

Carnivora	All families and species	Dogs, cats, jackals, foxes, wolves, bears, racoons, coatis, pandas, otters, weasels, martens, polecats, badgers, skunks, mink, ratels, genets, civets, linsangs, mongooses, hyaenas, ocelots, pumas, cheetahs, lions, tigers, leopards
Chiroptera	All families except Desmodontidae	Bats, flying foxes
Dermoptera		Flying lemurs
Edentata		Anteaters, sloths, armadillos
Hyracoidea		Hyraxes

---

[1] Schedule 1 to the 1974 Order. *See* pages 42–44 for further details.

[2] These names are for guidance only and do not form part of the Order (footnote to Schedule 1 to the 1974 Order). The effect is that the order will apply to any animal belonging to the orders of mammals listed in the first column (with any reservations made in the second column) whether or not its common name appears in the third column.

Insectivora		Solenodons, tenrecs, otter shrews, golden moles, hedgehogs, elephant shrews, shrews, moles, desmans
Lagomorpha		Pikas, rabbits, hares
Marsupialia		Opossums, marsupial mice, dasyures, marsupial moles, marsupial anteaters, bandicoots, rat opossums, cucuses, phalangers, koalas, wombats, wallabies, kangaroos.
Primates	All families except Hominidae (Man)	Tree-shrews, lemurs, indrises, sifakas, ayes-ayes, lorises, bush-babies, tarsiers, titis, uakaris, sakis, howlers, capuchins, squirrel monkeys, marmosets, tamarins, macaques, mangabeys, baboons, langurs, gibbons, great apes.
Rodentia		Gophers, squirrels, chipmunks, marmots, scalytailed squirrels, pocket mice, kangaroo-rats, beavers, mountain beavers, springhaas, mice, rats, hamsters, lemmings, voles, gerbils, water rats, dormice, jumping mice, jerboas, porcupines, cavies (including guinea-pigs), capybaras, chinchillas, spiny rats, gundis

PART III
Additional animals for contact purposes[1]

Artiodactyla	Pigs, peccaries, hippopotamuses, camels, llamas, chevrotains, deer, giraffes, pronghorns, cattle, antelopes, duikers, gazelles, goats, sheep
Monotremata	Echidnas, duck-billed platypuses
Perissodactyla	Horses, asses, zebras, tapirs, rhinoceroses
Pholidota	Pangolins
Proboscidea	Elephants
Tubulidentata	Aardvarks

[1] See p. 44.

APPENDIX D

Dangerous wild animals listed in the Dangerous Wild animals Act 1976[1]

Scientific name[2]	*Common name or names*[2]
Antilocapridae	Pronghorn
Bovidae except the species Cephalophus, Sylvicapra grimmia, Oreotragus oreotragus, Ourebia, Raphicerus, Nesotragus moschatus, Neotragus pygmeaus, Modaqua, any domestic form of Capra hircus, Dorcatragus megalotis, Ovis aries and all species of the genera Bos and Bubalus.	These include cattle, antelopes, gazelles, goats and sheep, except that duikers, grey duiker, klipspringer, oribi, grysbok, suni, royal antelope, dik-dik, domestic goat, Beira antelope, domestic sheep and domestic cattle are specifically excluded.
Camelidae except the species Lama glama and Lama pacos.	This kind includes the bactrian camel and Arabian camel except that llama and alpaca are specifically excluded.
Canidae except the species Canis familiaris, all species of the genera Vulpes, Alopex, Dusicyon and Otocyon.	This kind includes the wild dog, wolf, jackal, coyote except that the domestic dog and all foxes are specifically excluded.
Casuariidae	Cassowary
Cercopithecidae	Old world monkeys, including langur, colobus, macaque, guenon, patas, mangabey, baboon and mandrill.

---

[1] D.W.A. 1976, Schedule. The list may be varied from time to time by the Secretary of State. (D.W.A. 1976, s. 8). For the provisions relating to these animals, *see* Chapter 6.

[2] The second column above is included by way of explanation only; in the event of any dispute or proceedings, only the first column is to be taken into account (D.W.A. 1976, s. 7(5).)

Crocodylia	This kind includes the alligator, crocodile, gharial, false gharial and caiman.
Dromaiidae	Emu
Elapidae (including Hydrophiidae)	This kind includes the cobra, krait, mamba, coral snake and sea snake, and all Australian poisonous snakes including the death adder
Equidae except the species Equus caballus, Equus asinus and Equus caballus x Equus asinus	Horses except that the domestic horse, domestic donkey, mule and hinny are specifically excluded.
Felidae, except the species Felis catus	This kind includes the lynx, caracal, serval, bobcat, cheetah, lion, tiger, leopard, panther, jaguar, puma, cougar and ocelot, except that the domestic cat is specifically excluded
Giraffidae	This kind includes the giraffe and okapi
Helodermatidae	Gila monster and Mexican beaded lizard
Hippopotamidae	This kind includes the hippopotamus and pygmy hippopotamus
Hyaenidae except the species Proteles cristatus	Hyaenas except that the aardwolf is specifically excluded
Hylobatidae	Gibbon
Pongidae	Anthropoid apes including orang utan, gorilla and chimpanzee
Proboscidae	Elephants including the African and Indian elephant
Rhinocerotidae	Rhinoceros
Struthionidae	Ostrich
Suidae except any domestic form of Sus scrofa	Old world pigs except that the domestic pig is specifically excluded
Tapiridae	Tapirs
Tayassuidae	New world pigs including the collared peccary and white lipped peccary

Ursidae	This kind includes the polar bear, brown bear and grizzly bear
Viperidae (including Crotalidae)	This kind includes— (a) most snakes known as vipers and adders, and (b) the rattlesnakes, bushmaster, fer-de-lance, water moccasins and copperhead

APPENDIX E

Definition of "Animal" for the purposes of the Protection of Animals Acts[1]

"Animal" means any domestic or captive animal.

"Domestic animal" means any horse, ass, mule, bull, sheep, pig, goat, dog, cat or fowl or any other animal of whatsoever kind or species, and whether a quadruped or not, which is tame or which has been or is being sufficiently tamed to serve some purpose for the use of man.

"Captive animal" means any animal (not being a domestic animal) of whatsoever kind or species, and whether a quadruped or not, including any bird, fish or reptile, which is in captivity[2] or confinement, or which is maimed, pinioned or subjected to any appliance or contrivance for the purpose of hindering or preventing its escape from captivity or confinement.

"Horse" includes any mare, gelding, pony, foal, colt, filly or stallion

"Bull" includes any cow, bullock, heifer, calf, steer or ox.

"Sheep" includes any lamb, ewe or ram.

"Pig", includes any boar, hog or sow.

"Goat" includes a kid.

"Dog" includes any bitch, sapling[3] or puppy.

"Cat" includes a kitten.

"Fowl" includes any cock, hen, chicken, capon, turkey, goose, gander, duck, drake, guinea-fowl, peacock, peahen, swan or pigeon.

---

[1] P.A.A. 1911, s. 15(*a*)—(*d*).

[2] Mere temporary inability to get away is not a state of captivity. (*Rowley v. Murphy* (1964).) It will be seen that wild animals are not within the definition unless restrained in one of the says described in the definition of captive animal.

[3] A sapling is a greyhound in its first year.

[225]

APPENDIX F

Restrictions subject to which experiments calculated to give pain may be performed by a licensed person on any living vertebrate animal[1]

1. The experiment must be performed with a view to the advancement by new discovery of physiological knowledge or of knowledge which will be useful for saving or prolonging life or alleviating suffering,[2] although an experiment not performed directly for the advancement of such knowledge, but for the purpose of testing a particular former discovery alleged to have been made for the advancement of such knowledge, may be performed if a certificate[3] has been given stating that such testing is absolutely necessary for the effectual advancement of such knowledge.[4]

2. The experiment must be performed by a person holding a licence from the Secretary of State,[5] and where the licence is a conditional one or where the experiment is for the purpose of instruction, it must be performed in a registered place.[6]

3. During the whole of the experiment the animal must be under an anaesthetic, other than urari or curare,[7] of sufficient power to prevent its feeling pain,[8] unless a certificate[9] has been given stating that insensibility cannot be produced without frustrating the object of the experiment.[10h9]

---

[1] For experiments on living animals, *see* further p. 125.

[2] C.A.A. 1876, s. 3(1).

[3] The certificate must be signed by the president of one of certain named learned societies and also by a professor of medical subjects in a university or college incorporated by Royal Charter in Great Britain or Ireland (exclusive of the Irish Republic) unless the applicant is himself such a professor. (C.A.A. 1876, s. 11). The certificate may also be signed by a High Court judge in a case where he is satisfied that it is essential for the purpose of justice in a criminal case to make an experiment on living animals. (C.A.A. 1876, s. 12.).

[4] C.A.A. 1876, s. 3, proviso (4).

[5] *I.e.*, the Home Secretary.

[6] These are places, usually laboratories, registered by the Home Secretary and liable to inspection by inspectors appointed by him. (C.A.A. 1876, ss. 7, 10.)

[7] C.A.A. 1876, s. 4.

[8] C.A.A. 1876, s. 3(3).

[9] The certificate must be signed as described in note [3] above.

[10] C.A.A. 1876, s. 3, proviso (2).

4. If pain is likely to continue after the effect of the anaesthetic has ceased, or if any serious injury has been inflicted, the animal must be killed before it recovers from the influence of the anaesthetic,[1] unless a certificate[2] has been given stating that killing the animal would necessarily frustrate the object of the experiment, in which case the animal must be killed as soon as that object has been attained.[3]

5. The experiment must not be performed for the purpose of attaining manual skill.[4]

6. The experiment must not be performed as an illustration of lectures in a medical school, hospital, college or elsewhere,[5] unless a certificate[2] has been given stating that the proposed experiment is absolutely necessary for instruction with a view to the hearers acquiring physiological knowledge useful to them for saving or prolonging life or alleviating suffering.[6]

---

[1] C.A.A. 1876, s. 3(4).
[2] The certificate must be signed as described in note [3] on p. 226.
[3] C.A.A. 1876, s. 3, proviso (3).
[4] C.A.A. 1876, s. 3(6).
[5] C.A.A. 1876, s. 3(5).
[6] C.A.A. 1876, s. 3, proviso (1).

APPENDIX G

Spring traps approved by Government Ministers[1]

Type and make of trap	Conditions
Imbra Trap Mark I and Mark II, both manufactured by or under the authority of James S. Low & Sons Ltd., Atholl Smithy, Atholl Street, Blairgowrie, Perthshire.	The traps shall be used only— (a) for the purpose of killing or taking rabbits and set in rabbit holes, or (b) for the purpose of killing or taking grey squirrels or stoats, weasels, rats, mice or other small ground vermin, and set in artificial tunnels constructed for the purpose.
Fenn Vermin Trap Mark I, Vermin Trap Mark II, Vermin Trap Mark III, and Vermin Trap Mark IV (Heavy Duty) manufactured by or under the authority of Mr. A. A. Fenn of F.H.T. Works, High Street, Astwood Bank, Redditch, Worcester	The traps shall be used only— (a) for the purpose of killing or taking grey squirrels or stoats, weasels, rats, mice or other small vermin, and set in artificial tunnels constructed for the purpose and, in the case of the Vermin Trap Mark IV (Heavy Duty) in either natural or artificial tunnels, or (b) for the purpose of killing or taking rats or mice and set in the open on their runs.

---

[1] Spring Traps Approval Order 1975, Schedule. *See*, further, pp. 129–131.

Fenn Vermin Trap Mark VI (Dual Purpose) manufactured by or under the authority of Mr. A. A. Fenn (as above).

The trap shall be used only—
(a) for the purpose of killing or taking rabbits and set in rabbit holes, or
(b) for the purpose of killing or taking grey squirrels, mink, stoats, weasels, rats, mice or other small vermin, and set in natural tunnels or in artificial tunnels constructed for the purpose.

Fenn Rabbit Trap Mark I manufactured by or under the authority of Mr A. A. Fenn (as above).

The trap shall only be used for the killing or taking of rabbits and set in rabbit holes.

Juby Trap manufactured under the authority of the Ministry of Agriculture, Whitehall Place, London S.W.1.

As for the Imbra Traps above.

Fuller Trap manufactured by or under the authority of Fuller Industries, Three Trees, Loxwood Road, Bucks Green, Rudgwick, Sussex

The trap shall be used only for the purpose of killing or taking grey squirrels.

Sawyer Trap manufactured by or under the authority of James S. Low & Sons Ltd (as above).

The trap shall be used only—
(a) for the purpose of killing or taking grey squirrels or stoats, weasels, rats, mice or other small ground vermin and set in natural tunnels or in artificial tunnels constructed for the purpose, or
(b) for the purpose of killing or taking rats or mice and set in the open on their runs.

Lloyd Trap manufactured under the authority of the National Research Development Corporation

As for the Sawyer Trap above.

APPENDIX H

Specially protected wild animals[1]

Common Name[2]	Scientific Name
Adder[3]	Vipera berus
Bats, Horseshoe (all species)	Rhinolophidae
Bats, Typical (all species)	Vespertilionidae
Beetle, Rainbow Leaf	Chrysolina cerealis
Burbot	Lota lota
Butterfly, Chequered Skipper	Carterocephalus palaemon
Butterfly, Heath Fritillary	Mellicta athalia (otherwise known as Melitaea athalia)
Butterfly, Large Blue	Maculinea arion
Butterfly, Swallowtail	Papilio machaon
Cricket, Field	Gryllis campestris
Cricket, Mole	Gryllotalpa gryllotalpa
Dolphin, Bottle-nosed	Tursiops truncatus (otherwise known as Tursiops tursio)
Dolphin, Common	Delphinus delphis
Dragonfly, Norfolk Aeshna	Aeshna isosceles
Frog, Common[3]	Rana temporaria
Grasshopper, Wart-biter	Decticus verrucivorous
Lizard, Sand	Lacerta agilis
Lizard, Viviparous[3]	Lacerta vivipara
Moth, Barberry Carpet	Pareulype berbeata
Moth, Black-veined	Siona lineata (otherwise known as Idaea lineata)
Moth, Essex Emerald	Thetidia smaragdaria

---

[1] WCA 1981 Sch. 5. See, particularly, pp. 154–156 and 158–160 for further details.

[2] The common names are included by way of guidance only. In the event of any dispute or proceedings, these names shall not be taken into account (Footnote to WCA 1981 Sch. 5).

[3] These animals are only protected for the purpose of the offences described at items (3) and (4) on p. 159—see notes against the animals' names in WCA 1981, Sch. 5.

Moth, New Forest Burnet	Zygaena viciae
Moth, Reddish Buff	Acosmetia caliginosa
Newt, Great Crested (otherwise known as Warty newt)	Triturus cristatus
Newt, Palmate[1]	Triturus helveticus
Newt, Smooth[1]	Triturus vulgaris
Otter, Common	Lutra lutra
Porpoise, Harbour (otherwise known as Common porpoise)	Phocaena phocaena
Slow-worm[1]	Anguis fragilis
Snail, Carthusian	Monacha cartusiana
Snail, Glutinous	Myxas glutinosa
Snail, Sandbowl	Catinella arenaria
Snake, Grass[1]	Natrix helvetica
Snake, Smooth	Coronella austriaca
Spider, Fen Raft	Dolomedes plantarius
Spider, Ladybird	Eresis niger
Squirrel, Red	Sciurus vulgaris
Toad, Common[1]	Bufo bufo
Toad, Natterjack	Bufo calamita

---

[1] These animals are only protected for the purpose of the offences described at items (3) and (4) on p. 159—*see* notes against the animals' names in WCA 1981, Sch. 5.

APPENDIX I

Prohibited Methods of killing or taking wild animals[1]

Part I: Methods applicable to all wild animals[2]

1. Setting in position any self-locking snare which is of such a nature and so placed as to be calculated to cause bodily injury to any wild animal coming into contact with it.
2. [3] Using, for the purpose of killing or taking[4] any wild animal, any self-locking snare, whether or not of such a nature or so placed as described in paragraph 1 above, any bow or crossbow or any explosive other than ammunition for a firearm.[5]
3. [3] Using as a decoy, for the purpose of killing or taking any wild animal, any live mammal or bird whatever.

Part II: Methods applicable only to the wild animals included in Part III below[6]

4. Setting in position any of the following articles, being an article which is of such a nature and so placed as to be calculated to cause bodily injury to any wild animal which comes into contact with it:
   (*a*) any trap or snare;
   (*b*) any electrical device for killing or stunning;
   (*c*) any poisonous, poisoned or stupefying substance.
5. [3] Using, for the purpose of killing or taking a wild animal, any article described in paragraph 4 above, whether or not of such a nature and so placed as there described, or any net.

---

[1] For further details, see pp. 156–157. For the meaning of "wild animal", *see* pp. 153–154.

[2] WCA 1981, s. 11(1).

[3] In proceedings for an offence of using these methods, it shall be presumed that the animal in question was a wild animal unless the contrary is shown (WCA 1981, s. 11(5)).

[4] For an interpretation of "taking", see p. 100.

[5] For the meaning of "firearm", see note [4] on p. 139.

[6] WCA 1981 s. 11(2).

6. [1] Using, for the purpose of killing or taking a wild animal,—
    (*a*) any automatic or semi-automatic weapon;[2]
    (*b*) any device for illuminating a target or sighting device for night shooting;
    (*c*) any form of artificial light or any mirror or other dazzling device;
    (*d*) any gas or smoke not falling within the descriptions in paragraphs 4 or 5 above.
7. [1] Using as a decoy, for the purpose of killing or taking a wild animal, any sound recording.
8. [1] Using any mechanically propelled vehicle[3] in pursuit of a wild animal for the purpose of driving, killing or taking[4] it.

Part III: Wild animals protected from the methods described in Part II[5]

Common Name[6]	Scientific Name
Badger	Meles meles
Bats, Horseshoe (all species)	Rhinolophidae
Bats, Typical (all species)	Vespertilionidae
Cat, Wild	Felis silvestris
Dolphin, Bottle-nosed	Tursiops truncatus (otherwise known as Tursiops tursio)
Dolphin, Common	Delphinus delphis
Dormice (all species)	Gliridae
Hedgehog	Erinaceus europaeus
Marten, Pine	Martes martes
Otter, Common	Lutra lutra
Polecat	Mustela putorius
Porpoise, Harbour (otherwise known as Common porpoise)	Phocaena phocaena
Shrews (all species)	Soricidae
Squirrel, Red	Sciurus vulgaris

---

[1] Note [3] on the last page applies.
[2] These weapons do not include any weapon the magazine of which is incapable of holding more than two rounds (WCA 1981 s. 27(1)).
[3] "Vehicle" includes aircraft, hovercraft and boat (WCA 1981 s. 27(1)).
[4] For an interpretation of "taking", see p. 100.
[5] WCA 1981 Sch. 6.
[6] Note [2] to Appendix H applies (Footnote to WCA 1981 Sch. 6).

APPENDIX J

Animals which are not to be released or allowed to escape into the wild[1]

Common Name[2]	Scientific Name
Coypu	Myocastor coypus
Dormouse, Fat	Glis glis
Frog, Edible	Rana esculenta
Frog, European Tree (otherwise known as Common tree frog)	Hyla arborea
Frog, Marsh	Rana ridibunda
Gerbil, Mongolian	Meriones unguiculatus
Lizard, Common Wall	Podarcis muralis
Marmot, Prairie (otherwise known as Prairie dog)	Cynomys
Mink, American	Mustela vison
Newt, Alpine	Triturus alpestris
Porcupine, Crested	Hystrix cristata
Porcupine, Himalayan	Hystrix hodgsonii
Rat, Black	Rattus rattus
Squirrel, Grey	Sciurus carolinensis
Terrapin, European Pond	Emys orbicularis
Toad, African Clawed	Xenopus laevis
Toad, Midwife	Alytes obststricans
Toad, Yellow-bellied	Bombina variegata
Wallaby, Red-necked	Macropus rufogriseus

---

[1] WCA 1981, Sch. 9, Part I. See, further pp. 157–158. Birds and fishes included in Sch. 9 are omitted from this Appendix.

[2] The common names in the first column of this Appendix are included by way of guidance only; in the event of any dispute or proceedings, those names shall not be taken into account (Note to WCA 1981, Sch 9).

APPENDIX K

Licences for activities connected with wild animals[1]

Purposes for which licences may be granted	Issuing Authority
Scientific or educational Ringing or marking, or examining any ring or mark on, wild animals Conserving wild animals or introducing them to particular areas Protecting any zoological collection Photography	The Nature Conservancy Council[2]
Preventing the spread of disease[3] Preventing serious damage to livestock[5], foodstuffs, for livestock[5], crops, vegetables, fruit, growing timber or any other form of property, or to fisheries	The Minister of Agriculture,[4] the Secretary of State for Wales,[6] or the Secretary of State for Scotland,[7] as appropriate

---

[1] WCA 1981 ss. 16(3)(4)(9)(b)–(e), 27(1). For further particulars, see pp. 160–161.

[2] Applications for licences should be addressed to the Council at 19–20 Belgrave Square, London SW1X 9PY.

[3] This is not restricted to diseases of animals or otherwise.

[4] Applications for licences in England should be addressed to the local Divisional Office of the Ministry.

[5] For the definition of "livestock" see note [9] on p. 155.

[6] Applications for licences should be addressed to the Welsh Office, Crown Building, Cathays Park, Cardiff CF1 3NQ.

[7] Applications for licences should be addressed to the Department for Agriculture and Fisheries for Scotland, Chesser House, 500 Gorgie Road, Edinburgh EH11 3AW.

[235]

Preserving public health or
public safety.
To authorise the acts described
at items (3) and (4) on page 159.
To authorise a person to release,
or allow to escape into the wild,
certain animals[3]

The Secretary of State for the
Environment,[1] the Secretary of
State for Wales,[1] or the Secretary
of State for Scotland,[2] as
appropriate

---

[1] Applications for licences in both cases should be addressed to the Department of the Environment, Tollgate House, Houlton Street, Bristol BS2 9DJ.

[2] Applications for licences should be addressed to the Scottish Home and Health Dept, St. Andrews House, Edinburgh EH1 3DE.

[3] For details of these actions, which would otherwise be offences, see pp. 157–158.

APPENDIX L

**Special grounds of appeal against a notice requiring structural works
under Section 4 of the Prevention of Damage by Pests Act 1949[1]**

"(3) A person served with such a notice as aforesaid[2] may appeal to a
court of summary jurisdiction[3] on any of the following grounds which are
appropriate in the circumstances of the particular case:—

(a) that the notice or requirement is not justified by the terms of the
section under which it purports to have been given or made;

(b) that there has been some defect, informality or error in, or in
connection with, the notice;

(c) that the authority have refused unreasonably to approve the execution of alternative works, or that the works required by the notice
to be executed are otherwise unreasonable in character or extent,
or are unnecessary;

(d) that the time within which the works are to be executed is not
reasonably sufficient for the purpose;

(e) that the notice might lawfully have been served on the occupier of
the premises in question instead of on the owner, or on the owner
instead of on the occupier, and that it would have been equitable
for it to have been so served;

(f) where the work is work for the common benefits of the premises
in question and other premises, that some other person, being the
owner or occupier of premises to be benefited, ought to contribute
towards the expenses of executing any works required.

(4) If and so far as an appeal under this section is based on the ground
of some informality, defect or error in or in connection with the notice,

---

[1] P.H.A. 1936, s. 290(3)–(5); P.D.P.A. 1949, s. 4(5). For further details, *see*
pp. 194–195.
[2] That is, a notice from the district council requiring structural repairs or other
works to be done—*see* p. 194.
[3] *I.e.*, a magistrates' court.

the court shall dismiss the appeal, if it is satisfied that the informality, defect or error was not a material one.

(5) Where the grounds upon which an appeal under this section is brought include a ground specified in paragraph (*e*) or paragraph (*f*) of subsection (3) of this section, the appellant shall serve a copy of his notice of appeal on each other person referred to, and in the case of any appeal under this section may serve a copy of his notice of appeal on any other person having an estate or interest in the premises in question, and on the hearing of the appeal the court may make such order as it thinks fit with respect to the person by whom any work is to be executed and the contribution to be made by any other person towards the cost of the work, or as to the proportions in which any expenses which may become recoverable by the local authority are to be borne by the appellant and such other person.

In exercising its powers under this subsection, the court shall have regard—

(*a*) as between an owner and an occupier, to the terms and conditions, whether contractual or statutory, of the tenancy and to the nature of the works required; and

(*b*) in any case, to the degree of benefit to be derived by the different persons concerned."

INDEX

INDEX

A

D